NEW PATHWAYS

NEW PATHWAYS IN PSYCHOLOGY

Maslow and the Post-Freudian Revolution

by

COLIN WILSON

LONDON
VICTOR GOLLANCZ LTD
1979

150

© Colin Wilson 1972

ISBN 0 575 02796 7

First published 1972
This edition 1979

Printed in Great Britain by
St. Edmundsbury Press Limited
Haverhill, Suffolk

For Bertha Maslow

ACKNOWLEDGEMENTS

The idea for this book came from my friend Millen Brand, to whom I owe more than I can adequately express here. And the book could not have been written without the active and detailed cooperation of Abraham Maslow himself: since his death, his wife Bertha has offered the same friendly help and enthusiasm. I also wish to offer my thanks to Frank Goble, of the Jefferson Research Foundation, whose own book on Maslow had still not reached me (due to a postal strike) when the present manuscript was completed, but whose monthly news-letters have provided enormous stimulus.

I would also like to thank Messrs Macmillan for per-mission to quote from *The Collected Poems of W. B. Yeats*, the Washington Square Press for permission to quote from *Man's Search for Meaning* by Viktor Frankl, and Dan MacDougald of the Yonan Codex Foundation (now called Emotional Maturity Instruction) for help and information. Mrs Philip Magor was kind enough to draw my attention to the work of Assagioli, for which I am extremely grateful.

C.W.

CORNWALL,
MARCH 1971

CONTENTS

1*

fell out of love. Shaw's *Candida*: 'secret in the poet's heart'. The
power to 'focus'.

Freud's reticence. Mother fixation. Studies under Charcot. Hysteria. Vienna years. Development of psychoanalysis. Hartmann's
Philosophy of the Unconscious. The sexual theory. '*Whose* subconscious?' Psychoanalysing Freud. Freud versus religion. Cultural
pessimism. Alfred Adler. The social nature of man. Inferiority
as the root of neurosis. Adler on Dostoevsky. Adler's limitations.
Carl Jung. Jung's quarrel with Freud. Alchemy. Jung as phenomenologist. The four functions. Neurosis as imbalance of four
functions. Archetypes. Introvert and extravert. Otto Rank. *The
Trauma of Birth*. The importance of the will in curing neurosis.
Man's will to health. Man's supra-personal drives. The hero and
the artist. Jung's case of the business man. Creative stagnation as
the cause of neurosis. The 'robot': the destroyer of 'newness'.
Gestalt psychology. Wundt. The 'meaning faculty'.

PART TWO

'I consider myself as Freudian.' The reluctant rebel. Brooklyn
childhood. Anti-semitism. 'Angels.' Will Maslow. New York City
College. The New York scene—music, theatre, ideas. Decision
not to become lawyer. Cornell. Bertha. University of Wisconsin—
development of interest in psychology. Utopianism—'yearning
for the good life.' Professors. Pavlovian training. Timidity and
shyness. Graduation. Work under Thorndike. Thorndike's functionalism. Psychology in the thirties: Lewin, Goldstein, S–R
theory, Karen Horney and Erich Fromm. Wertheimer, Ruth
Benedict. The 'synergic society'. Revolt against S-R theory.
Fourteen years at Brooklyn College, working with underprivileged kids. Brandeis.

Harry Harlow's intellectual monkeys. Chickens who are good
choosers. Intelligence-testing apes. Cannibalism in dogs. More
monkey studies. First original research: synthesis of Freud and
Adler. Monkey dominance. Researches into dominance in
women. High-, medium- and low-dominance women. *A Theory*

PART THREE

Lane's breakdown. The blue flower. The robot's role in mental illness. Life failure. The importance of 'the beam of intentionality' in mental health. 'Preparedness'. The relationality of consciousness. Consciousness operates at too low a pressure for efficiency. Pessimism. Sartre's view of human motivation: necessary conflict. The self-image. Neurosis as a 'partial self-image'. Refutation of Sartre. Rubinstein and Best's planaria experiment. 'Anybody can become a peaker.' Use of the self-image to create peaks. Simone de Beauvoir and the mirror. The use of intentionality: Bell's *Before the Dawn*. Intentionality as the decoding of meaning.

NEW PATHWAYS IN PSYCHOLOGY

INTRODUCTORY

Personal Notes on Maslow

SOME TIME IN 1959, I received a letter from an American professor of psychology, Abraham H. Maslow, enclosing some of his papers. He said he had read my book *The Stature of Man*,[1] and liked my idea that much of the gloom and defeat of 20th century literature is due to what I called 'the fallacy of insignificance'. Maslow said this resembled an idea of his own, which he called 'the Jonah complex'. One day, he had asked his students: 'Which of you expects to achieve greatness in your chosen field?' The class looked at him blankly. After a long silence, Maslow said: 'If not you—*who* then?' And they began to see his point. This is the fallacy of insignificance, the certainty that you are unlucky and unimportant, the Jonah complex.

The papers he enclosed looked highly technical; their titles contained words like 'metamotivation', 'synergy', 'eupsychian'. I glanced at them and pushed them aside. Some months later I came across them again: this time, my eye was caught by the term 'peak experience' in one of the titles, and I started to read. It was immediately clear that I'd stumbled upon something important. Maslow explained that, some time in the late thirties, he had been struck by the thought that modern psychology is based on the study of sick people. But since there are more healthy people around than sick people, how can this psychology give a fair idea of the workings of the human mind? It struck him that it might be worthwhile to devote some time to the study of *healthy* people.

'When I started to explore the psychology of health, I picked out the finest, healthiest people, the best specimens of mankind

[1] In England *The Age of Defeat, 1958.*

I could find, and studied them to see what they were like. They were very different, in some ways startlingly different from the average . . .

'I learned many lessons from these people. But one in particular is our concern now. I found that these individuals tended to report having had something like mystic experiences, moments of great awe, moments of the most intense happiness, or even rapture, ecstasy or bliss . . .

'These moments were of pure, positive happiness, when all doubts, all fears, all inhibitions, all tensions, all weaknesses, were left behind. Now self-consciousness was lost. All separateness and distance from the world disappeared as they felt one with the world, fused with it, really belonging to it, instead of being outside, looking in. (One subject said, for instance, "I felt like a member of a family, not like an orphan".)

'Perhaps most important of all, however, was the report in these experiences of the feeling that they had really seen the ultimate truth, the essence of things, the secret of life, as if veils had been pulled aside. Alan Watts has described this feeling as "This is it!", as if you had finally got there, as if ordinary life was a striving and a straining to get some place and this was the arrival, this was Being There! . . . Everyone knows how it feels to want something and not know what. These mystic experiences feel like the ultimate satisfaction of vague, unsatisfied yearnings . . .

'But here I had already learned something new. The little that I had ever read about mystic experiences tied them in with religion, with visions of the supernatural. And, like most scientists, I had sniffed at them in disbelief and considered it all nonsense, maybe hallucinations, maybe hysteria—almost surely pathological.

'But the people telling me . . . about these experiences were not such people—they were the healthiest people! . . . And I may add that it taught me something about the limitations of the small . . . orthodox scientist who won't recognise as knowledge, or as reality, any information that doesn't fit into the already existent science.'[1]

[1] I have used an extract from a paper, 'Lessons from the Peak Experience', read in 1961 at the Western Behavioural Sciences Institute, La Jolla, California. It has not yet been printed in book form.

These experiences are not 'religious' in the ordinary sense. They are *natural*, and can be studied naturally. They are not 'ineffable' in the sense of incommunicable by language. Maslow also came to believe that they are far commoner than one might expect, that many people tend to suppress them, to ignore them, and certain people seem actually afraid of them, as if they were somehow feminine, illogical, dangerous. 'One sees such attitudes more often in engineers, in mathematicians, in analytic philosophers, in book-keepers and accountants, and generally in obsessional people.'

The peak experience tends to be a kind of bubbling-over of sheer delight, a moment of pure happiness. 'For instance, a young mother scurrying around her kitchen and getting breakfast for her husband and young children. The sun was streaming in, the children, clean and nicely dressed, were chattering as they ate. The husband was casually playing with the children: but as she looked at them she was suddenly so overwhelmed with their beauty and her great love for them, and her feeling of good fortune, that she went into a peak experience . . .

'A young man working his way through medical school by drumming in a jazz band reported many years later, that in all his drumming he had three peaks when he suddenly felt like a great drummer and his performance was perfect.

'A hostess after a dinner party where everything had gone perfectly and it had been a fine evening, said goodbye to her last guest, sat down in a chair, looked around at the mess, and went into a peak of great happiness and exhilaration.'

Maslow described another typical peak experience to me later, when I met him at his home in Waltham, Mass. A marine had been stationed in the Pacific and had not seen a woman for a couple of years. When he came back to the base camp, he saw a nurse, and it suddenly struck him with a kind of shock that women are different to men. The marine had told Maslow: 'We take them for granted, as if they were another kind of man. But they're quite different, with their soft curves and gentle natures . . .' He was suddenly flooded with the peak experience.

Observe that in most peak experiences (Maslow abbreviates it to P.E.'s, and I shall follow him), the person becomes suddenly *aware* of something that he had known about previously, but been inclined to take for granted, to discount. And

this matter had always been one of my own central preoccupations. My *Religion and the Rebel* (1957) had been largely a
study in the experiences of mystics, and in its autobiographical
preface, I had written about a boring office job: 'As soon as I
grew used to it, I began to work automatically. I fought hard
against this process. I would spend the evening reading poetry,
or writing, and would determine that, with sufficient mental
effort, I could stop myself from growing bored and indifferent
at work the next day. But the moment I stepped through the
office door in the morning, the familiar smell and appearance
would switch on the automatic pilot which controlled my
actions . . .' I was clearly aware that the problem was *automatism*. And in a paper I later wrote for a symposium of existential psychology,[1] I elaborated this theory of the automatic
pilot, speaking of it as 'the robot'. I wrote: 'I am writing this on
an electric typewriter. When I learned to type, I had to do it
painfully and with much nervous wear and tear. But at a certain stage, a miracle occurred, and this complicated operation
was 'learned' by a useful robot whom I conceal in my subconscious mind. Now I only have to think about what I want
to say: my robot secretary does the typing. He is really very
useful. He also drives the car for me, speaks French (not very
well), and occasionally gives lectures in American universities.

'He has one enormous disadvantage. If I discover a new
symphony that moves me deeply, or a poem or a painting,
this bloody robot promptly insists on getting in on the act. And
when I listen to the symphony for the third time, *he* begins to
anticipate every note. He begins to listen to it automatically,
and I lose all the pleasure. He is most annoying when I am tired,
because then he tends to take over most of my functions without
even asking me. I have even caught him making love to my
wife.

'My dog doesn't have this trouble. Admittedly, he can't
learn languages or how to type, but if I take him for a walk on
the cliffs, he obviously experiences every time just as if it is the
first. I can tell this by the ecstatic way he bounds about.
Descartes was all wrong about animals. It isn't the animals who
are robots; it's us.'

[1] 'Existential Psychology: A Novelist's Approach', in *Challenges of Humanistic
Psychology* edited by J. F. T. Bugental, McGraw Hill, 1967.

Heaven lies about us in our infancy, as Wordsworth pointed out, because the robot hasn't yet taken over. So a child experiences delightful things as more delightful, and horrid things as more horrid. Time goes slower, and mechanical tasks drag, because there is no robot to take over. When I asked my daughter if she meant to be a writer when she grew up, she said with horror that she got fed up before she'd written half a page of school-work, and couldn't even imagine the tedium of writing a whole book.

The robot is necessary. Without him, the wear and tear of everyday life would exhaust us within minutes. But he also acts as a filter that cuts out the freshness, the newness, of everyday life. If we are to remain psychologically healthy, we must have streams of 'newness' flowing into the mind—what J. B. Priestley calls 'delight' or 'magic'. In developing the robot, we have solved one enormous problem—and created another. But there is, after all, no reason why we should not solve that too: modify the robot until he admits the necessary amount of 'newness', while still taking over the menial tasks.

Now I was much struck by Maslow's comment on the possibility of *creating* peak experiences at will. Because his feeling was that it cannot be done. 'No! Or almost entirely no! In general, we are "Surprised by Joy", to use the title of C. S. Lewis's book on just this question. Peaks come unexpectedly . . . You can't count on them. And hunting them is like hunting happiness. It's best not done directly. It comes as a by-product, an epiphenomenon, for instance, of doing a fine job at a worthy task you can identify with.'

It seemed to me that this is only partly true. I will try to explain this briefly.

Novelists have to be psychologists. I think of myself as belonging to the school known as the phenomenological movement. The philosopher Edmund Husserl noted that all psychological acts are 'intentional'. Note what happens when you are about to tickle a child. The child begins to squirm and laugh before your hands have actually reached him. On the other hand, why doesn't it tickle when you tickle yourself? Obviously, because you know it's you. The tickling is not something *physical* that happens when your hands encounter flesh and make tickling motions. It seems to be 99% psychological. When the child screams with laughter, *he is tickling himself,* just as he might frighten himself by imagining ghosts in the dark. The paradoxical truth is that when someone tickles you, you tickle yourself. And when you tickle yourself, you don't tickle yourself, which is why it doesn't tickle.

Being tickled is a 'mental act', an 'intention'. So are all perceptions. I look *at* something, as I might fire a gun at it. If I glance at my watch while I am in conversation, I see the time, yet I don't *notice* what time it is. As well as merely 'seeing' I have to make a mental act of *grasping.*

Now the world is full of all kinds of things that I cannot afford to 'grasp' or notice. If I am absorbed in a book, I 'grasp' its content; my mind explores it as though my thoughts were fine, thin tentacles reaching every corner of the book. But when I put the book back on the shelf, it is standing among dozens of other books, which I have also explored at some time in the past. As I look at all these books, I cannot simultaneously grasp all of them. From being intimate friends, they have become mere nodding acquaintances. Perhaps one or two, of which I am very fond, mean more to me than the others. But of necessity, it has to be very few.

Consider Maslow's young mother getting the breakfast. She loves her husband and children, but all the same, she is directing her 'beam of interest' at making the coffee, buttering the toast, watching the eggs in the frying pan. She is treating her husband and children as if they were a row of books on a shelf. Still, her energies are high; she is looking forward to an interesting day. Then something triggers a new level of response. Perhaps it is the beam of sunlight streaming through the window, which seems to shake her arm and say: 'Look—isn't it all wonderful?' She suddenly looks *at* her husband and children as she would look at the clock to find out the time. She becomes self-conscious of the situation, using her beam of interest to 'scan' it, instead of to watch the coffee. And having put twice as much energy into her 'scanning', she experiences 'newness'.

The mental act of looking *at* her family, and thinking: 'I am lucky', is like an athlete gathering himself for a long jump, concentrating his energies.

What happens if somebody returns a book that he borrowed from me a long time ago? I look at the book with a kind of delight, as though it were a returned prodigal: perhaps I open it and read a chapter. Yet if the book had stayed on my shelf for six months I might not even have bothered to glance at it. The return of the book has made me focus my beam of interest, like an athlete gathering for a leap.

When something occupies my full attention, it is very *real* to me. When I have put the book back on the shelf, I have un-real-ised it, to some extent. I have pushed it back to a more abstract level of reality. But I have the power to real-ise it again. Consider the mental act I make when I feel glad to see the book again. I 'reach out' my invisible mental tentacles to it, as I might reach out my hand to a friend I am delighted to see, and I *focus* my beam of interest on it with a kind of intensity— the kind of intentness with which a sapper de-fuses an unexploded bomb.

We do this 'real-ising' and 'un-real-ising' all the time—so automatically that we fail to notice that *we* are doing it. It is not just 'happening'. Like the athlete gathering himself to leap, it is the deliberate compression of mental muscles.

All this suggests that Maslow is mistaken to believe that peak experiences have to 'come' without being sought. A little phenomenological analysis, like the kind we have conducted above, reveals that the P.E. has a structure that can be duplicated. It is the culmination of a series of mental acts, each of which can be clearly defined.

The first pre-condition is 'energy', because the P.E. is essentially an overflowing of energy. This does not mean ordinary physical energy; Maslow points out that sick people can have P.E's as easily as healthy ones, if the conditions are right. If you say to a child: 'I'll take you to the pantomime tonight if you'll tidy your bedroom', he immediately seethes with a bustling energy. The normally boring act of tidying a room is performed with enthusiasm. And this is because he—figuratively— 'takes a deep breath'. He is so determined that the tidying shall be satisfactory that he is prepared to devote attention to every square inch of the floor. And the 'mental act' that lies behind this is a certain concentration and 'summoning of energy', like calling 'All hands on deck'. If I am asked to do a job that bores me, I summon only a small quantity of energy, and if the job is complicated, I skimp it. If I am determined to do it thoroughly, I place the whole of my interior army and navy 'on call'. It is this state—of vigilance, alertness, *preparedness*—that is the basis of the peak experience.

Healthy people—like Maslow's housewife—are people with a high level of 'preparedness'. This can be expressed in a simple image. My 'surplus energy' is stored in my subconscious mind, in the realm of the robot: this is like money that has been invested in stocks and shares. Nearer the surface of everyday consciousness, there are 'surplus energy tanks', energy which is ready-for-use, like money in my personal account at the bank. When I anticipate some emergency, or some delightful event (like a holiday) which I shall need energy to enjoy to the full, I transfer large quantities of 'ready energy' to these surface tanks, just as I might draw a large sum out of the bank before I go on holiday.

'Peakers' are people with large quantities of energy in the ready-energy tanks. Bored or miserable people are people who keep only small amounts of energy for immediate use.

But it must be borne in mind that both types of people have large amounts of energy available in their '*deep* storage tanks' in the realm of the robot. It is merely a matter of transferring it to your 'current account'.

In a paper called 'The Need to Know and the Fear of Knowing', Maslow describes one of his crucial cases.

'Around 1938, a college girl patient presented herself complaining vaguely of insomnia, lack of appetite, disturbed menstruation, sexual frigidity, and a general malaise which soon turned into a complaint of boredom with life and an inability to enjoy *anything*. Life seemed meaningless to her. Her symptoms closely paralleled those described by Abraham Myerson in his book *When Life Loses Its Zest* . . . As she went on talking, she seemed puzzled. She had graduated about a year ago and by a fantastic stroke of luck—this was the depression, remember —she had immediately got a job. And what a job! Fifty dollars a week! She was taking care of her whole unemployed family with the money and was the envy of all her friends. But what was the job? She worked as a sub-personnel manager in a chewing-gum factory. And after some hours of talking, it became more and more clear that she felt she was wasting her life. She had been a brilliant student of psychology and was very happy and successful in college, but her family's financial situation made it impossible for her to go on into graduate studies. She was greatly drawn to intellectual work, not altogether consciously at first because she felt she *ought* to feel fortunate with her job and the money it brought her. Half-consciously then she saw a whole lifetime of greyness stretching out ahead of her. I suggested that she might be feeling profoundly frustrated and angry simply because she was not being her own very intelligent self, that she was not using her intelligence and her talent for psychology and that this might well be a major reason for her boredom with life and her body's boredom with the normal pleasures of life. Any talent, any capacity, I thought, was also a motivation, a need, an impulse. With this she agreed, and I suggested that she could continue her graduate studies at night after her work. In brief, she was able to arrange this and it worked well. She became more alive, more happy and zestful, and most of her physical symptoms had disappeared at my last contact with her.'

It is significant that Maslow, although trained as a Freudian, did not try to get back into the subject's childhood and find out whether she experienced penis-envy of her brothers or a desire to murder her mother and marry her father. He followed his instinct—his feeling that creativeness and the desire for a *meaningful existence* are as important as any subconscious sexual drives.

Anyone who knows my own work will see why Maslow's approach appealed so much to me—and why mine, apparently, appealed to Maslow. My first book, *The Outsider*, written when I was 23, was about people like Maslow's girl patient—men driven by an obscure creative urge that made them dissatisfied with everyday life, and which in some cases—T. E. Lawrence, for example—caused them to behave in a manner that seemed masochistic. The book sprang from my own obsession with the problem of 'life failure'. Auden wrote:

'Put the car away; when life fails
What's the good of going to Wales?'

Eliot asks in *The Rock*: 'Where is the life we have lost in living?' And Shaw says of the Ancients in *Back to Methuselah*: 'Even at the moment of death, their life does not fail them.' Maslow's patient was suicidal because she felt she was losing her life in the process of living it. Quite clearly, we were talking about the same thing. I had asked repeatedly in *The Outsider*: '*Why* does life fail?' Maslow was replying, in effect: Because human beings have needs and cravings that go beyond the need for security, sex, territory. He states it clearly in the preface to the Japanese edition of *Eupsychian Management*, asserting that 'human nature has been sold short, that man has a higher nature which is just as 'instinctoid' as his lower nature, and that this higher nature includes the need for meaningful work, for responsibility, for creativeness, for being fair and just, for doing what is worthwhile and for preferring to do it well.'

I must outline my own approach to this problem, as I explained it in subsequent correspondence with Maslow. *The Outsider* had developed from my interest in the romantics of the 19th century—Goethe, Schiller, Novalis, Wagner, Nietzsche, Van Gogh. What fascinated me was their *world rejection*. It was summed up by Villiers de l'Isle-Adam's hero Axel in the words 'Live? Our servants can do that for us.' Axel asserted that 'real life' is always a disappointment. The heroine, Sarah, has a long speech in which she speaks of all the marvellous places they might visit now they have found the treasure. Axel replies that the cold snows of Norway *sound* marvellous, but when you actually get there, it's just cold and wet. L. H. Myers had made the same point with fine precision in *The Near and the Far*, where the young Prince Jali stares at a splendid sunset over the desert, and reflects that there are two deserts: one that is a glory to the eye, and one that is a weariness to the feet. If you tried rushing towards that sunset, you would only get your shoes full of sand. It seems impossible to grasp 'the promise of the horizon'. And it was this feeling of despair about the near and the far—the feeling that they can never be reconciled—that led to so many early deaths among the romantics: suicide, insanity, tuberculosis. Obermann, in Senancour's novel of that name, says that the rain depresses him, yet when the sun comes out it strikes him as 'useless'. *This* is life-failure.

But man's achievement is to have created a world of the mind, of the intellect and imagination, which is as real in its way as any actual country on the map. Sir Karl Popper, in one of his most important papers, calls it 'the third world.'[1] The first world is the objective world of things. The second world is my inner subjective world. But, says Popper, there is a third world, *the world of objective contents of thoughts*. If some catastrophe destroyed all the machines and tools on this earth, but *not* the libraries, a new generation would slowly rebuild civilisation. If the libraries are all destroyed too, there could be no re-emergence of civilisation, for all our carefully stored knowledge would have gone, and man would have to start regaining it from scratch. Teilhard de Chardin calls this 'third world' the noösphere—the world of mind. It includes the works of Newton, Einstein, Beethoven, Tolstoy, Plato; it is the most important part of our human heritage.

A cow inhabits the physical world. It has almost no mind, to speak of. Man also inhabits the physical world, and has to cope with its problems. But he has built civilisation because *the physical world is not enough*. Nothing is so boring as to be stuck in the present. Primitive man loved stories for the same reason that young children do. Because they afforded an escape from the present, because they freed his memory and imagination from mere 'reality'. Einstein made the same point: '. . . one of the strongest motives that lead men to art and science is to escape from everyday life, with its painful crudity and hopeless dreariness . . . A finely tempered nature longs to escape from personal life into the world of objective perception and thought; this desire may be compared to the townsman's irresistible longing to escape from his noisy, cramped surroundings into the silence of high mountains . . .'[2]

But my central point is this. Man is a very *young* creature: his remotest ancestors only date back two million years. (The shark has remained unchanged for 150,000,000 years.) And although he longs for this 'third world' as his natural home, he only catches brief glimpses of it. For it can only be 'focused' by a kind of mental eye. This morning, as I cleaned my teeth in the bathroom a fragment of Brahms drifted through my head

1 *Epistemology without a Knowing Subject*, Amsterdam 1968.
2 Einstein, *Ideas and Opinions*, London, 1956, p. 227.

and caused that sudden feeling of inner-warmth. The person labelled 'Colin Wilson' ceased to matter: it was almost as if I had floated out of my body and left him behind, as if the real 'I' had taken up a position somewhere midway between myself and Brahms. In the same way, when I am working well, I seem to lose my identity, 'identifying' instead with the ideas or people I am writing about. But very often, I cannot even begin to focus the 'third world'; the real world distracts me, and keeps my attention fixed on its banal 'actualities' like some idiot on a train who prevents you from reading by talking in a loud voice.

All the same, this 'third world' is a *place*; it is there all the time, like China or the moon; and it ought to be possible for me to go there at any time, leaving behind the boring person who is called by my name. It is fundamentally a world of pure *meaning*. It is true that my small personal world is also a world of meaning; but of trivial, personal meaning, distorted and one-sided, a worm's eye view of meaning.

It is man's evolutionary destiny to become a citizen of the third world, to explore it as he might now explore Switzerland on a holiday.

It is impossible to predict what will happen to human beings when that time comes: for this reason. Meaning stimulates the will, fills one with a desire to reach out to new horizons. When a man in love sees the girl approaching, his heart 'leaps'. When I hear a phrase of music that means something to me, my heart leaps. That 'leap' is vitality from my depths, leaping up to meet the 'meaning'. And the more 'meaning' I perceive, the more vitality rushes up to meet it. As his access to the world of meaning increases, man's vitality will increase towards the superman level; that much seems clear.

Boredom cripples the will. Meaning stimulates it. The peak experience is a sudden surge of meaning. The question that arises now is: how can I *choose* meaning? If Maslow is correct, I can't. I must be 'surprised' by it. It is a by-product of effort.

At this point, I was able to point out to Maslow a possibility that he had overlooked, a concept I called 'the indifference threshold' or 'St Neot margin'. It is fundamentally a recognition *that crises or difficulties can often produce a sense of meaning when more pleasant stimuli have failed.* Sartre remarks that he had never felt so free as during the war when, as a member of the French Resistance, he was likely to be arrested and shot at any time. It seems a paradox: that danger can make you feel free when peace and serenity fail to arouse any response. It does this by forcing you to concentrate.

I stumbled on this concept in the following manner. In 1954, I was hitch-hiking to Peterborough on a hot Saturday afternoon. I felt listless, bored and resentful: I didn't want to go to Peterborough—it was a kind of business trip—and I didn't particularly long to be back in London either. There was hardly any traffic on the road, but eventually I got a lift. Within ten minutes, there was an odd noise in the engine of the lorry. The driver said: 'I'm afraid something's gone wrong— I'll have to drop you off at the next garage.' I was too listless to care. I walked on, and eventually a second lorry stopped for me. Then occurred the absurd coincidence. After ten minutes or so, there was a knocking noise from *his* gearbox. When he said: 'It sounds as if something's wrong', I thought: 'Oh *no!*' and then caught myself thinking it, and thought: 'That's the first definite reaction I've experienced today.' We drove on slowly—he was anxious to get to Peterborough, *and by this time, so was I.* He found that if he dropped speed to just under twenty miles an hour, the knocking noise stopped; as soon as he exceeded it, it started again. We both listened intently for any resumption of the trouble. Finally, as we were passing through a town called St Neots, he said: 'Well, I think if we stay at this speed, we should make it.' And I felt a surge of delight. Then I thought: 'This is absurd. My situation hasn't *improved* since I got into the lorry—in fact, it has got worse, since he is now crawling along. All that has happened is that an inconvenience has been threatened, and then the threat withdrawn. And suddenly, my boredom and indifference have vanished.' I formulated then the notion that there is a borderland or threshold of the mind that can be stimulated by pain or inconvenience, but not pleasure. (After all, the lorry originally stopping for me failed to arouse a response of gratitude.) I labelled it 'the indifference threshold' or—after the place I was travelling through at the time—the St Neot margin.

All that had happened, of course, was that the threat of a

second breakdown had made me *concentrate my attention*. I spent a quarter of an hour listening intently to the engine. The threatened 'crisis' made me use my focusing-muscle, instead of allowing it to remain passive. Relaxing it—when he said we could probably make it—caused a rush of pleasure.

The same applies to Sartre. The constant danger of arrest kept him at a high level of *alertness*, of tension. Maslow's girl patient became so bored with her job in the chewing gum factory that she allowing the focusing-muscle to go permanently flaccid.

If you allow the will to remain passive for long periods, it has the same effect as leaving your car in the garage for the winter. The batteries go flat. When the batteries go flat, 'life fails'.

These 'focusing muscles' must be used if we are to stay healthy, for they are the means by which the mind focuses on values, just as the eye muscles enable the eye to focus on distant objects. If we fail to use them for long periods, the result is a kind of mental short-sightedness, a gradual loss of the feeling of the reality of values, of meaning. This explains what happens if you watch television for too long, or read a very long book on a dull winter day until your eyes are aching. Your 'meaning focus' relaxes as your interest flags, and if you then go for a walk, everything seems oddly meaningless and dull. It just 'is', and it doesn't arouse any response.

The Greek poet Demetrios Capetanakis wrote in the early forties: '"Well," I thought when the war started, trying to hope for the best, "it will be horrible, but if it will be so horrible as to frighten and wake up the mind, it will be the salvation of many. Many are going to die, *but those who are going to survive will have a real life, with the mind awake*" . . . But I was mistaken . . . The war is very frightening, but it is not frightening enough.'

The same thought struck me when I read the article Camus wrote for the resistance paper *Combat* when the Germans were being driven out of Paris.[1] It is called 'The Night of Truth' and is full of noble phrases. The skyline of Paris is blazing, he says, but these are the flames of freedom. 'Those who never despaired of themselves or of their country find their reward under this sky . . . the great virile brotherhood of recent years will never forsake us . . . man's greatness . . . lies in his decision to be

[1] Reprinted in *Resistance, Rebellion and Death*.

stronger than his condition', and so on. But Simone de Beauvoir's novel *The Mandarins* begins shortly after the liberation,
and Camus is one of the characters. And they drift around the
night spots of St Germain and drink too much and smoke too
much and waste time on pointless adulteries. What had happened to the Night of Truth?

The answer is simple. Without the danger and injustice to
keep the mind alert, they allowed a kind of inner-laziness to
descend.

But didn't Camus *remember* their feelings about a completely
different kind of future? The answer is: in the real sense of the
word, no. Real memory brings a sense of meanings and values
with it. False memory recalls the 'facts', but without their inner
content of meaning. It must be squarely recognised that man
suffers from *a very real form of amnesia*. This is not a figure of
speech but a reality. For the 'meaning' depends upon the
mind's power of 'focusing'.

Must we, then, draw the pessimistic conclusion that mankind
needs war and injustice to prevent him from lapsing into a condition of boredom, or at least, of preoccupation with trivialities?

The answer, fortunately, is no. 'Focusing' is a muscle, and it
can be strengthened like any other muscle. Graham Greene, in
an essay I have often quoted, describes how, in his teens, he sank
into a condition of extreme boredom and depression, during
which life became meaningless. He tried playing Russian roulette with his brother's revolver, inserting only one bullet,
spinning the chambers, pointing it at his head and pulling the
trigger. When there was just a click, he was overwhelmed by a
feeling of delight, and a sense of the meaningfulness of life. The
situation is fundamentally the same as in my 'St Neot margin'
experience in the lorry, except that Greene's concentration was
more intense, because the negative stimulus was greater. At a
later stage, I discovered that a mild peak experience could
easily be induced merely by concentrating hard on a pencil,
then relaxing the attention, then concentrating again ... After
doing this a dozen or so times, the attention becomes fatigued—
if you are doing it with the right degree of concentration—and
a few more efforts—deliberately ignoring the fatigue—trigger
the peak experience. After all, concentration has the effect of
summoning energy from your depths. It is the 'pumping'

motion—of expanding and contracting the attention—that causes the peak experience.

Another interesting point arose when I was lecturing to Maslow's class at Brandeis University in early 1967. I was speaking about the peculiar power of the human imagination. I can imagine trapping my thumb in the door, and wince as if I had actually done it. I can go to see a film, and come out of the cinema feeling as if I have been on a long journey. Even so, it must be admitted that imagination only provides a dim carbon copy of the original experience. I may try to recall a particularly happy day, and even re-experience some of its pleasures; but compared to the original experience, it is like paste jewellery compared to the real thing. The hero of Barbusse's novel *Hell*, trying to recall the experience of watching a woman undress, admits: 'These words are all dead. They leave untouched, powerless to affect it, the intensity of what was'. Proust, tasting a madeleine dipped in tea, recalls with sudden intensity the reality of his childhood: but that is a fluke. He cannot do it by an ordinary act of imagination.

Yet the matter of sex appears to be an exception to this rule. A man can conjure up some imaginary scene with a girl undressing, and he responds physically as if there *were* a girl undressing in the room: his imagination can even carry him to the point of a sexual climax. In this one respect, man has completely surpassed the animals: here is a case where the mental 'act' needs no object . . .

At this point, Maslow interrupted me to point out that this is not quite true; monkeys often masturbate. I asked him if he had ever seen a monkey masturbating in total isolation, without the stimulus of a female monkey anywhere in the vicinity. He thought for a moment, then said he hadn't.

Even if he had, it would not have basically affected my point. If monkeys can do problems for fun, perhaps they have more imagination than we give them credit for. But the interesting point is that in the matter of sex, man can achieve repeatedly what Proust achieved momentarily tasting the madeleine: a physical response *as if* to reality. Absurd as it sounds, masturbation is one of the highest faculties mankind has yet achieved. But its importance is in what it presages: that one day, the imagination will be able to achieve this result in *all* fields. If all perception is 'intentional', due to a 'reaching out', a 'focusing', on the part of the perceiver, then it ought to be possible to reconstruct any reality by making the necessary effort of focusing. We have only been kept from this recognition by the old, false theory of 'passive perception'.

Anyone who did chemistry at school will recall what happens if you mix sulphur and iron filings, and then heat them in a crucible. A small area of the sulphur melts and fuses with the iron. At that point, you can remove the flame of the bunsen burner; the reaction will continue of its own accord; the glow slowly spreads throughout the mixture until the whole crucible is red hot, and the end result is a chunk of iron sulphide. The same process goes on in the mind when we become deeply interested in anything. The warm glow produced by favourite poetry or music is often the beginning of this fusing process.

We are all familiar with the process of a wider glimpse of 'meaning' leading to the revitalising of the will. This, in fact, is why people need holidays. As life drags on repetitively, they get tired; they stop making effort; it is the *will* that gets run down. The holiday 'reminds' them of wider meanings, reminds them that the universe is a vast spider's web of meaning, stretching infinitely in all directions. And quite suddenly they are enjoying *everything* more: eating, reading, walking, listening to music, having a beer before dinner. The 'meaning' sharpens the appetite for life—that is, the will to live.

It is our misfortune that we are not equally familiar with the reverse process: that a deliberate increase in willed concentration can *also* start the 'fusion' process working. This is, in fact, common sense. The deeper my sense of the 'meaningfulness' of the world, the fiercer and more persistent my will. And increased effort of will leads in turn to increased sense of meaning. It is a chain reaction. So is the reverse, when 'discouragement' leads me to stop willing, and the passivity leads to a narrowed sense of meaning, and the gradual loss of 'meaning' leads to further relaxation of the will. The result is a kind of 'down staircase' of apathy. On the other hand, any intense glimpse of meaning can cause a transfer to the 'up staircase'. This is most strikingly illustrated in an experiment that Maslow's colleague,

Dr. A Hoffer, carried out with alcoholics.[1] Hoffer reasoned that alcoholics may be people of more-than-average intelligence and sensitivity. Because of this, they find that life is too much for them, and they drink because at first it produces peak experiences. But as often as not it doesn't; then they drink more to increase the stimulus, and become involved in guilt and depression. Hoffer tried giving these alcoholics mescalin—producing a far more powerful 'lift' than alcohol—and then deliberately induced peak experiences by means of music, poetry, painting—whatever used to produce P.E's before the subject became alcoholic. The startling result was that more than 50% were cured. The peak experience is an explosion of *meaning*, and meaning arouses the will, which in turn reaches out towards further horizons of meaning. The alcoholic drinks because he wants peak experiences, but he is, in fact, running away from them as fast as he can go. Once his sense of direction had been restored, he ceased to be alcoholic, recognising that *peak experiences are in direct proportion to the intensity of the will.*

And what should be quite clear is that there is no theoretical limit to the 'chain reaction'. Why does a man get depressed? Because at a certain point, he feels that a certain difficulty is 'not worth the effort'. As he becomes more discouraged, molehills turn into mountains until, as William James says, life turns into one tissue of impossibilities, and the process called nervous breakdown begins. Having recognised that the cause of the trouble lies in the collapse of the will, there is no theoretical reason why the ex-alcoholic should come to a halt with the achievement of 'normality'.

There is, of course, a practical reason. The will needs a *purpose*. Why do we feel so cheerful when we are planning a holiday—looking at maps, working out what to pack? Because we have long-distance purpose. One can understand how Balzac must have felt when he first conceived the idea of creating the *Comédie Humain*, the excitement of working out a series of novels about military life, a series about provincial life, a series about

[1] See Maslow's paper 'Fusions of Facts and Values' (1963). See also: 'The Psychedelic Experience—A New Concept in Psychotherapy' by J. N. Sherwood, M. J. Stolaroff and W. W. Harman, *Journal of Neuropsychiatry*, Vol. 4, No. 2, Dec. 1962, and 'Personality Change Associated with Psychedelic (LSD) Therapy: A Preliminary Report' by Robert E. Mogar and Charles Savage, *Psychotherapy*, Vol. 1, No. 4, Autumn 1964.

the aristocracy . . . 'Building castles in the air', this activity is
called; but with a little effort, they actually get built. Man
seems to need long-range purpose to get the best out of himself.
And once the alcoholic has achieved 'normality' again, he may
well say: 'All right, where do I go from here?'

If this were true, it would represent a kind of dead end. For
undoubtedly, our civilisation tends to deprive us of the kind of
long-range purpose that our pioneer ancestors must have enjoyed. But it provides us with something else: the ability to live
on the plane of the mind, the imagination.

And there is a still more important matter we have overlooked: the mind's capacity to *reach out* for meaning. This is
perfectly illustrated by a story told in Romain Gary's novel *The
Roots of Heaven*. In a German concentration camp during the
war, the French prisoners are becoming increasingly demora-
lised: they are on a down-staircase. A man called Robert de-
vises a way to arrest the decline. He suggests that they imagine
an invisible girl in the billet. If one of them swears or farts, he
must bow and apologise to the 'girl'; when they undress, they
must hang up a blanket so she can't see them. Oddly enough,
this absurd game works: they enter into the spirit of the thing,
and morale suddenly rises. The Germans become suspicious of
the men, and by eavesdropping they find out about the invisible girl. The Commandant fancies himself as a psychologist.
He goes along to the billet with two guards, and tells the men:
'I know you have a girl here. That is forbidden. Tomorrow, I
shall come here with these guards, and you will hand her over
to me. She will be taken to the local brothel for German
officers.' When he has gone, the men are dismayed; they know
that if they 'hand her over', they won't be able to re-create her.
The next day the Commandant appears with his two soldiers.
Robert, as the spokesman, says: 'We have decided not to hand
her over'. And the Commandant knows he is beaten: nothing
he can do can force them to hand her over. Robert is arrested
and placed in solitary confinement; they all think they have
seen the last of him, but weeks later, he reappears, very thin
and worn. He explains that he has found the way to resist solitary confinement—their game with the invisible girl has taught
him that the imagination is the power to reach out to *other
realities,* realities not physically present. He has kept himself

from breakdown by imagining great herds of elephants trampling over endless plains . . .

The irony, in the novel, is that it is Robert who later becomes a hunter of elephants. But that is beside the point. The point is that the will *can* make an act of reaching towards meaning, towards 'other realities'.

In phenomenological terms, what actually happened when the prisoners began apologising to the imaginary girl? First of all, they threw off their apathy and entered into a communal game. It was like a coach-load of football fans whiling away a tedious journey with community singing. But having raised their spirits by entering into the game, they also *reminded themselves* of circumstances in which they would normally be 'at their best'. Gorky's story *Twenty Six Men and a Girl* may be regarded as a parable about the same thing: the twenty-six overworked bakers keep up their spirits by idealising the girl, treating her as a goddess. . . . And thereby *reminding themselves* of the response appropriate to a goddess.

And this leads naturally to a concept that has become the core of my own existential psychology: the Self-Image. A man could not climb a vertical cliff without cutting hand-holds in the rock. Similarly, I cannot achieve a state of 'intenser consciousness' merely by wanting to; at least, it is extremely difficult without training. We tend to climb towards higher states of self-awareness by means of a series of self-images. We create a certain imaginary image of the sort of person we would like to be, and then try to live up to the image. 'The great man is the play-actor of his ideals,' says Nietzsche.

One of the clearest expositions of the self-image idea can be found in a story called *The Looking Glass* by the Brazilian novelist Machado de Assis. A young man who has lived all his life in a small village in Brazil is called up for military service. In due course he becomes a lieutenant. When he returns home in his uniform he is the envy of the village; his mother calls him 'My lieutenant'. One of his aunts is particularly delighted with him: she invites him to her remote farm, and insists on addressing him as 'Senhor Lieutenant'. Her brother-in-law and all the slaves follow suit. At first, the youth is embarrassed; he doesn't *feel* like a lieutenant. But gradually he gets used to the idea. 'The petting, the attention, the deference, produced a transformation in me . . .' He begins to feel like a lieutenant.

But one day, the aunt goes away to the bedside of a sick daughter, and takes the brother-in-law with her. The lieutenant is left alone with the slaves. And the next morning, they have all deserted, leaving him alone.

Suddenly, there is no one to feed his ego. He feels lost. In his room there is an enormous mirror, placed there by his aunt. One day he looks in the mirror—and his outline seems blurred and confused. The sense of unreality increases until he is afraid he is going insane. And then he has an inspiration. He takes his lieutenant's uniform from the wardrobe and puts it on. And immediately, his image in the mirror becomes solid and clear. His feeling of sanity and self-respect returns.

Every day thereafter, he puts on the uniform, and sits in front of the mirror. And he is able to stay sane through the remaining week before his aunt returns . . .[1]

Machado subtitles his story 'Rough draft of a new theory of the human soul'. And so it is, for a story written in 1882. His hero explains to his auditors that he believes man has two souls: one inside, looking out, the other outside, looking in. But this is crude psychology. He means that the subjective 'I' gains its sense of identity from actions and outward objects. But this implies that the 'inner me' remains unchanged. This in turn implies that the shy, nervous 'inner self' is the permanent substratum of one's more confident layers of personality, and this is obviously untrue. Shyness is simply a disinclination to express oneself out of fear that it will turn out badly; confidence— such as he gained through the petting and admiration—is the ability to act decisively.

The key sentence is: 'The petting, the attention, the deference, produced a transformation in me.' For this type of transformation, I coined the word 'promotion'. It is, in effect, a promotion of the personality to a higher level. All poetic experience is a 'promotion' experience, since it raises the personality to a higher level. One has a sense of becoming a stronger, or more mature, or more competent, or more serious person.

---

[1] *The Psychiatrist and Other Stories*, translated by William L. Grossman and Helen Caldwell, University of California Press, 1963.

If he had been a lieutenant for several years, being alone in the house would not have eroded his sense of identity. The trouble is that he is young, and that he is only just trying-on a new personality, the 'Senhor Lieutenant'. The image of himself in the looking glass provides the reinforcement he needs.

The resemblance between this story and Romain Gary's story of the prison camp need hardly be pointed out. In both cases, moral decline is arrested by *reminding oneself* of something that re-creates the self-image. The weakness of Machado's theory of two souls becomes clear when we consider that Robert keeps himself sane in solitary confinement by an effort of inner-strength, of imagination, not by evoking a more 'successful' level of his personality. The elephants are an image of freedom. The sensation of freedom is always accompanied by a feeling of *contraction* of one's inner-being. Such a contraction occurs when we concentrate intently upon anything. It also occurs in sexual excitement, and explains why the orgasm is perhaps the most fundamental—at least the most common— 'promotion' experience.

Donald Aldous, the technical editor of a well-known record magazine, told me a story that makes the role of the self-image even clearer. Before the war, the B.B.C. hired a famous conductor to broadcast a series of concerts. They were to be relayed from the new sound-proof studios. The orchestra had never played there before, and the rehearsals lacked vitality. They explained that the studio was too dead: they could not hear the echo of their own playing. Donald Aldous was given the interesting job of arranging a system of loudspeakers around the walls that relayed the sound back to the orchestra a split second after they had played it, like an echo. As soon as they could 'hear themselves', the playing of the orchestra improved enormously.

What is at issue in all such cases is a certain inner-strength. Captain Shotover in *Heartbreak House* tells Ellie Dunne that as a young man, he 'sought danger, hardship, horror and death'—as captain of a whaler—'that I might feel the life in me more intensely'. That is to say, he sought conditions that would keep him at a high level of tension and alertness, so as to develop the inner-muscle of concentration. And note that the function of this muscle is to produce a sense of inner-freedom. When it is feeble, I am easily bored, depressed, made to feel sorry for myself. I am a moral hypochondriac. When it has been strengthened by a long period of alertness and effort, I feel equal to most emergencies, and this is the same as to say that I feel inner-freedom.

The self-image notion is of immediate relevance to Maslovian psychology. And here we touch upon the very heart of the matter, the most important point of all.

Let us consider the question: what is the mechanism by which a 'self-image' produces 'promotion'? The answer is: it provides me with a kind of artificial standard of objective values. It gives me a sense of external *meaning*. Why did the peak experience under mescalin cure the alcoholics? Because the peak experience is a flood of meaning, obviously pouring in from outside. As it pours in, you ask yourself the question: Why doesn't this happen all the time, if the meaning is always there? And the answer is obvious: because I allow the will to become passive, and the senses close up. If I want more meaning, then I must force my senses wide open by an increased effort of will. We might think of the senses as spring-loaded shutters that must be forced open, and which close again when you let them go.

It must be clearly understood that we live in a kind of room of subjective emotions and values. If I am not very careful, the shutters close, and I lose my objective standards. At this point, I may wildly exaggerate the importance of my emotions, my private ups and downs, and there is no feeling of objective reality to contradict me. A child beset by misery is more bewildered than an adult because he has nothing to measure it by; he doesn't know how serious it is. As soon as his mother kisses him and says, 'There, it doesn't really matter . . .', he relaxes. If I get myself 'into a state' about some trivial worry, and then I hear that some old friend has died of cancer, I instantly 'snap out' of my black mood, for my emotions are cut down to their proper size by comparison with a more serious reality.

Moods and emotions are a kind of fever produced by lack of contact with reality. The shutters are closed, and the temperature in the rooms rises. It *can* rise to a degree where it becomes a serious fever, where the emotions have got so out-of-control that reality *cannot* break in. These are states of psychotic delusion—or perhaps merely of nervous overstrain. The characteristic of these states is exaggeration: every minor worry turns into a monstrous bogey. Inevitably, I cease to make efforts of will—for the will is at its healthiest when I have a firm sense of reality and of purpose. And we have seen what happens when the will becomes passive: the vital forces sink, and, at a certain point, physical health is affected. The 'existential psychologist' Viktor Frankl—of whom I shall speak at length later—remarked on 'how close is the connection between a man's state of mind—his courage and hope, or lack of them—and the state of immunity of his body', and tells a story that makes the point forcefully. Frankl was a Jew who spent most of the war in a German concentration camp:

'I once had a dramatic demonstration of the close link between the loss of faith in the future and this dangerous giving up. F——, my senior block warden, a fairly well-known composer and librettist, confided in me one day: "I would like to tell you something, Doctor. I have had a strange dream. A voice told me that I could wish for something, that I should only say what I wanted to know, and all my questions would be answered. What do you think I asked? That I would like to know when the war would be over for me. You know what I mean, Doctor—for me! I wanted to know when we, when our camp, would be liberated and our sufferings come to an end."

'"And when did you have this dream?" I asked.

'"In February, 1945", he answered. It was then the beginning of March.

'"What did your dream voice answer?"

'Furtively he whispered to me, "March thirtieth."

'When F——told me about his dream, he was still full of hope and convinced that the voice of his dream would be right. But as the promised day drew nearer, the war news which reached our camp made it appear very unlikely that we would be free on the promised date. On March twenty-ninth, F—— suddenly became very ill and ran a high temperature. On March thirtieth, the day his prophecy had told him that the war and suffering would be over for him, he became delirious and lost consciousness. On March thirty-first, he was dead. To all outward appearances he had died of typhus.'[1]

Frankl's composer friend was physically near the end of his resources; this is why the collapse of his will made such a difference. (Frankl also mentions the unprecedentedly high death rate in the camp between Christmas 1944 and New Year 1945, because so many prisoners had pinned their hopes on being home for Christmas.) It took a year of work in the chewing-gum factory to deplete Maslow's girl patient to the point where she ceased to menstruate. Normally healthy people possess a 'cushion' of energy to absorb shocks and disappointments, and this cushion is identical to the 'surplus energy tanks' of which we have spoken. It is maintained by will-power fired by the sense of meaning. We are only aware of this *direct* action of the will upon the body in physical extremes: for example, if I am feeling sick, I can disperse the sickness by 'snapping out' of my feeling of nausea and summoning subconscious forces of health. If we were more clearly aware of this connection between 'positive consciousness' and physical health, we would treat mental passivity as a form of illness. Another anecdote of Frankl's—from the same book—may be said to provide the foundation of an 'attitude psychology' closely related to Maslow's. The prisoners were transferred from Auschwitz to Dachau. The journey took two days and three nights, during which they were packed so tight that few could sit down, and half starved. At Dachau, they had to stand in line all night and throughout the next morning in freezing rain, as punishment because one man had fallen asleep and missed the roll call. Yet they were all immensely happy, laughing and making jokes: *because Dachau had no incinerator chimney.*

To summarise: man evolves through a sense of external meaning. When his sense of meaning is strong, he maintains a high level of will-drive and of general health. Without this sense of external meaning, he becomes the victim of subjective emotions, a kind of dream that tends to degenerate into nightmare. His uncontrolled fantasies and worries turn into an octopus that strangles him.

[1] *From Death Camp to Existentialism.* Beacon Press, 1962. Later republished as *Man's Search for Meaning,* revised and enlarged. All quotations are from this later edition.

Man has evolved various ways of preventing this from happening. The most important is religion. This *tells* a man that certain objective standards are permanently true, and that his own nature is weak and sinful. The chief trouble with authoritarian religion is that it works best for intellectually-uncomplicated people, and fails to carry much conviction for the highly sophisticated and neurotic—who are the very ones who need it most.

In certain respects, art succeeds where religion fails. A great symphony or poem is an *active reminder* of the reality of meaning: it provides a stimulus like an electric shock, re-animating the will and the appetite for life. Its disadvantage is that we all assume that art is 'subjective' by nature, that it tells us about the emotions of the artist, not about the objective world. And so 'when life fails', the effectiveness of art diminishes.

Men of imagination have always tended to use the self-image method to prevent them from becoming victims of the octopus of subjectivity. It is essentially a method for pushing problems and disappointments to arm's length. Yeats has described how, when he was sure no one was looking, he used to walk about London with the peculiar strut of Henry Irving's Hamlet. In *Heartbreak House,* Hector whiles away an idle moment by pretending to fight a duel with an imaginary antagonist and then making love to an imaginary woman. But the self-image also plays a central role in all human creativity. The young artist, lacking certainty of his own identity, projects a mental image of himself that blurs into an image of the artist he most admires. Brahms's self-image is half-Beethoven; Yeats's is half-Shelley. And the ultimate value of their work—its inner-consistency and strength—depends upon how deeply they commit themselves to acting out the self-image.

According to Freud and Karl Marx, fantasy is an escape from reality and responsibility. According to Maslow, fantasy is the means by which a determined man masters reality.

'Reality' is the key word in existential psychology. It poses no philosophical problems. It means objective meaning, as opposed to subjective values. Eliot wrote: 'We each think of the key, each in his prison', implying that there is no escape from one's subjective prison. Blake knew better: he agreed that 'five windows light the caverned man', but added that through one of them, he can pass out whenever he wants to. That is to say that by an effort of reaching out to meaning, he can re-establish contact with reality. The situation could be compared to a child who becomes confused during a game of blind man's buff, but who has only to remove the bandage in order to re-orient himself to the room. And the most important point for psychotherapy is that he can do this *by an act of will*. Mental illness is a kind of amnesia, in which the patient has forgotten his own powers. The task of the therapist is to somehow renew the patient's contact with reality.

The first thing that will be observed about this 'third force psychology' I have outlined is that it is a great deal more optimistic than that of Freud, or even Jung. It implies that *all* human beings are closer to more intense states of consciousness than they realise. Somewhere in his autobiography, Stephen Spender remarks that everyone nowadays is neurotic, because it is inevitable at this stage in civilisation. Maslow's feeling seems to be that neurosis is definitely abnormal, and that there is no reason why most people should not be capable of a high level of mental health and of peak experiences.

Among intelligent people, our cultural premises are certainly largely responsible for the prevailing pessimism. The Victorians went in for moral uplift and the belief in man's higher nature. Darwin and Freud changed all that. Darwin showed that we do not need the postulate of a creator to explain why man is superior to the ape. Freud denounced religion as a delusion based upon the child's fear of the father, and asserted that neurosis is due to the frustration of man's animal nature—specifically, his sex drives. After the First World War, despair and frustration became the keynote of literature; the optimists of the previous decade—Shaw, Wells, Chesterton—became almost unmentionable. In science, philosophy, psychology, there was an increasing tendency to 'reductionism'—which Arthur Koestler has defined as the belief that all human activities can be explained in terms of the elementary responses of the lower animals, such as the psychologist's laboratory rat. This reductionism should not be construed as a materialistic jibe at idealism —although it often looks like that—but as *a desire to get things done*, accompanied by the fear that nothing will get done if too much is attempted. Maslow told me once that a respectable psychologist had leapt to his feet at a meeting of the American Psychological Association, and shouted at him—Maslow—'You are an evil man. You want to destroy psychology.' The irony of the story is that by the time Maslow told it to me, he was president of the American Psychological Association! The old reductionist climate began to change in the early sixties. In Europe, the school of existential psychology was already well established. Sir Karl Popper—one of the original founders of the school of Logical Positivism—was arguing that science is not a plodding, logical, investigation of the universe, but that it proceeds by flashes of intuition, like poetry. Popper's most distinguished follower, Michael Polanyi, published in 1958 his revolutionary book *Personal Knowledge*, a carefully reasoned attack on the 'timetable or telephone directory conception of science'—i.e. the view that all future books on science could be written by an electronic brain, if it was big enough. Polanyi stated that what drives the scientist is *an increasing sense of contact with reality*—that is to say, precisely what drives the poet or the saint. In biology, the old rigid Darwinism began to relax; in 1965, Sir Alister Hardy, an orthodox Darwinian, and Professor of Zoology at Oxford, asserted in his Gifford Lectures that the genes might be influenced by telepathy, and that certain biological phenomena are only explainable on the assumption of some kind of 'group mind'. 'Reductionism' was breaking apart.

It was in 1968 that an American publisher suggested to me that I should write a book about Maslow. I asked him how he felt about the idea, and he approved—pointing out, at the same time, that another friend, Frank Goble, was also writing one. I decided to go ahead all the same, and Maslow patiently answered the questions I threw at him through 1969, although a heart attack had slowed him up considerably. At my suggestion, he made a pile of tapes, full of biographical and personal details, some for publication, some not. Meanwhile, I was reading my way steadily through a hundred or so papers he had sent me, dating back to the early thirties, when he was working on monkeys with Harry Harlow. But when I started writing the book, in Majorca, in the autumn of 1969, I realised that it was going to be more difficult than I had expected. I had intended to make it a straight account of Maslow's life and work, a short book that would stick to my subject. But, after all, Viktor Frankl was also part of the subject, and so were Erwin Straus, Medard Boss, William Glasser, Ronald Laing, and many other existential psychologists. Worse still, it was hard to keep myself out of it, since Maslow's work had exerted so much influence on my own ideas, and since we had been engaged in a fragmentary dialogue for the past ten years.

In June, 1969, I told Maslow in a letter that it looked as if my book about him was going to be part of a larger book about the revolution in psychology, and asked more questions, which he answered on tape. A few days before this last batch of tapes arrived, I received a letter from his secretary telling me that he had died of a heart attack on June 8, 1970. Listening to his voice, it was hard to get used to the idea that he was dead.

I am still not certain whether this is the best way to write the book; but I can see no other. In this introduction I have tried to give a sketchy outline of the ideas that preoccupied Maslow— and myself—during the past ten years. In the first part of the book, I have tried to give a picture of the major trends in psychology from its beginnings in the 19th century, through the Freudian revolution, down to Maslow. Part Two deals exclusively with Maslow; it is the book I intended to write to begin with. Part Three discusses existential psychology in general, and attempts to state some general conclusions about the movement. Inevitably, this is the most personal part of the book, and may be regarded as a continuation of this introduction. The ultimate question is not one of psychology so much as of philosophy, or even religion. Viktor Frankl talks about 'the existential vacuum', writing: 'More and more patients are crowding our clinics and consulting rooms complaining of an inner emptiness, a sense of total and ultimate meaninglessness of their lives'. I coined the term 'nothingness neurosis' to describe this state. But in discussing it, I have tried to avoid generalisations, and to remain faithful to the phenomenological—the descriptive—method. That was always Maslow's own approach.

PART ONE

I

The Age of Machinery:
from Descartes to Mill

ACCORDING TO MASLOW, mental health depends upon the will fired by a sense of purpose. When human beings lose their forward drive, the will batteries become flat, just as a car's batteries become flat if it is left in the garage all winter. The result is a feeling of 'life failure', a loss of instinctive values. In Maslow's psychology, the central place is given to the sense of values the human response to *what is worthwhile*.

It is one of the absurd paradoxes of psychology that it has taken three centuries to reach the conclusion that man actually possesses a mind and a will.

Some time in the 1630s, the philosopher Descartes was intrigued by the automata in the royal gardens at Versailles. When the water supply was turned on, musical instruments played: nymphs vanished into the bushes, and a menacing figure of Neptune advanced on the intruder waving a trident. It was not long since Harvey had discovered the circulation of the blood, and many physiologists believed that the nerves were tubes that conducted the 'animal spirits' round the body. Descartes found himself speculating about what distinguishes a man from an automaton, and concluded that it is simply that his mechanisms are more subtle. There was no question, of course, of believing that man is *merely* a machine; as a good Catholic, he knew that man possesses an immortal soul. But it seemed to him highly likely that plants and animals are nothing more than automata, driven by their sensations and desires. Even in man, he wasn't certain where the mechanism ended and the soul began; he decided that the body and soul interact in the brain's pineal gland. The mind, according to Descartes, can exist and think quite apart from the brain.

Descartes was timid by nature. When he heard that Galileo had been seized by the Inquisition for declaring that the earth revolves around the sun, he decided against publishing his own system, contained in a book called *Le Monde*. An expurgated version appeared after his death.

Other thinkers were bolder. Thomas Hobbes, an Englishman and a Protestant, visited Galileo in 1636; although Galileo had recanted his heretical ideas three years before, he was still under house arrest. Hobbes began working on his own system of nature, and it was intended as a blow against religious bigotry. The mind, he said, does not exist, for it is a contradiction to talk about an 'immaterial substance'. Even God, if he exists, must be made of *something*. It follows that thoughts are the motion of some refined substance in the head. Imagination is basically the same thing as memory—a kind of faded snapshot of past events. Both memory and imagination are no more than 'decaying sense', like the after-image you get if you close your eyes after staring at a bright window frame. Moreover, said Hobbes (still defying the Pope), the driving motives of human existence are fear and the desire for power. Generosity and disinterestedness are only more subtle forms of the will to power.

Hobbes, it must be remembered, was a contemporary of Shakespeare and Milton; he lived in an age when the burning of witches—and atheists—was still commonplace. Any scientific man with a mind of his own felt the need to tilt at the colossus of bigotry that still ruled the lives of most people in Europe. The best way of undermining superstition was to continue the work of men like Giordano Bruno and Francis Bacon: to write books glorifying the power of reason. Philosophy, Hobbes said, is a form of calculation that uses words instead of numbers. It has no business with belief or superstitition, only with what can be *known for certain*. Anything worth understanding can be understood scientifically. The scientific definition of a man is not an immortal spirit (saved from damnation by Jesus), but a group of material particles in motion.

All this is not an expression of intellectual defeat or nihilism, but the defiant expression of a credo of freedom. (And even in England, the publication of such ideas was not without its dangers; Hobbes anticipated charges of heresy by fleeing to Paris.) To begin with, 'reductionism' was forged as a weapon of free thought.

Hobbes's friend Lord Herbert of Cherbury wrote books on philosophy that were closer in spirit to Descartes. For Descartes accepted that man has certain ideas that are *not* learned from experience; for example, the idea of God, of right and wrong, of the self, of cause and effect. . . . Herbert of Cherbury interpreted this to mean that God has provided man with certain faculties by means of which he can attain to infallible truth. He is born with innate truth written on his soul, so to speak. This means that he has no need of religious revelation; the use of these faculties is enough to prove the truth of religion. (This doctrine became known as Deism, or Natural Religion.)

John Locke, a younger contemporary of Hobbes, set out to refute this theory. Locke was a member of a club that met to discuss questions of religion and morality. Cherbury's views caused some controversy. Locke supported the view that man has no knowledge that is not learned from experience. At the beginning of his life, the human mind is like a sheet of blank paper, and experience writes on it. Locke wrote an essay explaining this idea and read it to the club; it was received with applause. He decided to expand it, and the result was *An Essay Concerning Human Understanding* (1690), which attempted to do for the human mind what Isaac Newton had recently done for the solar system in his *Principia*: to explain it in terms of *laws*.

Nearly half a century later, Locke's views were carried to new extremes by David Hume—who, for our purposes, is one of the most significant figures in the history of psychology. For Hume's model of the human mind, has influenced every psychologist—directly or otherwise—since the publication of *A Treatise of Human Nature* (1739). Hume went even further than Hobbes in denying the existence of the mind. When he looked inside himself, he said, he did not discover a soul, the 'essential David Hume', but merely sensations and ideas, drifting around like leaves in the wind. Why should there be an essential David Hume, or anybody else? The personality of man is totally shaped by his experience, as mountains are shaped by wind and rain. He derives the idea of his identity from his intercourse with other people. His mental life is only a dim carbon copy of his physical life. What he calls thinking is actually only association of ideas. It follows, of course, that free will is an illusion. It must be, because man has no 'self' to do the willing.

And it was these ideas—that thinking and willing are illusions—that came to mean so much to the psychology of the next two centuries. It certainly looks plausible enough. If I stare out of the window of a train, my thoughts drift along, one thing reminding me of another. Readers of Sherlock Holmes will remember his trick of startling Watson by suddenly breaking in on his thoughts with a remark that proves he knows what Watson is thinking. He does it by watching Watson's eyes wandering round the room, and inferring his 'train of thought' from the expression on his face. And what is a 'train of thought', after all, but an association of ideas? Can we deny that this is how we do most of our thinking?

But surely, we might object, *real* thinking is quite different from daydreaming or free-associating? It *feels* different. I have a sensation of putting more will into it—in fact, of putting more of 'myself' into it than into daydreaming. Hume will, of course, deny this. He will say that 'real thinking' is also association of ideas, and that how much I put into it is neither here nor there. I could not put more into it unless what I was thinking about stimulated and excited me. Everything can be explained in terms of stimulus and response . . .

And this is, I think, the point to state flatly that Hume's theory is ultimately unacceptable. One stage further, and he will be assuring me that I am not alive at all, and that there is no such thing as consciousness. (In fact, William James wrote an essay entitled 'Does "Consciousness" Exist?', and the behavioural psychologist J. B. Watson answered the question in the negative.) It is true that you *could* interpret all thinking as a mechanical process, just as a paranoiac can interpret everything that happens to him as evidence that the whole world is plotting against him. And Archbishop Whately made the same

point in a delightful book called *Historic Doubts Relative to Napoleon Buonaparte*, in which he proves conclusively, by Hume's
method, that Napoleon never existed. With a little skill and
casuistry, *any* proposition can be doubted. It would be possible
for a Martian to argue that the Empire State Building is a
product of the wind and weather, and his arguments would be
irrefutable unless Martians could come to earth and investigate
for themselves. And if we are going to explain the mind as some
kind of 'natural formation', how about the body? What it
amounts to is that our human world is full of *meaningful* objects
—chairs, tables, houses, books—and Hume has invented a
party game whose rules consist in explaining them away as
meaningless, the products of chance. It is amusing as an intellectual exercise, but should not be taken seriously.

As in the case of Hobbes, it is important to understand
Hume's reasons for insisting on the seriousness of his particular
game. By the time he wrote the *Treatise*, witches were no longer
burned, and Isaac Newton had settled the matter of the earth
revolving round the sun once and for all; but the thought of the
age was still dominated by religion. Volumes of sermons were
as popular as novels are today—readers of Boswell will recall
Dr Johnson's discourse on the relative merits of the sermons of
Jortin, Sherlock, Atterbury, Tillotson, South, Seed and Small-
ridge. Hume produced a sceptical essay on miracles whose
avowed intention was to act as 'a check to the most arrogant
bigotry and superstition'. He enjoys baiting the clergy, com-
menting that a wise man proportions his belief to the evidence,
and that a miracle would only be acceptable if the reasons
against it should be more incredible than the reasons in its
favour. In the *Enquiry Concerning the Principles of Morals* (1751)
he asserts—predictably—that moral judgements are purely a
matter of emotion, not of reason. The word 'good' means
either useful or agreeable. It must have given Hume considerable pleasure to read some of the indignant sermons directed
against him. A society dominated by the clergy must have been
almost as intolerable to his precise intellect as a society dominated by television advertisements or women's magazines
would have been. Michael Polanyi's comment about Marxism
applies to Hume's scepticism: '. . . it enables the modern mind,
tortured by moral self-doubt, to indulge its moral passions in

terms which also satisfy its passion for ruthless objectivity'.[1] Hume's feeling for logic and reason *was* a passion.

But did Hume literally believe his demonstration that man possesses no self and no will? If by belief we mean a principle that one lives by, the answer is no. He was a philosopher, and this restricted his field of intellectual vision. If he had been a racing driver, he would have been more aware of the reality of his will and freedom of choice, for a man involved in such a dangerous activity, requiring split-second timing, is aware of dozens of choices that he *could* make—overtaking, braking, cutting-in, accelerating. A racing driver is aware that what does the choosing is not a robot, but a 'self' that looks out from behind his eyes. And as he takes a corner at eighty miles an hour, he knows perfectly well that this self is not merely the sum of all his past sensations and experiences, but that it is somehow over and above them, their *ruler*. Sedentary philosophers fail to notice the importance of the will because thinking uses so little of it. A zoologist whose only knowledge of tigers came from the stuffed ones in museums might be forgiven for failing to emphasise their speed and savagery. It takes an upsurge of powerful feeling to make the mind aware of the importance of willed effort.

It is not even true that it makes no difference to leave the will out of account in psychology, as William James discovered. James was much inclined to Hume's type of sceptical analysis. At the age of twenty-eight, when in a state of depression, he experienced a panic-attack followed by nervous collapse. He describes[2] how he was suddenly struck by 'a horrible fear of my own existence'. He found himself recalling an imbecilic patient he had seen in an asylum, and thinking 'That shape am I, potentially. Nothing that I possess can defend me against that fate, if the hour for it should strike for me as it struck for him.' For months he experienced continual panic, until, on April 29, 1870, he read Renouvier's essay on freedom, and was suddenly convinced by his definition of free will—'the sustaining of a thought *because I choose to* when I might have other thoughts'. He decided that his first act of will would be to believe in free will. A slow recovery commenced. The case bears obvious resemblances to Maslow's case of the girl who ceased to menstruate,

[1] *Personal Knowledge*, p. 228.
[2] *Varieties of Religious Experience*, Chapter 6.

and the element that makes the difference between neurosis and health is again optimistic forward drive. If Hume had really believed in his own theories, he would have ended in mental collapse.

Again, consider the matter of sexual response. At first there seems to be no difficulty in the way of explaining this in terms of associationist psychology. A healthy male sees a strange girl undressing; the image is conveyed to the retina of his eye, to his brain, to his sexual nerves; there is a release of hormones, and the stimulus produces a predictable effect on the sexual organs. It *seems* straightforward enough, until we look more closely. Sex between two intelligent human beings is never as simple as this; they are responding on many levels, and both have other things at the back of their minds. It is far more complicated than any Pavlov-dog mechanism—as one can see, for example, in reading D. H. Lawrence. The various impulses must be channelled, directed, perhaps taken past certain obstacles. There is a story of Maupassant's called *The Unknown* in which a man who is completely obsessed and infatuated with a girl experiences total sexual failure with her—because she has a fine line of black hair down the centre of her back which he sees as she undresses. The Pavlov-dog mechanism only applies to the simplest kind of sex. More complex varieties may require as much 'steering' and judgement as a football player needs as he dribbles the ball towards the goal. The act is *not* preordained for success; there are a hundred possibilities, between supreme success and total failure, and the whole act sweeps forward *on the point of the will*, like a surf rider on a wave. Even the simple process of sexual tumescence is not Pavlovian, as one can see in the Maupassant story; it depends upon mental acts *carried forward* by the will, step by step, and the whole process could be reversed or arrested at any of the steps.

Man already spends most of his time in a state of passivity, hardly aware of his capacity for freedom; this is the price he has paid for his complexity. If Hume's associationism ever came to be *totally* accepted as a picture of the workings of the human mind, all flashes of non-passivity, all peak experiences, would cease.

On the other hand, if man can ever come to grasp how completely he sustains his minute-to-minute, second-to-second existence by means of his will, the result will be a total change in the quality of human consciousness. Consider what happens if I am feeling vaguely sick, and I somehow repress the nausea by an act of will. What exactly do I do? The simplest method is to focus on something that interests me deeply, to try to forget my sickness. For the very act of focusing awakens my impersonal will. And the effect upon the body is instantaneous. It could be compared to those ghosts in M. R. James who get inside the bed sheet and make the sheet rise up and float around the room. When the will is passive, the sheet lies innocently on the bed; the will awakens, and the sheet suddenly rises up with a human shape inside it.

At this point, another aspect of Hume's philosophy must be considered: his belief that we *add* meaning to the world—just as you add milk to a bowl of cornflakes, which would otherwise be dry and uneatable.

Again, the evidence looks convincing. If I hear a tune that reminds me of some happy time in the past, I feel a ripple of pleasure. A child who is with me does not experience the same pleasure, for he is hearing it for the first time, with an 'innocent ear', so to speak. I am getting the pleasure from a certain meaning which I *add* to the tune. A man in love sees all kinds of charms in the lady of his affections; his friends strongly suspect that it is a kind of self-hypnosis, for to them she appears to be just another girl . . . On a spring morning, I go for a walk and see everything as delightful; on my walk I meet a friend who works a night shift in a factory, and he obviously fails to appreciate the charm of the morning because he is tired. In other words, it is my *energy* that makes the difference between delight and indifference, just as a glass of whisky can brighten a dull day.

That is Hume's position. The world is just moving matter. It is pointless to ask whether a sunset is really beautiful, just as it is pointless to ask if it is really red. Redness is a wavelength of light which my eyes *interpret* as redness, and beauty is also 'in the eye of the beholder', not out there.

This leads to what is known as the sense-datum theory of perception. When I say, 'I see that pencil', I mean literally that I perceive a real, solid object. But if someone puts the pencil in a glass of water, it appears to bend in the middle. Would it be true to say, 'I see a bent pencil'? Obviously not: the pencil itself isn't bent. So what is it that I see? The answer is 'a sense datum', an appearance. Sense data can vary. A bar of chocolate tastes sweet to me and bitter to a man with jaundice. Is the chocolate really sweet or bitter? The question is meaningless, says Hume. All I know about the chocolate is what my senses tell me, and my senses are quite capable of telling me lies. For example, they may tell me that a mirage is an oasis.

According to this view, the senses are like an interpreter who accompanies a tourist in a foreign country. The tourist cannot speak the language, so he has to rely on the interpreter for all communication with the natives. And he has no way of knowing how far the interpreter distorts what people say to him or what he tries to say to them. For all he knows, the interpreter may have a malicious sense of humour, and give an absurd twist to everything. If that is so, man can never *know* anything definite; his most cherished certainties may be illusions.

This view, however, is based to some extent upon verbal confusion. The words 'sense data' *mean* that I am aware of something. If I am looking at a red book, then my awareness of red is a sense datum. To say I am 'aware of a sense datum' is to say I am aware of my awareness of red, which is tautologous.[1]

One of Hume's earliest and most penetrating critics rejected the sense datum theory. This was Thomas Reid (1710–1796), another hard-headed Scot, who was also a clergyman. Reid had been much impressed by the arguments of Locke and Bishop Berkeley, but when he read Hume, his common sense revolted. Hume says that consciousness is a series of sensations and impressions that appear to be joined up together because they follow one another. In reality, there is no connection. Consciousness is not even a string of beads; it is a row of beads without a string. Reid denied this: he declared that man's intuition of his consciousness reveals that it is a creative unity, capable of purpose. There *is* a string. And my mind doesn't 'add' meaning to a bowl of dry sense data. It has a direct sense of meaning, of reality. It is common sense for the tourist to assume that his interpreter is translating him more or less

[1] For a more detailed demolition of the theory, see *Sense and Sensibilia* by J. L. Austin (1962).

accurately—certainly more sensible than assuming, on no evidence whatever, that he is wilfully distorting. Besides, the tourist has a pair of eyes, and his instincts would soon tell him if the interpreter was distorting to any great extent. This is Reid's argument, abstracted from his rather obscure *Inquiry into the Human Mind on the Principles of Common Sense* (1764). He convinced many people at the time, but Hume remained the greater influence on psychology.

In the twentieth century, Alfred North Whitehead used similar arguments against Hume. Whitehead argued that we have two kinds of perception, 'immediacy perception' and 'meaning perception', which operate together just as my two eyes operate to give me depth perception. (Whitehead called them 'presentational immediacy' and 'causal efficacy'.) Hume's 'string of sensations' is immediacy perception; but more important, from the point of view of my will and creative drives, is 'meaning perception'. Meaning perception shows us what is important; immediacy perception shows us what is trivial. One is a telescope; the other, a microscope. Significantly, Whitehead illustrates the theory by mentioning William Pitt, the Prime Minister of England, who was heard on his death-bed to murmur: 'What shades we are, what shadows we pursue.' Whitehead points out that what has happened here is that the exhausted Pitt has *lost* meaning perception, and grasps the world only as the meaningless repetition of immediate experience. The significance of this illustration for our present purposes should be clear. If immediacy perception is associated with despair, and mental health depends upon the sense of meaning, then a psychology that allows no room for meaning perception is seriously deficient *as a science*.

From the point of view of Maslow's psychology, the real objection to Hume is this: that his psychology cannot define the difference between narrow consciousness and 'intensity consciousness', which, as far as human beings are concerned, is the most important difference in the world. The consciousness of a very tired man is almost entirely 'subjective'. He sees things, but somehow they don't 'get through' to him. The quality of his everyday experience is not much higher than a daydream. (Most people have had to ask themselves at some time: 'Did that actually happen to me, or was it just something

I dreamed or imagined?') There are other states when everything seems curiously *new* and fresh, and impressions seem to
fall into the senses like a stone into a pool, producing ripples.
We have all experienced these two states—the feeling of narrowness seldom leaves us. But Hume's psychology cannot distinguish between them (any more than Freud's can, as we shall
see). He might say that in states of 'intensity consciousness', one
is simply more wide-awake and therefore receives more impressions and sensations than when tired. But this is not true,
for intensity consciousness can happen to me when I am tired.
No, the real difference between these two states is a difference
of what I put *into* them. When I am bored, I close my senses as
I might close a window. If something 'awakens my interest' I
open my senses and somehow 'reach out' towards reality. This
is impossible, according to Hume, because (a) I do not possess
the will-power to 'reach out'; will is an illusion, and (b) I cannot, in any case, 'reach out' to reality; I am trapped behind my
senses as if in a prison, and all I can 'know' is the sense data that
get in through the bars of my cell.

It is worth noting, before we leave Hume, that one of the
reasons that he was convinced of the correctness of his 'associationism' was that he was unaware of the existence of the subconscious mind. The most powerful forces that move men and
animals tend to work on a level below normal consciousness:
the sexual impulse is an obvious example. And an instinctive
activity *seems* to be automatic—that is to say, mechanical. Only
as a fuller understanding of the subconscious mind began to
develop, in the early 19th century, was it possible to grasp the
difference between a mechanism and a subconscious or
instinctive drive.

On the Continent, it was a contemporary of Hume's, the
Abbé de Condillac (1715–1780), who popularised the idea that
man is 99% machine. One of his most celebrated and per-
suasive arguments makes use of a statue as illustration. Imagine,
says Condillac, a statue which nevertheless possesses just one
single faculty, the sense of smell. A pungent smell impinges on
this sense, and the result is 'attention'. More smells follow, and
now that attention has developed, the difference between them
is noted—that is to say, memory also develops. And from then

on, anything can happen: that is to say, according to Condillac, the statue will develop a kind of mind based upon the sense of smell. The complex develops out of the simple. Allow the statue five senses—as man actually has—and the possibilities for increased complexity are endless, Condillac goes on to explain how his statue develops the power of reflection, imagination, reason, as well as passions, hopes and sense of purpose (will). Man does not need *free* will, says Condillac, since he can only desire what is good for him anyway—or what he thinks is good for him. What else would he desire even if he had free will? The complexities of the human mind are due to natural laws. It is as if snowflakes believed that they choose their own shapes, pointing to the differences between them as evidence of free choice. Until a snowflake psychologist explains to them that their shapes are strictly a matter of the laws of nature, and could not be altered even if they wanted. (The image is not Condillac's, but it is in his spirit.)

It was a disciple of Condillac, Pierre Cabanis (1757–1808), who took some of the most decisive steps in the history of psychology. It is true that Cabanis is basically a materialist, asserting that the brain is an organ for producing thought as the stomach is an organ for digesting food, and that all mental processes are in reality physical. But he was also a practical physiologist who made a study of the nervous system. His conclusion was that there is an 'inner man' and an 'outer man'. The outer man is Hume's conscious, rational being; the inner man is more complex, for he consists of lower centres of consciousness associated with the brain and nervous system. This is, in fact, the first true appearance of the subconscious mind in psychology.[1] Cabanis also believed in the existence of a 'moi centrale', a central ego, and recognised that perception is a *transaction* between this central ego and the outside world. In the case of hallucinations or delusions, the 'inner man' does far more than his proper share of the transaction, overwhelming the external stimuli.

---

[1] It should be mentioned here that the idea of the subconscious mind floated in the air of the 19th century. It pervades Schopenhauer's *World as Will and Idea* (1816–1820). In Gogol's story *The Miraculous Revenge* (1830), the young bride Katerina has dreams in which her father tries to persuade her to commit incest. When she tells her husband, he says: 'You do not know a tenth part of what your soul knows.' The first definitive analysis of the unconscious occurs in Hartmann's *Philosophy of the Unconscious* (1869—see p. 118).

And so, in spite of thinking of himself as a materialist, Cabanis took several huge strides beyond Hume and Condillac. He recognised that perception is a *mental act*, a reaching out. In that case, what does the reaching? The very 'inner man', the essential 'me' that Hume denies. Add to this his intuitive recognition of the subconscious mind, and he becomes one of the key figures in the history of psychology. However, history, with its usual irony, has preserved his name mainly as the founder of physiological psychology, the laboratory study of the way we react to sensations, etc. In the 19th century, this aspect of his work was continued by Hermann von Helmholtz, E. H. Weber and Theodor Fechner. Helmholtz was the first man to measure the speed of a nerve impulse, while Fechner did important work on the measurement of the intensity of sensations. Wilhelm Wundt, who continued this work, coined the valuable term 'apperception', meaning the way that new experiences blend with the mass of old experiences, forming a new whole.[1] The value of this concept will be seen later.

Associationism received its most dogmatic statement in the work of James Mill, who asserted flatly that the mind is a machine and its laws mechanical laws. His son John Stuart Mill was altogether less of a determinist, and when he revised and edited his father's work, he suggested that perhaps the laws of the mind are *chemical* rather than mechanical; elements blend, strange combinations take place. The poet in Mill was in revolt against the depressing notion that all our feelings and insights are nothing more than the permutations of a computer. And there are times when he seems to recognise that even the complex, mysterious reactions of chemicals fail to explain the alchemy of the will. In economics, he rejected the determinism of Adam Smith and Ricardo, asserting that even if there are rigid laws of production of wealth, there are no rigid laws of distribution; society can make up its own mind what to do with its resources. But in psychology, he never worked up the courage to take the revolutionary step.

The philosopher Hermann Lotze (1817–1881) should be mentioned as an important transitional figure in psychology,

[1] In philosophy—as used by Liebnitz and Kant—apperception simply meant perception of one's inner states—introspection.

and a spiritual forebear of Maslow. Lotze recognised that most of the laws of the universe—and the mind—are mechanical; but, he insisted, mechanism does not have the last word. Human hopes point beyond mere mechanism to a universe of values. No doubt the structure of the world—and the mind—*is* 'atomistic'; but perhaps even the atoms themselves are not dead matter; they *could* be sentient. Fechner himself had made the same suggestion: if trees and plants are alive, but much *less* alive than human beings, then why should stones not be alive, but less so than trees? In the 20th century, Whitehead incorporated a similar view into his 'philosophy of organism', and Bernard Shaw's evolutionism is based on the same concept.

In spite of Lotze, and various other psychologists who accepted the reality of the will, psychology remained mechanistic. On the one hand there were experimental psychologists, measuring the intensity of sensations and the speed of reactions; on the other, systematic psychologists like Alexander Bain and Theodor Lipps, who accepted a modified associationism, allowing for various degrees of free will. James Ward and G. F. Stout, two British psychologists, argued powerfully against associationism, insisting on the reality of the 'moi centrale', the unifying ego, and its drive towards satisfactions. But by that time—the late 19th and early 20th centuries—the great Freudian revolution was under way, and these discussions were regarded as academic. There seemed to be a general feeling that since psychology had attained the rank of a science, it had better stick to analysis and definition. The will (or 'conation', as it came to be called) was allowed a small place among feelings, cognitions, memories, and so on, but it had to take its place at the back of the queue.

II

Towards a Psychology of the Will:
Brentano to James

IN THE MIDST of all this systematising, no one paid much attention to another weighty textbook, issued in 1874. Its author, Franz Brentano, was known to have been a spoiled priest, and this in itself made him an object of suspicion among scientists; a defence of the soul and the will was surely to be expected. . . ? In fact, the psychology expounded in *Psychology from the Empirical Standpoint* was founded upon a flat denial of Humeian associationism.

Hume had said that the apparently 'purposive' movements of our thoughts and feelings are like the movement of leaves on a windy autumn day: a matter of natural laws. Brentano observed his own thoughts and feelings, and decided this was untrue. For what *is* a thought or feeling? Surely, it is a kind of *action*, like reaching out to pick up an apple from the table? My thought or feeling has an object, like the apple; I love something or someone, I think *about* something. But the thought or feeling itself is the *act* of reaching out to whatever I am thinking or feeling about. No object, no thought. Hume, Condillac, Cabanis and the rest had tried to explain acts of will as a kind of natural outflow or reflex; if I am hungry, I can't help 'willing' to satisfy it, so to speak. My hand is drawn towards the apple by hunger, as if by some gravitational force. This isn't really 'will', any more than the steam that drives the steam engine is will. Brentano would accept this illustration. The steam that drives the steam engine has no *object*: it is being driven from behind, by the hot coals. But a thought or a feeling always reaches out *towards* an object; they could not exist without this element of purpose.

An illustration will make this clear. An acquaintance told me recently about a murder case in which the killer had arranged his victim's clothing in neat piles around her. When caught, the murderer proved to be suffering from a brain disease called lepto-meningitis. Murderers suffering from lepto-meningitis *always* arrange the victims' clothing in neat piles, said my friend.

There is no doubt some element of truth in this; I can recall other cases with the identical feature. But my friend failed to recognise the illogicality of his assertion. The decision to fold clothes and arrange them around the victim's body is a highly complex one; it involves a number of choices. Lepto-meningitis might, for all I know, produce an obsession with neatness; but this would still not be a predisposition to arrange clothes in neat piles. No brain disease could dictate the exact form of a complex series of choices. It is like saying that hailstorms always make Hungarians stand on the left foot and whistle the first seven bars of the Radetzky March.

This illustration makes clear the absurdity of some of the 19th-century theories about the direct link between physical and mental processes. There is no mental process without its accompanying physical process, says Bain. The reverse seems to follow naturally: there is no thought or feeling that is not the outcome of a physical process. We can imagine certain physical processes—lepto-meningitis, for example—triggering certain mental processes: perhaps a craving for neatness, order, simplicity, to counterbalance a feeling of disintegration. But beyond that, we move into the world of choice and free will, the realm of the mind and its responses.

Nowadays Brentano's 'act psychology' is remembered chiefly as the inspiration of his pupil, Edmund Husserl, the creator of phenomenology. Husserl carried Brentano's ideas to their logical conclusion. If all thoughts are mental acts, like your hand reaching out to pick up an apple, then we must accept the existence of a body to which the arm belongs. If thoughts are not blown around like leaves on a windy day, but directed by a sense of purpose, then who does the directing?

Husserl decided in favour of the 'moi centrale', which he preferred to call by Kant's term, 'the transcendental ego'. That is
to say, there *is* an 'essential David Hume', whether I notice
him through introspection or not. Perhaps I am too close to
see him. If I look at a newspaper photograph through a powerful magnifier, I see only a series of dots. If I remove the magnifier, I see a recognisable face with a recognisable expression.

More important is the use Husserl made of Brentano's
assertion that a thought or feeling is always *about* something. It
reaches out to things. It is intentional. I look *at* something: that
is, I do half the work. If I am tired or absent-minded, I may
look at something—in the sense of allowing my eyes to rest on
it—yet fail to notice it. I may look absent-mindedly at my
watch and fail to notice the time. For looking at my watch and
observing the time are two separate acts, as distinct as taking a
bite out of an apple, chewing it and swallowing it. This is the
'apperception' I spoke of earlier. The process of perceiving
reality is an active process, like chewing and swallowing.

Many earlier psychologists had noted the role of 'attention' in
mental life, but no one had recognised that it disproves Hume
and James Mill. Because although some external events may
jerk me into attention, the kind of attention I pay to a book as
I read it is a kind of 'pressure' that I exert towards the book.
And I am doing the pushing: it is coming from inside, and
going outwards.

Like Hume, Husserl was not primarily a psychologist, but a
philosopher. Ever since Locke, European philosophers had
taken the view that 'meaning' is in the eye of the beholder. The
universe is devoid of meanings and values. The grass is not
really green; it just happens to reflect light of a certain wavelength which my eye interprets as green. My so-called values
all arise out of the need to survive. Hot food feels 'good' to an
empty stomach because I need it; a girl strikes me as pretty because I also have biological needs. Why a sunset strikes me as
beautiful is more difficult to explain; that is due to some complex association of ideas. Perhaps it reminds me of fried eggs.

Husserl was a 'realist'—that is, he believed that our senses
do give us more-or-less direct knowledge of the world. But it is
true that the intentional element in perception—the part *I* put
into it—often distorts what my senses convey. Sometimes this

is simply a matter of prejudice; for example, I may feel that a person I dislike is genuinely ugly, or at least unpleasant, without realising that I am being influenced by my feelings. In other cases, the distortion is more subtle. In the Muller-Lyer illusion, two lines of equal length appear to be unequal, because one of them has a V shape capping either end and the other has a Y shape. There are dozens of other visual illusions of the same sort—straight lines appear curved, curved lines appear straight. Weber discovered that an icy cold penny, placed on the forehead, felt twice as heavy as a warm penny. In the same way, if a man expects to be touched with a hot poker, and he is touched with an icicle, he may be convinced that it is the hot poker. (If he is very suggestible he may even blister.) A blindfolded man, made to take alternate sips of strong beer and water, may end up identifying the beer as water and vice versa. In all these cases, we cannot say that the senses are telling lies: it is our interpretation of what they tell us that is wrong.

Husserl's basic assertion could be summarised as follows: Philosophy has no chance of making a true statement about anything until it can distinguish between what the senses really *tell* us—the undistorted perception—and how we interpret it. A newspaper editor who was ordered to engage a highly emotional and opinionated man would carefully check his articles for distortions, and would try to train him in objective reporting before giving him any important assignment. And the philosophical method that Husserl called 'pure phenomenology' is an attempt to teach the mind to be objective. Consequently, it should be understood as a training course for philosophers rather than as a philosophical system.

Husserl was fundamentally a kind of mystic. He once referred to himself as 'one who has had the misfortune to fall in love with philosophy'. The act of trying to see things 'without prejudice', purely as themselves, was known as the 'phenomenological reduction', and the ultimate aim of the reduction is to discover the transcendental ego, or pure consciousness. The transcendental ego is the self that lies behind and above the 'self' we regard as our identity, the 'personal self'. It is impersonal. And the realm of pure consciousness is the realm of which the transcendental ego is king; the aim of the reduction is to give the philosopher direct intuitive knowledge of this king-dom. Husserl's obsession with descriptive accuracy was ob-viously due to some recurring vision or insight, not unlike D. H. Lawrence's vision of a 'non-personal' consciousness in the sexual orgasm.

At the time Husserl was studying under Brentano in Vienna, William James was creating his own kind of intuitive psycho-logy in America. He discovered the concept of intentionality at about the same time as Husserl, but he made less practical use of it in his philosophy. Speaking about his hat:

'If it were present on this table, the hat would occasion a movement of my hand: I would pick it up. In the same way, this hat as a concept, this idea hat [in the cloakroom] will presently determine the direction of my steps. I will go retrieve it.'[1]

James recognised that thinking about his hat and picking it up are basically the same kind of activity, both with a real hat (*not* a sense datum) as object.

James is not such an important figure as Husserl. The philosophy with which his name is identified—pragmatism—has long been a dead issue. But one must qualify that by saying that he is in many ways a more interesting figure than Husserl. To begin with, he is the heir of a sceptical tradition, the heritage of Hume, Comte, Darwin . . . America in the 1880s and 1890s was a country with a strong religious tradition; there was still plenty of puritan bigotry about. Both emotionally and prac-tically speaking, James was committed to the scientific method. (He began as a physiologist.) But then, there is more than a little of the poet and the artist in him—as much as in his brother Henry. His father was a follower of Swedenborg, whose doctrine is healthy, hopeful and undogmatic. By temperament, William is something of a mystic, a tough-minded mystic. (James invented the term 'tough-minded', meaning someone who hungers for logical precision.) But the most respectable psychologists of the day assure him that everything a man does is selfishly motivated, that thought is mere association of ideas, that our mental life is as mechanical as our physical reflexes.

[1] *Essays in Radical Empiricism*, pp. 206–233. Quoted in *The Writings of William James* edited by J. McDermott, Random House, 1967, p. 184.

His own observation assures him of the truth of much of this, for he is perceptive enough to see that there *is* a close correspondence between physical states and emotions. In *Principles of Psychology* (1890) he calls the body a 'sounding board', which vibrates subtly to emotions. His meaning is more easily grasped if we think of the body as a church organ on which you can play anything from Pop goes the Weasel to a Handel sonata. But for all its subtlety, an organ is a machine. Of course, in the case of a church organ there is an organist and a composer; but many of our physical emotions are produced by 'the world', external stimuli . . .

It was this clash between a strong creative impulse and his self-destructive scepticism that produced in James—as in many intelligent young people—the strain that brought him to the edge of nervous breakdown. It is worth quoting a passage that James cites in his *Varieties of Religious Experience*, the case of Theodore Simon Jouffroy (who was himself an enthusiastic advocate of Reid's psychology):

'I shall never forget that night of December in which the veil that concealed me from my own incredulity was torn. I hear again my footsteps in that narrow naked chamber where long after the hour of sleep had come I had the habit of walking up and down . . . Anxiously I followed my thoughts, as from layer to layer, they descended towards the foundation of my consciousness, and, scattering one by one all the illusions which until then had screened its windings from my view, made them every moment more clearly visible.

'Vainly I clung to these last beliefs as a shipwrecked sailor clings to the fragments of his vessel; vainly, frightened at the unknown void into which I was about to float, I turned with them towards my childhood, my family, my country, all that was dear and sacred to me: the inflexible current of my thoughts was too strong—parents, family, memory, beliefs, it forced me to let go of everything. The investigation went on more obstinate and more severe as it drew near its term, and did not stop until the end was reached. I knew then that in the depth of my mind nothing was left that stood erect.

'This moment was a frightful one; and when towards morning I threw myself exhausted on my bed, I seemed to feel my earlier life, so smiling and full, go out like a fire, and before me another life opened, sombre and unpeopled, where in future I must live alone, alone with my fatal thought which had exiled me thither, and which I was tempted to curse. The days which followed this discovery were the saddest of my life.'[1]

What Jouffroy has done here is to apply a ruthless reductionism to his emotions, seeing them all in their worst light. ('He's always generous when he's drunk', etc.) All perceptive people know how easily this can be done; one only needs to get into a negative mood to see everything and everybody as hollow and selfish. Jouffroy, like James, had to rescue himself by accepting a psychology that left room for the will.

When James came to write his *Principles of Psychology*, nearly twenty years after his breakdown, he began by observing that if the cerebral hemispheres of a frog or a pigeon are cut out, the creature can still *respond* normally to all the usual stimuli (i.e. like a machine), but it loses all capacity for spontaneous movements. Left without stimuli it sinks into a state of lethargy. That is to say, it is now reduced to one of Hume's 'machines'.

Obviously, we are here only one step away from Maslow. It is worth recalling that when James had his attack of panic, due to the memory of the catatonic patient in the asylum, he was in 'a state of philosophic pessimism', i.e. Jouffroy's state of total reductionism, non-belief in the reality of the will. If you do not believe you possess free will, you do not feel that anything is worth doing. And for all practical purposes your state is that of the frog with its brain hemispheres cut out. And in this state, nervous collapse is possible, as actually happened in James's case, or that of Maslow's girl patient who stopped menstruating. Creative activity cannot flourish in an atmosphere of reductionism and determinism. Conversely, the higher the level of man's creative activities, the greater his degree of freedom.

James could have gone on to argue—from the frogs and pigeons—that man's capacity for spontaneous or creative action proves the existence of free will. He takes the more cautious road and argues only that the higher faculties involve a more complicated pattern than stimulus-response. In man, the pattern is complicated by *ideas*, which intervene between stimulus and response.

[1] *Varieties of Religious Experience*, p. 173, from *New Philosophical Miscellanies* by Jouffroy.

But although James asserted that there can be no psycho-logical proof of free will, he nevertheless goes straight to the heart of the matter when he points out that we become aware of free will when we are *making an effort*. For it is then that we be-come aware that we can increase or decrease the effort. If Hume's determinism is true, then 'effort' is something that is called forth by the object itself, just as my appetite might be called up by delicious-smelling food and destroyed by stale food. 'Will' is the lobotomised frog's response to a stimulus.

James has actually stumbled on the concept of intentionality, yet he fails to make proper use of it. Let me suggest briefly what I mean by 'proper use'. The question of effort applies particu-larly to matters involving meaning. If, in the middle of a general conversation, someone lifted up his hand and said urgently: 'Listen', everyone would make an effort of focusing the attention, listening intently. That is, they would deliber-ately *put more effort* into attention. In order to grasp meanings, I must 'focus'—concentrate, 'contract' my attention muscles. Perception is intentional, and the more energy (or effort) I put into the act of 'concentrating', the more meaning I grasp. What happens to the lobotomised pigeon when no stimulus is present? '. . . when left to himself', says James, 'he spends most of his time crouched on the ground with his head sunk between his shoulders as if asleep'. He is not asleep, but his attention is vague, broad, diffused, unfocused, like a bored schoolboy staring blankly out of a window, ignoring the drone of the teacher's voice. No 'meaning' is present to consciousness. We must admit that, for 99% of their lives, most human beings are in a state not far from that of lobotomised pigeons. When faced with some crisis or emergency, their sense of meaning becomes strong; so does their feeling of freedom. They fight and struggle with concentrated attention, and every minute gain produces a sense of triumph. Without emergency to keep them 'on their toes', their general level of intensity diminishes; they take their comfort for granted; their responses become dulled. And, in a vague, distressed way they wonder what went wrong, why life is suddenly so unexciting? Was it all a delusion—the excitement, the sense of meaning? Why has life failed?

This is one of the most urgent problems for civilised man. He has created civilisation to give himself security. Security for what? For boredom? His chief problem seems to be that most human beings need a certain amount of challenge, of external stimulus, to stop them from sinking into the blank stare and blank consciousness of the idiot. The answer must lie in the higher levels of consciousness, those levels where, as James says, the idea slips between stimulus and response. The higher one ascends on this scale, the more *self-sustaining* consciousness becomes. Maslow's preoccupation with creativity can be seen as a logical step beyond James and Husserl.

James is not yet ready for these flights. *The Principles of Psychology* is an astonishing book. He accepts that the correct procedure for the psychologist is introspection, and his fourteen-hundred-page book is a perfect example of what Husserl means by phenomenology—the descriptive analysis of mental states. He rejects Hume's notion that consciousness is a series of 'states' linked together like beads, and insists that it is more like a stream than a string of beads. (James is responsible for the phrase 'stream of consciousness'.) But his analyses never carry him far into the realm of values and free will.

In fact, James's most valuable observations in the area of existential psychology occur in a number of scattered papers— which may, perhaps, account for their lack of influence. There is also the fact that James is known as a pragmatist, and pragmatism is generally regarded as a thinly disguised version of positivism or materialism—which, indeed, it is. Before I speak of James as a forerunner of 'third force psychology', it may be an idea to say something about his pragmatism.

James begins his lecture on pragmatism with a typically down-to-earth illustration. He describes coming back from a walk in the Adirondacks to find the camping party divided on a philosophical question. The question was this. Suppose there is a squirrel on the bark of a tree, and a man who is trying to catch the squirrel. However, as fast as the man runs around the tree, the squirrel also runs round it, so that it is always on the opposite side from its pursuer. The question is: Does the man go round the squirrel? The party, said James, was unable to reach an agreement, until he settled the matter with a further definition. It depends, he said, upon what you mean by 'going round'. If you mean that the man is first to the north, then the east, then the south, then the west of the squirrel, yes, he goes round it. If you mean he is first to the right, then the left of the squirrel, no, he doesn't. This, says James, is the pragmatic approach. You don't try to solve the problem in some absolute, logical sense, as if it were a problem in mathematics, but simply bring it down to earth, relate it to experience. To approach a question pragmatically is to ask what practical difference it would make if one answer or the other were true. If it makes no difference, then both are equally true or false.

It is necessary to understand James's reasons for taking such a view. He lived in the post-Hegelian age when philosophers spend much time arguing about God, Design, the Idea, and so on. James's objection to this was much the same as Kierkegaard's fifty years earlier; he wanted to bring philosophy back into the realm of human *experience*. 'You must bring out of each word its practical cash-value, set it at work within the stream of experience.' James's pragmatism sprang out of his *feeling for reality*.

But having noted its value as an antidote to abstract philosophising, it is necessary to point out that it is inadequate as a theory of meaning. Take the case of the squirrel on the tree. One's first reaction is to say: The man does not actually pass the squirrel, therefore he doesn't go round it in any sense at all. But as usual, common sense is deceptive. Put the question in another way. The moon goes round the earth. Suppose a man in a jet plane also went round the earth, always keeping on the opposite side from the moon, would the moon be going round him too? The answer is now self-evidently yes. It makes no difference what the man is doing; he can be standing on his head or turning himself inside out. If he is on the earth, then the moon goes round him, no matter what his position on the earth. The same applies to the man and the squirrel, as we quickly see if we forget the tree—which is really irrelevant—or imagine it to be perfectly transparent.

It was James's misfortune that he decided to bring philosophy back to earth by espousing the pragmatist position; his philosophy is broader and subtler than the label suggests. In general outlook and approach, he is close to Husserl; yet he takes up a philosophical position which is the reverse of Husserl's. For Husserl's basic aim was to bring certainty back to philosophy, to overcome ambiguity and relativism. A man who is in love with philosophy—or science—cannot do with relativism. He cannot accept the idea that a meaning is any less a meaning because I am not aware of it. Are there people on Mars? There is no way of verifying it or otherwise, says James, so it is meaningless. It is true that, in these days of space travel, it might easily be verified (or falsified) so a pragmatic definition is not excluded. Very well, make it Alpha Centauri, where there is no possible chance of verifying it. I still have a feeling that the question 'Are there men on Alpha Centauri?' is *meaningful*, even though it is unlikely we shall ever find out. In the same way, James would treat the question: 'Is Buddhism truer than Christianity?' as a matter of relativism: 'It depends what you mean by true . . .' But I have a strong intuition that it *is* a meaningful question, and that although it is beset with thorns, we could work out a method for approaching it rationally, without relativism.

Once we have allowed this notion that 'abstract truth' is a meaningless phrase, which ought to be replaced by 'what is true *for me*', the next step is to start talking about the psychological mechanisms by which I apprehend 'meaning', and equating them with the meaning itself. This tendency is known as 'psychologism', and was Husserl's *bête noir*. (It is worth noting that C. S. Pierce, James's mentor in pragmatism, also deplored psychologism.)

But when we pass from James's philosophical stance to his work in general, it becomes possible to see why Whitehead referred to him as 'that adorable genius'; there is a concrete-ness, a clarity, a freshness about his writing that produces a heady sensation in the reader. He is always illuminating, turning a floodlight on any question he considers, totally indifferent to style as such (as all the best writers are). James has provided more insights into the actual working of the human mind than any other psychologist or philosopher. He may occasionally fail to think issues out to their ultimate end, but this is because he proceeds by flashes of insight and intuition, and is unwilling to venture where his intuition cannot light the way.

We come upon the essence of James in an essay called 'On a Certain Blindness in Human Beings', where he has a long quotation from R. L. Stevenson about the bull's-eye lanterns they used to carry as boys, objects that 'smelt noisomely of blistered tin'. Stevenson recalls the immense delight that came from the possession of these lanterns on winter nights, and goes on to speak of the fable of the monk who stopped in a wood to listen to the singing of a bird, and discovered, when he got back to the monastery, that he had been away for fifty years. This is the most important thing about human life, the moments of enchantment or delight—what J. B. Priestley calls 'magic'. It is like a flow of electricity into the heart: it arouses a sense of total affirmation and boundless longing. By comparison, our thinking activities seem odourless and bloodless. This is, of course, precisely the objection that D. H. Lawrence made to the activities of the intellect in its search for 'meaning'; in fact, Lawrence asserted that the meanings that really matter cannot be grasped by the intellect, but must be experienced by the whole human being, so to speak. This is why James wants to keep philosophy 'with its feet in the stream of experience'.

The whole of James's essay is concerned with these moments of intense, ecstatic 'meaning', and he quotes with approval Wordsworth's line, 'Authentic tidings of invisible things', apparently unaware that to accept the existence of these invisible meanings is to contradict the letter of his pragmatic philosophy. The 'certain blindness' of his title is the blindness that comes from our one-sided view of the universe. He describes a journey in North Carolina when he felt depressed by the patches of civilisation among the mountains: charred tree stumps, squalid huts, rickety fences. He asked his mountaineer driver about the people who made such clearings, and the man's reply, full of pride in their 'cultivation', made James aware that for him, these clearings were a source of intense satisfaction, representing hard work and the conquest of nature.

The recognition of the 'certain blindness' is the beginning of phenomenology. In order to conquer reality, we must filter it and bully it. It is like wearing sun-glasses to watch an eclipse. But the consequence is that we cannot get back to the primal, clean perception. T. E. Lawrence writes:

'We started on one of those clear dawns that wake up the senses with the sun, while the intellect, tired after the thinking of the night, was yet abed. For an hour or two, on such a morning, the sounds, scents and colours of the world struck man individually and directly, not filtered through or made typical by thought; they seemed to exist sufficiently by themselves . . .'

It is not only thought that prevents us from achieving this primal perception when we like; it is preoccupation of any kind. A farmer ploughing a field is as unlikely to have 'primal perception' as a professor lecturing to his class.

But at this point, Husserl has a vital contribution to make to the discussion. All perception is intentional. Since 'primal perception' is more rich and complex than ordinary perception, it must take more 'intending'. If we cannot achieve this state of almost visionary clarity at will, *this is because we do not know how to intend it.* It is as difficult to catch as some foreign station on the radio. Sometimes it comes through accidentally; but if we want to find it at will, we had better know the exact wave-band, the best position of the aerial, and so on.

This is an important recognition. D. H. Lawrence takes the position that since primal perception *is* primal, then it is no use trying to reach it by means of thought; one must begin by ceasing to think, by switching off the 'old mill of the mind, consuming its rag and bone . . .' We can see now that this is a fallacy, depending upon the notion that primal perception can only be achieved by simplicity, when, in fact, it requires a *more* complex act of 'intentionality' than ordinary thinking. Ordinary thinking may not be of much use, but it is a step in the right direction. Because at least thinking is an attempt to 'intend' or focus a thought-object, and is better than passivity. We grasp meaning by intending it correctly, just as you see a distant object by correctly adjusting the binoculars.

The essay 'On a Certain Blindness in Human Beings' is James's statement of his basic philosophical credo; this is something that philosophy must never lose sight of, this *richness* of perception that made the monk listen oblivious for fifty years. From there we may turn to the essay 'The Energies of Man' for a further exploration of the psychology of the vital forces. Here he is preoccupied with the phenomenon of 'second wind': how one can reach the point of exhaustion, press on, and suddenly find oneself feeling fresh again, full of energy. Quite clearly, our conscious insight into our energy-levels is deficient. We might say that human beings have an 'energy indicator' like the petrol gauge in a car. When confronted by some new task, I glance quickly inside myself, to see how my energies stand. If something goes wrong with my tape recorder late at night, I put off further investigation until the next morning, because I know I shall botch the job if I attempt it when I am tired. But my energy indicator often tells me lies; it may tell me I am good for nothing but sleep when an interesting conversation will keep me wide awake for another three hours.

James remarks: 'Everyone is familiar with the phenomenon of feeling more or less alive on different days. Everyone knows on any given day that there are energies slumbering in him which the incitements of that day do not call forth, but which he might display if these were greater. Most of us feel as if a sort of cloud weighed upon us, keeping us below our highest notch of clearness in discernment, sureness in reasoning or firmness in deciding. Compared to what we ought to be, we are only half awake. Our fires are damped, our drafts are checked. We are making use of only a small part of our possible mental and physical resources. In some persons this sense of being cut off from their rightful resources is extreme, and we then get the formidable neurasthenic and psychasthenic conditions, with life grown into one tissue of impossibilities . . .'

'Stating the thing broadly, the human individual thus lives usually far within his limits; he possesses power of various sorts which he habitually fails to use. He energizes below his *maximum,* and he behaves below his *optimum.* In elementary faculty, in co-ordination . . . his life is contracted like the field of vision of an hysteric subject—but with less excuse, for the poor hysteric is diseased, while in the rest of us, it is only an inveterate *habit*—the habit of inferiority to our full self—that is bad.'

At the beginning of this important passage, he has already indicated the basic nature of the problem when he mentions energies *'which the incitements of that day do not call forth'*. That is, he recognises that the problem for most human beings is that they are like the lobotomised pigeon: they require *stimulus* to get the best out of them, to make them 'pull themselves together'. As Sartre says of the café proprietor in *Nausea*: 'When his café empties, his head empties too.'

Gurdjieff,[1] a psychologist of the 20th century, liked to compare man to an enormous mansion with reception rooms, dining rooms, bedrooms, libraries; who for some reason, is un-

[1] See part 3. p. 208.

aware of all this, and prefers to inhabit the basement, which he assumes to be the only room in the house.

James goes on to ask: what happens in the moments when man suddenly feels 'more alive', when he seems to wake up and expand. How do such moments come about? He answers that men experience the feeling of expansion when some unusual stimulus fills them with emotional excitement, or when some unusual *idea of necessity* induces them to make an additional effort of will. He cites the case of a colonel during the Indian Mutiny who, in spite of wounds and exhaustion, drove himself for weeks on little else but brandy, without once feeling in the least drunk. Emergencies cause us to make use of departments of the will of which we are normally unconscious. '*Excitements, ideas and efforts*, in a word, are what carry us over the dam.'

It is typical of James to throw out this image of the dam in the excitement of exposition, without bothering to explore it. He goes on:

'In those "hyperesthetic" conditions which chronic invalidism so often brings in its train, the dam has changed its normal place. The slightest functional exercise gives a distress which the patient yields to and stops. In such cases of 'habit-neurosis' a new range of power often comes in consequence of the 'bullying treatment', of efforts which the doctor obliges the patient, much against his will, to make. First comes the very extremity of distress, then follows unexpected relief. There seems to be no doubt that *we are each and all of us to some extent victims of habit-neurosis* . . . We live subject to arrest by degrees of fatigue which we have come only from habit to obey. Most of us may learn to push the barrier farther off, and to live in perfect comfort on much higher levels of power.'

This enables one to see what he had in mind in speaking of a dam. A dam is built in a river to create a reservoir or lake. The lake in this case is consciousness, and the energies it involves. But it is a shifting dam. Some excitement or fresh stimulus or crisis can make the dam move down-river, creating a larger lake than usual. In that case, one's powers reach a higher level. Consciousness is enriched, shot through with a sense of other times and other places—of 'otherness' in general. This means that it is less dependent on external stimulus to keep it going. A stimulus is nothing else than a *suggestion for a mental act* (or any other kind of act), and an enriched consciousness contains its own suggestions within itself. Perhaps the most interesting point is that when we cease to make efforts, when we become passive or depressed, the dam tends to move the *other* way, turning the lake into a duck pond, so that consciousness reveals only a dreary, narrow universe, and nothing seems worth the effort.

James's example of the chronic invalid makes it quite clear that the act of 'pushing back the dam' amounts to nothing more or less than *calling the bluff of consciousness*. Like an old soldier, skilled in 'swinging the lead', consciousness can put on a pathetic and convincing show of exhaustion; then, sparked by some bugle call, it can explode into violent activity, revealing the deception.

A few pages later, James comes close to the heart of the matter when he discusses certain cases of 'morbid' compulsion. 'One is a girl who eats, eats, eats all day. Another walks, walks, walks, and gets her food from an automobile that escorts her. Another is a dipsomaniac. A fourth pulls out her hair. A fifth wounds her flesh and burns her skin . . . all are what [Janet] calls psychasthenics, or victims of a chronic sense of weakness, torpor, lethargy, fatigue, insufficiency, impossibility, unreality, and powerlessness of will; and that in each and all of them the particular activity pursued, deleterious though it be, has the temporary result of raising the sense of vitality and making the patient feel alive again.'

The analysis is accurate, but it could go deeper. What we have here are five cases of 'lobotomised pigeons', people whose inner-pressure has sunk to such an extent that 'life has failed them'. No one likes to live on this level of boredom and non-feeling. We all instinctively turn towards *meaning*, towards situations that will stimulate us, as a flower turns to the sun. We are trying to build up that inner-pressure where the chain reaction begins, where meaning begins to glow and rise in us and we suddenly feel more purposeful and sure of our direction. For any external 'meaning' which causes me to concentrate, to make a long, intense effort, has the effect of 'warming me up', stimulating my *general sense of meaning* as well as my sense of this particular meaning. The sapper who has concentrated every nerve to defuse an unexploded bomb finds himself looking at the sunset with twice his normal appreciation, and inhaling his cigarette with something like ecstasy. If there is some activity that *always* produces in me this intense inner-glow, then it will become the centre of my life. 'Walter', the author of the anonymous Victorian autobiography *My Secret Life* achieved this kind of 'higher consciousness' from sex, and spent his whole life in pursuit of it. Janet's patient responded to food as 'Walter' responded to sex, and ate compulsively because the act of concentrating upon food set up the inner glow of meaning. The patient who had to keep walking derived a sense of meaning from purposeful forward movement, as well as walking off nervous excitement, in the way that the father-to-be walks up and down outside the maternity ward. The cases of women who pull out their hair and burn their skin are more negative; these might be regarded as giving exaggerated expression to the same impulse that makes others bite their nails. Schizophrenia is dissociation of the thinking and feeling aspects of the personality; these 'psychasthenic' patients are, as James perceives, attempting to unite the whole being, to 'pull themselves together'—literally—by some action that *makes* them focus.

James has hit upon some vital insights, and he returns to them again and again in the course of his writing, without necessarily deepening them. He recognises that the whole phenomenon of 'second wind' means that man possesses, in effect, 'superman' levels, which lie in the realm of potentiality. Once tapped, these 'hidden powers' may produce physical effects; he speaks of a friend who has cured himself of a dangerous brain condition by the practice of Hatha-yoga, which, as James remarks, seems 'to conjure the further will-power needed out of itself'—the chain reaction, meaning leading to further effort, effort leading to further meaning. He also understands what I have called 'promotion': 'A new position of responsibility will usually show a man to be a far stronger creature than was supposed. Cromwell's and Grant's careers are stock examples of how war will wake a man up'. And his essays are fascinating simply because he keeps returning to this problem of 'intensity', mental pressure. In 'What Makes a Life Significant?', he describes a week spent at the Co-operative community near Chautauqua Lake, where all conditions are ideal: the town is beautifully laid out in the forest; an atmosphere of prosperity and cheerfulness reigns; there is an excellent college, fine music, cultural activities, athletic activities, everything to make life delightful. 'And yet what was my own astonishment, on emerging into the dark and wicked world again, to catch myself quite unexpectedly and involuntarily saying: "Ouf! what a relief! Now for something primordial and savage, even though it were as bad as an Armenian massacre, to set the balance straight again. This order is too tame. . . ."'

But, typically, James fails to reach the correct conclusion. He explains how he travelled home feeling that the pessimists are right about modern civilisation; it is getting flat and boring. What is needed is heroism, struggle . . . (It would be interesting to know what James thought of Nietzsche.) But at this moment he saw a workman high on a scaffold, and realised that *this* is the heroism of modern life: this is what gives it its contact with reality. 'On freight-trains, on the decks of vessels, in cattle-yards and mines, on lumber-rafts, among the firemen and the policemen, the demand for courage is incessant . . .' He goes on to consider Tolstoy's doctrine of the supreme dignity of labour, and to reject it on the grounds that hard work in itself is no solution. But he ends the essay without reaching a solution. And in the fine essay 'The Moral Equivalent of War', he can get no further than to say that we must find intellectual and spiritual activities to bring out the warlike virtues of courage and bravery in us. This is a vital insight, but he fails to analyse the question *phenomenologically*. Why does a week spent in the utopian Chautauqua community produce a vague sense of moral suffocation? Because there is a lack of crisis, of emergency; as James says, the place is just resting on its oars. The vicious circle begins—or rather, the vicious downward spiral. In the atmosphere of high-minded triviality, the will relaxes, our 'control-cable' slackens, and the sense of meaning diminishes. There is nothing to keep us up to the mark. The mental pressure sinks, like a tyre with a puncture. Of course, if you could find the 'moral equivalent of war', some crisis to make you grim and serious, the pressure would rise again. But that is precisely the human problem: the negative nature of consciousness, which means that without some positive pressure, we tend to lose drive and sense of meaning. I open casually an article on Arch-duke Rudolph of Hapsburg, the son of the Emperor Franz

Joseph of Austria, who committed suicide in 1889, and it mentions his boredom, and the way he 'seemed to doubt the validity of everything he did'. In the army, he took his military duties seriously for a while, then relaxed, and became bored again . . . Quite. There was no compulsion to be a good officer; he was the Crown Prince. If he had been the son of a poor government clerk, trying to make a career in the army, he would have made use of his undoubted abilities and fought upwards. But there was no 'upwards' to fight; he was already at the top. He rested on his oars, let his sense of meaning relax. And the downward spiral began, the attempt to find a meaning for his life in debauchery, seductions, half-hearted revolutionary activities . . . Without a moral compass, without the intellect to grasp that his own lack of *concentration* was reducing his sense of meaning, he could only drift towards suicide. (Dostoevsky created a similar character, Stavrogin, in *The Devils*.)[1]

We might say that the higher the 'mental pressure', the faster the chain-reaction; the more 'meanings' tend to connect up with other meanings, spreading outwards like ripples on a pond. But ripples cannot travel in a vacuum. As the mind's inner pressure drops towards the point of the lobotomised pigeon, individual meanings die away before they have time to awake echoes, to stimulate the will to more meaning.

Anything that raises the mental pressure, that causes man to focus and concentrate, is good. But again, we must criticise James for failing to follow-through to the end. He allows this insight to lead him towards moral relativism. Since belief produces this mental pressure, then belief is good in itself, and it does not much matter whether it is true or not. The will to believe is the important thing. If it produces creative results, then it is, by the pragmatism definition, true. This can easily be read as a justification of the view that any means are justifiable to achieve a certain end—a lesson that Mussolini claimed to have learned from James. James overlooked the more important consequence of his insight that we need a moral equivalent of war. Think of the sapper defusing the bomb; he makes a determined act of focusing, of total concentration, with the result that he gains a feeling of inner warmth and tension, of increased pressure. We do not necessarily require crisis to produce this

[1] See Part 3, p. 225. See also my *Order of Assassins* (1972), Chap. 4.

result. Anything that interests us deeply can do it, from a mathematical problem to great music. And what is observable —especially in the case of the music—is that *the spreading inner-glow is built-up intentionally*. Any poetry-loving teenager knows how to do this, getting a certain faint 'shock of recognition' with a favourite poem, blowing delicately on the spark as he turns from poem to poem until the glow has turned into a regular camp-fire. By mental discipline we can learn to focus meaning, which 'seems to conjure the further will-power needed out of itself'. Meaning is an external reality: it is always there, unchangeable: the mind grasps it by building up a certain inner-warmth and pressure. James's Hatha-yoga friend remarked in a letter. 'You are quite right in thinking that religious crises, love crises, indignation crises, may awaken in a very short time powers similar to those reached by years of patient Yoga-practice.'

To return to the case of Archduke Rudolph. It is obviously preposterous that his good fortune in being born Crown Prince should be a disadvantage. If unborn souls in heaven were allowed to choose their station in life, then being a peasant in a backward land would be near the bottom of the list, and being a Crown Prince near the top. What strange mechnical fault in the human engine can lead to this reversal of values?

The answer is simple. Like all animals, man has evolved through fighting and struggling. It is at a very recent point in his history that he invented civilisation. Fighting and struggling have become a habit, and he finds it difficult to adjust to a life without them. Lack of struggle does not affect most animals because they live closer to their instincts; their life-rhythms are the rhythms of the blood. But man has cut himself off from this level, by his development of intellectual consciousness. He is in a difficult position, neither one thing nor the other, no longer an animal, but a long way from being a god, or even a wise and self-controlled being.

Why did he develop consciousness? Because it is the most efficient instrument yet devised for *solving problems*. Man is at his best when solving problems. He concentrates, he focuses, he takes a tight grip on his values and doesn't let them go, he maintains a high level of discipline and *a high pressure of consciousness*. It is true that he still has more than enough problems to solve. But at this point in evolution, the most obvious deficiency of the human race is in *foresight*. We are splendid at solving short-term problems; but after solving each problem, we have a curious habit of relaxing on our oars, ceasing to make an effort, and allowing the pressure to drop. That is what is wrong with the Chautauqua community: with its lack of interesting challenge, it allows its members to become victims of this annoying habit of economising on concentration.

Although James fails to grasp the meaning-will equation, he extends his phenomenology in another direction. James's most important book is *The Varieties of Religious Experience*, a detailed exploration of the 'moral equivalent of war'. It may well be the most important single volume in the history of psychology, since it is a direct attack upon the problem of man's spiritual evolution. Certain of its formulations go further than anything else in James's work.

What interests James about religious conversion is that it seems to be an example of an *inner* process, a kind of intense chemical reaction that takes place without continuous stimuli from the outside world. Its very nature contradicts the associationist and materialist views. In associationism, the character is something fixed and stable, created by a lifetime of experience, as a mountain is shaped by the weather. But in religious conversion, the mountain is riven apart; it explodes and belches fire. The phenomenon of 'promotion' can be seen with peculiar clarity.

Since James himself had passed through a serious moral crisis, he was particularly interested in the men who see 'too deep and too much', who are oversensitive to the world's suffering and misery. There can be no doubt that the ordinary man is condemned to a form of blindness by his habit-bound existence; he plods through life like a blinkered horse, never seeing far beyond the end of his nose. He is like a sleepwalker. But what about the man who wakes up? What kind of a world meets his eyes? The evidence seems contradictory. You might say that both Wordsworth and Louis-Ferdinand Céline have a wider range of consciousness than the ordinary man; yet one is certain of the 'reality of the unseen', while the other sees the world as a kind of cesspool. Which is *truer—The Prelude* or

Journey to the End of Night? In *The Energies of Man,* James had recognised that the powers and faculties of most of us are 'contracted like the field of vision of a hysteric subject'; we all suffer from 'a certain blindness'. Once this is recognised, we can see that religion is basically only another name for being dissatisfied with this constricted vision. Intensely religious people want to escape the 'cloud' that weighs upon us. What interests James is the possibility of escaping the normal narrowness. In an important essay, 'A Suggestion about Mysticism', written not long before his death, James suggested that so-called mystical experience is not, in fact, abnormal or super-normal, but is a perfectly ordinary extension of our normal field of consciousness. This is in line with a statement he makes in *Varieties of Religious Experience* to the effect that the state of mind induced by alcohol, or even a good dinner, is a low-level mystical experience. Ordinary consciousness focuses upon certain objects or 'facts' in the same way that the eyes do; beyond these central facts, there are other things of which consciousness is half-aware, things that lie at the margin. But consciousness can suddenly widen, so that things that were at the margin are suddenly grasped and absorbed. There is no fixed limit, says James, between what is 'central' and what is 'marginal' in consciousness. I have only to move my eyes or turn my head to actually see things that were previously on the edge of my field of vision. In the same way, what strikes me as 'real' is whatever is physically present to me, the things I can actually see and touch. The more dull and tired I get, the narrower becomes my sense of 'reality'. But sometimes, my consciousness seems to turn its head, and I suddenly become sharply aware of the reality of something that had been shadowy and abstract a moment before. I may talk about some time in my past, without really becoming aware of its reality; and then some smell or tune *brings it alive,* makes it as real as the present moment. James describes a number of occasions on which he has experienced this sense of expanding reality. 'In each of the . . . cases, . . . the experience broke in abruptly upon a perfectly commonplace situation and lasted perhaps less than two minutes' . . . 'What happened each time was that I seemed all at once to be reminded of a past experience; and this reminiscence . . . developed into something further that belonged with it, this in turn into something further still, and so on, until the process faded out, leaving me amazed at the sudden vision of increasing ranges of distant fact . . .'

Religion, then, according to James, is not necessarily a sense of 'other realities', beyond our present world, but only a heightened sense of the realities that surround us. The less awake I am, the narrower my sense of reality. Which raises the interesting question: How can I become more awake?

James had already given a partial answer to this question in *The Energies of Man*:

'Either some unusual stimulus fills them with emotional excitement, or some unusual idea of necessity induces them to make an extra effort of will. *Excitements, ideas and efforts* . . . are what carry us over the dam'.

The Varieties of Religious Experience is basically a study in 'the excitement, ideas and efforts'. A typical case, from the chapter on 'The Divided Self', may be taken as illustration. A young man wastes his inheritance on riotous living until he is in a condition of poverty and misery. He goes to a hilltop with the intention of killing himself. There, it strikes him that if he is going to do something so utterly drastic, he may as well turn his desperation to better purpose: he will regain every penny of his lost fortune. He goes down the hill in a state of excitement and asks a householder for some menial job. He is paid a few pennies, and given something to eat. From then on he takes every job, avoiding spending a penny unnecessarily. He ends very rich—and a miser.

The story parallels Greene's account of how he 'snapped himself out' of a condition of chronic apathy by playing Russian Roulette with his brother's revolver. The man has allowed himself to become a drifting alcoholic; he feels that nothing is worth doing. The decision to kill himself shakes him into wakefulness. If I ask myself whether some effort 'is worth it', I am balancing my convenience, my comfort, against the outlay of effort it will require. When a man has decided to kill himself, his own convenience becomes infinitely light, and *any* effort becomes worthwhile. Ask a man who is about to be executed if he would care to delay his death for a few hours while he cleans out a cesspool, and he will leap at the chance. Raskolnikov in *Crime and Punishment* says he would rather stand on a narrow ledge for ever, in darkness and tempest, than die at once. Our usual response to reality is conditional; but the response of a healthy creature to the prospect of death is unconditional. The will stiffens in protest. And, in this case, the result was a kind of conversion; of dubious validity, since it changed a drunk into a miser. But at least it replaced a drifting creature with a purposeful one.

Equally interesting, from the same chapter, is the case of a man who suddenly fell out of love. He was infatuated with a coquette, consumed by jealousy, yet utterly obsessed by her. One day, on his way to work, brooding on the girl as usual, something in him revolted; he rushed home, destroyed all her letters and relics, and from that time onward, ceased to feel anything for her. 'I felt as if a load of disease had suddenly been removed from me . . .' James observes that this is a case of two conflicting levels of personality, but fails to see the full significance of the case. The man is passive and negative; he knows the girl is a flirt, that she is playing with him, that she will never say yes; that she would make an awful wife. But he is too feeble to resist a pretty face. *There is no counter-force*, and he is passive. Over two years, minor humiliations occasionally 'wake up' a more determined level, but the deciding factor seems to have been the misery caused by his jealousy of another man. His 'higher purposive level' lacks the power to take-over, but under the pressure of minor annoyances and humiliations, it consolidates its position. And then one day comes the *coup d'état*; everything is ready. The girl is rejected by his mind as a healthy body rejects a splinter. 'Promotion' occurs, and he is suddenly free of her.

It is interesting to compare this with what happens at the end of Shaw's *Candida*. The young poet has been rejected by Candida; he should be feeling suicidal. 'But', says Shaw, as Marchbanks walks out into 'Tristan's holy night', 'they do not know the secret in the poet's heart.' What secret? That he knows he is destined for greater things than comfortable domesticity with Candida. After all, the stars are still there . . .

This is more important than it looks at first sight. Marchbanks is doing—more or less deliberately—what James did accidentally: turning his head, and becoming immediately aware of *wider horizons of reality*. And if this is true of poets in general—even to the smallest extent—then poets have started to make the evolutionary advance that mankind has been trying to make since civilisation began. The only way we can wholly accept civilisation, escape the compulsion to fight and struggle for mastery, is to overcome the basic disadvantage of consciousness: its tendency to remain focused upon the present. It must become a searchlight that can scan distant horizons of reality. It is James's instinctive understanding of this that fills *The Varieties of Religious Experience* with creative tension and excitement.

There is not space here to attempt an adequate account of the book, but some of its central concepts must be listed. The concept of the 'threshold' was already known in psychology before James used it; but James gave it an interesting twist. A person with a high noise threshold is a person who can stand a lot of noise; Fechner devised ways of measuring 'sensation thresholds' in the laboratory. James speaks of the 'pain threshold'—not meaning how much pain people can stand, but how far they are aware of the pain in the world. 'Misery will never end', said Van Gogh, immediately before committing suicide; this is an example of a low pain threshold. Ivan Karamazov in Dostoevsky's novel says he wants to 'give God back his entrance ticket' because the amount of pain in the world means that life is fundamentally not worth living. Anyone who is too much aware of the world's pain, and his own inability to remedy it, is likely to sink into a state of life failure, or 'anhedonia', as James prefers to call it: a state in which life completely fails to arouse any kind of response of pleasure. Anhedonia is the most dangerous form of schizophrenia. To a person with a low pain threshold, it seems that anhedonia would be the inevitable state of all human beings, if they were not too stupid to draw the correct conclusions from their experience. But would it? The logical or rational answer to the question would seem to be yes. But on the other side of the balance, we have to take into account peak experiences and mystical experiences, whose nature seems to be an explosive, total affirmation. Dostoevsky's Kirilov has a vision in which he suddenly sees that 'everything's good', and that even pain and misery make no difference to this objective fact. Dürrenmatt's angel in *An Angel Comes to Babylon* asserts that he has flown all over the earth and never observed the slightest sign of misery; his own intensity is so great that he cannot recognise it when he sees it. How can we reconcile these totally opposed points of view? James makes an interesting beginning by quoting Professor Starbuck:

'An athlete . . . sometimes awakens suddenly to an understanding of the fine points of the game and to a real enjoyment of it, just as the convert awakens to an appreciation of religion. If he keeps on engaging in the sport, there may come a day when all at once the game plays itself through him—when he loses himself in some great contest. In the same way, a musician may suddenly reach a point at which pleasure in the technique of the art entirely falls away, and in some moment of inspiration he becomes the instrument through which music flows . . .' (P.169)

James grasps that what happens in such cases is that 'conscious strainings are letting loose subconscious allies behind the scenes'. He speaks of 'centres of personal energy'—meaning by that, whatever we feel *is most worthwhile*. This is an important concept; for clearly, a man who lacks a strong personal centre of gravity is bound to be weak and self-divided; whereas the word 'saved' always means possessing a strong personal centre of gravity; Newton is 'saved' by his love of science. Beethoven by his love of music, and so on. All the same, the concept is less important than it seems at first sight. For it is already covered by the notion of the 'sense of reality' we have already discussed. A musician may play his instrument perfectly—in the technical sense—but he is not fully alive to the meaning—the reality—of the music until the day it seems to play *through* him. He turns his head slightly, and something that had been an abstraction suddenly becomes a reality. What human beings need to develop is this power to 'focus' realities by a kind of mental turn of the head.

James was not a systematic psychologist—in spite of the size of his major work—and so it is difficult to summarise his contribution. He was full of dazzling insights; but they are often to be found in essays printed in his miscellanies, instead of in their proper place—at the core of *Principles of Psychology*. But for our present purposes, his ideas may be summarised as follows:

There is something *wrong* with 'normal' human consciousness. For some odd reason, we seldom get the best out of it.
The main trouble seems to lie with our sense of values, which
only seems to come alive in moments of great excitement or
crisis. Otherwise it snores hoggishly, and we only live at half-
pressure. The trouble seems to lie in the co-operation of the
conscious and subconscious mind. If you keep up a certain
conscious straining, you will 'let loose subconscious allies behind the scenes'; this happens most notably in religious experience. We are certainly capable of a far broader and deeper
sense of reality than the one we are accustomed to. The fascinating area, for psychology, lies in this realm of 'values'; and this
in turn seems to be a matter of the collaboration of the conscious and subconscious parts of the mind—a collaboration
that, ideally, would be *directed* by the conscious mind and
powered by the subconscious. The conscious mind must learn to
understand the subconscious—not only how to call its bluff
when it shams fatigue, but how to make the best possible
creative use out of it.

This summary of James—inadequate, but accurate as far as
it goes—reveals how close he is to Maslow's position. It is
ironical that he should have left no successors; that after his
death, in 1910, psychology should have been dominated by a
new kind of determinism, that had no place for 'will' or 'values'.

III

Freud and After

It must be stated at once that in turning from Mill, Husserl and James to Freud, we are turning from the views of professors of philosophy to those of a practising physician who has to deal with sick patients every day. In effect, we are surveying a different field. It would be less true to say that Freud's views conflict with those of James than to say that they hardly ever come into contact.

Freud was born in 1856—in the same year as Bernard Shaw, and into the same era of progress and expansion, of scientific liberalism and political conservatism. It was the age of Darwin, and also of Mary Baker Eddy; of Karl Marx, and also of spirit-rapping and table-turning. Freud, the eldest son of a middle-class Jewish family, grew up in the atmosphere of conservatism. When Freud was four, the family moved to Vienna—and Vienna in the twelfth year of the reign of Franz Joseph was the nearest thing in the world to the London of Queen Victoria. And Freud's family was, perhaps, the nearest thing to the middle-class Victorian family. His father married twice, and had two children by the first marriage, seven by the second. When Freud was born, his father was forty-one, his mother twenty-one. Freud's eldest stepbrother was the same age as his mother; his nephew, John, was actually a year older than Freud himself. As Ira Progoff has pointed out, Freud was bound to feel that, from the point of view of age, it was as reasonable for his mother to be *his* wife.

Revealing details about Freud's personal life have come to light only in recent years, with the publication of Ernest Jones's three-volume biography. Jones—a friend and disciple of Freud

—writes in the preface that he is aware that Freud would dis-
approve of the project; he felt that he had disclosed all that was
necessary about himself in a reticent autobiographical sketch.
The founder of psychoanalysis was a shy, reserved man who
gave the impression of coldness. He spent his life tearing down
veils, but he drew the line where he himself was concerned; it
was left for Jones to perform that service—in a respectful, but
frank and thorough manner. From Jones we learn of Freud's
passionate attachment to his mother, of the emotional upset
over her second pregnancy, of his feeling of awe the first time
he saw her naked. We also learn how Freud was struck by a
remark—made when he was nineteen—that his family actually
consisted of three generations, since his father should really
have been (from point of view of age) his grandfather. It ver-
balised Freud's own early feelings.

Freud was a clever child, his mother's favourite; she was
convinced from the beginning that her son would be a great
man, and made him aware of it. He remarked later: 'A man
who has been the indisputable favourite of his mother keeps for
life the feeling of a conqueror, that confidence of success that
often induces real success.' Freud needed the confidence; his
apprenticeship was as long as Shaw's. Success began to come
only as he approached fifty.

Freud's attachment to his nephew John was powerful throughout childhood: 'We had loved each other and fought each
other, and . . . this childish relation has determined all my
feelings in my intercourse with persons of my own age.' He
goes on to make this point more explicit: 'An intimate friend
and a hated enemy have always been indispensable to my
emotional life; I have always been able to create them anew,
and not infrequently . . . friend and enemy have coincided in
the same person; but not simultaneously, of course, as was the
case in my early childhood.' Freud's whole career is marked by
passionate friendships—in which there is a strong element of
reliance on Freud's side—which change to equally violent
enmity: Breuer, Fliess, Adler, Jung, Rank. In at least two of
these cases—Fliess and Jung—there were strong 'libidinal
undertones'—to borrow Progoff's phrase. The whole of Jones's
biography of Freud conveys the impression that Freud was a
man of strong emotions; and that, unlike many other eminent

men of science—Darwin and Einstein, for example—he was by no means in total control of them. A repetitive pattern of intense—almost erotic—friendship, followed by hatred, is not the sign of a mature and integrated personality.

On the other hand, there can be no doubt that Freud was driven, all his life, by what Jones calls 'a divine passion for knowledge'. He was fluent in seven languages as well as German; (they included Latin and Greek); and he had a passion for English literature, which he read in the original. Together with this intellectual brilliance went an immense self-confidence. In childhood, he seems to have dreamed of being a great general; at the age of fourteen he expounded to his sisters the positions of the armies in the Franco-Prussian war. The desire to be a 'man of eminence' never left him.

Jones speculates on why Freud's interest switched from military strategy to science; was it, perhaps, the result of a completely abortive love affair with a fourteen-year-old girl, or a logical recognition that the intellect is superior to force? The speculation is surely unnecessary. The scientific temperament delights in facts and ideas, which enable one to gain mastery over the chaotic personal world, to fix the eyes on the distant impersonal horizon, upon the 'far' rather than the 'near'. It is the same force that drives the poet, except that the scientist is fortunate in being able to take pleasure in the 'cold facts' that repel more romantic temperaments. Besides, Freud was not happy in Vienna—he always hated the city—and science was a refuge as well as a sensible choice for a career.

His inclination was towards creative work—which in science means research. Unfortunately, the opportunities for making a career out of research were limited. Although he had no particular wish to become a doctor, it seemed, on the whole, to be the best all-round choice; he entered the Vienna Faculty of Medicine at the age of seventeen, and managed to remain a medical student for eight years, studying also philosophy, biology and zoology. During this period he was able to satisfy his desire for research, working in the laboratory of Ernst Brücke on such problems as the nervous systems of crayfish and petromyzons (a parasite-fish), and the reproductive system of eels. But work of this kind was unremunerative. When he fell in love, at the age of twenty-six, he decided—reluctantly—that it was time to start pursuing his medical career. The girl, Martha Bernhays, seems to have been gentle and intelligent, and they became engaged—secretly—only two months after meeting. There followed four years of frustration, when her mother insisted on moving her from Vienna to place temptation beyond the reach of the young couple. They finally married when Freud was thirty; she was the only love of Freud's life, and the marriage was an exceptionally happy one.

For a year before his marriage, Freud was in Paris, studying under Charcot, who was probably the greatest nerve specialist in the world. Charcot was interested in hypnosis—which would have been regarded as highly suspicious by the Academy of Sciences if Charcot's authority as a neurologist had been less impressive. The 'magician' Mesmer had discovered 'animal magnetism' in the 1770s; he cured patients by stroking them with magnets or with his 'magnetised' hands. (All he had actually discovered, of course, was the power of suggestion; but it would be more than another century before this was recognised by medicine.) Mesmer had been discredited, and the Academy condemned magnetism. It also condemned a discovery of a disciple of Mesmer's—hypnotism; the Marquis de Puysegur had accidentally hypnotised a peasant lad in the course of stroking him 'magnetically'. Charcot managed to avoid being classified with the charlatan Mesmer by attempting to account for illness in terms of nerve physiology. His materialistic approach seemed to be satisfactorily scientific. But his medical curiosity and his remarkable intuition carried him beyond his self-imposed limitations. Charcot was fascinated by the phenomena of hysteria—which was prevalent among upper-class women in Paris. Hysteria had been one of the basic causes of the witch craze that had convulsed Europe from the 13th to the 17th centuries: nuns who believed themselves possessed by devils, women who developed strange witch's marks—spots where they felt no pain—at the suggestion of their inquisitors. But while the 17th century thought hysteria a sign of the devil's influence, the 18th tended to regard it as either imagination or play-acting. It was Charcot who recognised that hysteria could be genuinely 'unconscious', and could produce observable physical symptoms—pains, phantom pregnancies, and so on. Charcot's rival, Hyppolyte Bernheim, whose 'school' was at

Nancy, went even further in many respects, recognising clearly
for the first time the immense importance of suggestion in cases
of hysteria, and how the hypnotist himself might complicate the
case by means of inadvertent suggestions. Bernheim had, in
fact, discovered the vital importance of 'intentionality' a quarter of a century before Husserl.[1] If Freud had studied under
him instead of under Charcot, the history of psychology in the
20th century might have been very different.

As it was, Freud's 'realistic obsession' found itself perfectly at
home in the atmosphere of Charcot's Salpêtrière. Freud loved
'facts'. The romantic in him clung to facts as his salvation.
Hysteria was a fact, and the results that could be produced in
hysteric subjects through hypnosis were also facts. Freud
sensed that a revolution in psychology was about to occur, and
he knew that he could play a major part in it. Small hints were
enough to trigger his adventurous intellect. He heard Charcot
telling his assistant that many nervous disorders can be traced
to 'the genital thing'. Charcot's brilliant pupil Janet spoke
casually of 'unconscious mental acts', and Freud made a note of
the phrase. (Later, Janet explained that it was only 'a manner
of speaking'; he meant automatic acts. Illogically, Freud regarded this as a stab in the back.) A gynaecologist in Vienna,
on Freud's return from Paris, remarked that what a certain
neurotic woman really needed was 'repeated doses of a normal
penis'—her husband was impotent. He added that this was one
thing he could not prescribe. But Freud, with his mixture of
innocence and daring, could see no reason why not. Doctors
said these things in private, as if they were indecent smoking
room stories; but they weren't; they were science—cold, pure,
beautifully sterile. Why should a sincere, dedicated scientist be
afraid to tell the truth about them? On his return to Vienna,
Freud proceeded to do exactly this. He was fortunate in having
a position from which he could make himself heard. For in the
previous year he had been appointed a *Privatdozent*, a lecturer
in neurology in Vienna, on the basis of some brilliant diagnoses.
As Gerard Lauzun remarks, it was like wheeling the Trojan

---

[1] It must be emphasised that Brentano's idea of intentionality fell short of
Husserl's in important respects; he stated only that mental acts must have an
'object'; Husserl grasped the *creative* nature of the intention. Sartre, of whom I shall
speak later, is a follower of Brentano rather than Husserl.

Horse within the walls of the citadel. Now, when he proceeded to describe his Paris experiences, and lecture on male hysteria, the Medical Society of Vienna was forced to give him a hearing. They hated every word of it—it savoured too much of the chicanery of Mesmer, who had been expelled from Vienna. They listened with irritable scepticism, and challenged Freud to produce a single case of male hysteria. It took Freud five weeks to produce one—due to the obstructive attitude of hospital doctors—and although the Society applauded his second paper, they were clearly unconvinced, and proceeded to forget it immediately. Meynert, who had been one of Freud's sponsors for the lecturing job, wrote a paper attacking Charcot, and closed his laboratory to Freud. It was not long before Freud found himself out in the cold, as far as Viennese medical society was concerned. His method of treating hysterical disorders with hypnosis was reminiscent of Mesmer, and his increasing insistence on sexual factors was regarded as a sign of some morbid aberration. Freud worked as the director of the neurological department of an Institute of Child Diseases, refrained from lecturing, and continued to pursue his ideas in relative isolation.

The psycho-analytic method developed in a number of steps. First, there was the hypnotic method developed by Charcot. Next, Freud became interested in the 'cathartic' method, in which the patient was encouraged to talk about the symptoms and their possible cause. Then he discovered the method of free-association, in which the patient was asked to lie down and say whatever came into his—or her—head. These last two methods are obviously closely connected, and developed from one of Breuer's cases. An attractive young girl named Bertha Pappenheim—later to become known as 'Anna O'—developed various hysterical symptoms: paralysis, stuttering, a nervous cough, inability to eat. The girl also showed signs of dual personality, having periods during which she was transformed from a responsible and intelligent girl into a badly behaved child. She became fixated on Breuer—who was called in to deal with her cough. She would describe her symptoms to him at length— hallucinations, muscular constrictions and so on and would experience relief. Breuer quickly perceived the value of the 'talking cure', and in due course, Bertha became almost normal again. (Unfortunately, she had a relapse when Breuer's wife became jealous and compelled him to give up the case.) Freud was greatly struck by all this, and he persuaded Breuer to write about it in *Studies in Hysteria* (1895), a book that appeared under their joint authorship. It was in this work that another important Freudian concept made its appearance—that of repression. This was in the case of a governess who displayed hysterical symptoms, which turned out to be due to her attempt to repress her violent attachment to her employer.

In all essentials, the Freudian theory was now complete. It stated that nervous diseases (neuroses), which had always been assumed to be *physical* diseases of the nervous system, were usually emotional in origin, and that the root cause was normally sex. (At an early stage, he was inclined to believe that it was the seduction of children by adults that was the major cause of the trouble; it was only after the *Studies in Hysteria* that he came to recognise that the child may harbour strong sexual desires towards the parent of the opposite sex. Typically, he made this discovery through self-analysis.)

No one who has studied reports of possessed nuns, such as those of Loudun and Aix-en-Provence, can doubt the importance of Freud's insight. The witch-finders and inquisitors had observed with horror the way the writhing nuns blasphemed, exposed their genitals, and made obviously sexual movements with their hips: they assumed it was the devil's work. Freud recognised the same symptoms in his own female patients, and understood the explosive power of the sexual impulses that were being suppressed. He recognised the importance of sexuality in children.

All this was due to the power of the subconscious mind, which Freud was the first to recognise clearly. This is perhaps his most remarkable achievement. It may be compared to the discovery by geologists that the earth is not a cold, solid ball, but is full of molten rock at enormous temperatures and pressures. Until that time, geologists had believed volcanoes to be due to small local fires of coal or wood under the ground, but this theory could not explain earthquakes, geysers, and the sudden appearance of whole islands in the ocean. The new theory could. And Freud's theory could explain the hysterical convulsions of the human personality, by recognising that the personality is no more than a crust over a region of fire and molten rock.

It was this aspect of Freud that caused the psychologist William McDougall to classify Freud with Goethe, Schopenhauer, Bergson and Nietzsche as a 'vitalist' (or Dionysian), in contrast to 'mechanists' such as Locke, Mill and Bain. To the modern reader, the classification seems curious; this is because we are more conscious of Freud's determinism than of his revolutionary stride beyond Victorian rationalism. But Freud was both a vitalist and a determinist. In an essay on Freud, Thomas Mann speaks of him as a poet of the subconscious, and compares him to Schopenhauer. The comparison is apt; for Freud is both a romantic and a pessimist. In 1869, a brilliant young German, Edouard von Hartmann, published *The Philosophy of the Unconscious*, in which the ground of all existence is seen to be a vast subconscious will, that acts out of a monstrous irrationality—an irrationality that has made it evolve its own enemy, rational consciousness; the result, Hartmann believes, must be destruction. Freud has taken over Hartmann's irrational consciousness, a great invisible octopus writhing in the depths of the mind, and pointed out that the force that moves it is the force of sex. The pessimism remains, for it is unavoidable if one views the subconscious as magnificently irrational. In that case, what about the rational mind of the psychologist and philosopher that tries to expound the subconscious root of all things? It must recognise its own absurdity. The philosopher's correct relation to the subconscious is that of a priest to his god, the dark god that has created him through an aberration, and that merely tolerates his existence as an elephant might tolerate a gnat.

For Freud, psychoanalysis *was* a kind of religious conception. Jung tells a curious story of Freud saying: 'My dear Jung, promise me never to abandon the sexual theory . . .' in the tone of a father saying to his son: 'Promise me to go to church every Sunday'. The sexual theory seemed to Freud a mountain of truth towering above the foothills of 19th-century rationalism and occultism; he was committed to it like the worshipper to his God. He was the Moses who had been chosen to bring the tables of the law. (Jones mentions that the figure of Moses came to obsess Freud from the 1890s on.)

It is difficult to blame Freud for his one-sidedness. Why should he not be emotionally committed to a discovery so tremendous? His conceptions were incomparably deeper than those of James Mill or Alexander Bain. Any attempt to displace sex from the centre of the stage was bound to be an attempt to replace it with something less impersonal, more human; and that would be allowing the old shallow rationalism to creep back.

But the basic fallacy of Freud's position should be clear to anyone who read the last chapter with attention. Hume said he looked inside himself and found only ideas and impressions. Freud says he looks inside himself and finds the swirling forces of the subconscious. And again, the question of the 'controller' arises. *Whose* subconscious? According to Freud, it is simply *the* subconscious, an impersonal force. He, Sigmund Freud, is the superficial ego, the face that looks at him out of the mirror. This superficial ego *thinks* it has opinions, makes decisions; in reality, it only reflects unseen forces. Its 'rational' judgements and actions are really expressions of these inner forces. Man's only chance of freedom is to understand these forces and come to terms with them. Man is a tiny rider on a gigantic black horse. But again, we must ask the question: Whose horse?

For we are again faced with the paradox of the 'robot': that although it is not inaccurate to speak of 'my robot', the robot *is* me. In those moments, described by Starbuck, when the game begins to play the athlete, when the music begins to play the musician, 'I' merge into the robot; the subconscious forces are far more completely and subtly at my command than in everyday consciousness. Freud habitually thought of the 'me' as the conscious ego (as Hume did), and the subconscious as the 'It' (or the Id, which seems a case of a Freudian pun).

It would seem, then, that Freud himself presents an interesting case for his own type of analysis. He is a member of a large Jewish family unit, and his father is old enough to be his grandfather—underlining the patriarchal role. He is emotionally obsessed by his much younger mother. He is a person of strong emotions, but has difficulty in expressing them. He possesses a definite homosexual leaning, which appears in relations with various close friends—relationships which veer between love and hatred. (In later life, says Jones, he succeeded in diverting the homosexual component into more acceptable channels, forming friendships with women who possessed a dominant streak—his wife's sister, and Lou Andreas Salome, for example.) A man of strong sexual impulses, he nevertheless remains a virgin until he is thirty. It is not until he is in his mid-forties— towards the end of the century—that he overcomes the tendency to emotional ups and downs, and gains a degree of serenity. And even so, the emotions continue to run strong under the somewhat rigid surface. Because his emotional patterns remain unchanged, he is inclined to relive the pattern of events of his past, in different settings, with different individuals. In due course, all these strictly personal patterns were stated in the form of generalities, and applied dogmatically to the rest of the human race. The relation between all parents and children is an erotic one with powerful elements of hostility. The basic drive in all men is sexual and aggressive, but they prefer to re-press or rationalise this knowledge. The so-called 'higher nature' of man is based upon religions and social moralities, which in turn are expressions of unconscious forces. Man tends to relive past emotional patterns, and these lie behind all his so-called logical thinking. (It is a pity that Freud has left no psychoanalytic study of Shaw; it would be interesting to know what he made of a man whose life was not dictated by repressed emotions. The few references in Jones indicate a predictable hostility.)

This is the fundamental criticism of Freud: that there is a strongly emotional element in his 'reductionism'. And an emo-tional assertion is not to be trusted. Towards the end of a strait-laced century, he was the first man to grasp something of the explosive power of the sexual impulse. The insight so dazzled him that he proceeded to apply it to every problem that arose. Religion, artistic creation, wit, altruism, they were all 'rationa-lised' manifestations of the sexual impulse. Children may ex-perience their first erotic sensations at six months; a glimpse of the parents engaged in intercourse at this age may trigger all kinds of later complications, for it appears to be an act of aggression of the father towards the mother. Girls experience penis envy for their brothers, while the boys are stricken with castration anxiety by the sight of their sisters' loins . . . It was perhaps inevitable that Freud should eventually discover, at the root of subconscious life, an even more powerful destructive principle, *thanatos*: the death urge, the urge to aggression and chaos,[1] the murderous drive that makes nonsense of man's desire for civilisation and order. War is not an aberration, due to the frustration of creative impulses, but the emergence of man's true nature.[2]

To summarise, Freud was the first to understand the mystery and depth of the subconscious, and the first to assign adequate importance to the sexual impulse. Others followed—Wedekind in Germany, D. H. Lawrence in England. They recognised sex as a mystical force, capable of giving man a glimpse of the god-like. But they were imaginative artists. Freud was a clinician, working every day with emotionally crippled human beings. Frustration of the sexual impulse struck him as perfectly adequate to explain most neurosis. (Although he is by no means as dogmatic as many anti-Freudians would have us believe; he genuinely did his best to keep an open mind.) He derived great pleasure from his contact with harsh reality, in rather the same manner that many police pathologists derive a tough-minded enjoyment from their gruesome work, and enjoy shocking gentler and more squeamish spirits. And anyone who has read Freud knows that there is a kind of hard poetry in his realism, an exhilaration in its stern eye-to-business. No matter how far psychology moves beyond 'the sexual theory', Freud can never be dismissed; for the odd reason that his achievement was artistic as much as scientific. As in the operas written by Bert Brecht and Kurt Weill, the tough-mindedness is an essential part of the achievement.

However, the limitation of his approach becomes apparent in a work like *Civilisation and Its Discontents* (1929). In *The Future of an Illusion* (1927) he had dismissed religion as an illusion based upon man's desire for a father figure. Romain Rolland objected that, for him, religion was founded upon a feeling which he called 'the oceanic feeling' (using a phrase of Whitman's)—by which he obviously meant a broad, overwhelming sense of *meaning*, such as William James described in speaking of 'horizons' of fact. Freud's extremely restricted philosophical approach meant that he had no phenomenology for dealing with

---

[1] *Beyond the Pleasure Principle*, written 1918.
[2] See p. 238.

such a notion. Philosophically speaking, his feet were firmly cemented into 'the natural standpoint', the 'triviality of everydayness'. What precisely can Rolland mean by 'oceanic feeling'?, asks Freud. Adults have a sharp sense of their own limits which keeps them confined in a personal ego. Only babies—or the mentally sick—lack this clear dividing line. A baby is not consciously aware of where his own face ends and his mother's breast begins; it is all one warm, hazy cloud. Thus, Freud concludes triumphantly, we can explain the 'oceanic feeling' as a throwback to early childhood, and see clearly that it has nothing to do with religion. . . . Here one can see the essence of the reductionist method: to solve a subtle problem by pretending that it is, in fact, a crude and obvious one.

Freud's psychology is purely clinical, derived from the consulting room. It lacks what all previous psychologies had possessed: an account of the way we apprehend 'meaning'. Meaning is essentially what the philosopher Bernard Lonergan calls 'insight'. A schoolboy might use an algebraic formula every day for solving problems. One day, he finds he has forgotten it and decides to work it out for himself. As a result, he *understands* it for the first time. This is insight: the difference between 'knowing' something in an abstract kind of way, and grasping it *as a reality*. Insights always have the effect of 'awakening' me, sharpening my sense of reality, like some smell that reminds me of autumn during my childhood. Occasionally, as James describes, insights may pour in so fast that consciousness seems to expand at a bewildering rate. This is the oceanic feeling; and the description given in this paragraph is an example of phenomenological thinking.

The remainder of Freud's essay contains one of his best known formulations: the notion that there is a basic conflict between civilisation and man's deeper impulses. The fundamental human drive, says Freud, is the search for happiness. All men would like unrestricted gratification of all their desires, in the manner of De Sade's anti-heroes. But being part of a community offers such enormous advantages that men are willing to forego this aggressive desire to gratify all needs, and abide by social laws. So civilisation is almost synonymous with frustration. *Thanatos*, the aggressive, destructive impulse, is muzzled by conscience, or the 'super ego', which turns its aggressiveness against the conscious ego; this leads to the desire for self-punishment, so typical of saints and highly moral men. The price we pay for civilisation is guilt and the forfeiture of happiness.

It is typical of Freud's almost masochistic pessimism that he should regard the super-ego (or 'higher self', as it would once have been called) as a matter of self-restraint and dreary moral observances, rather than as the part of man capable of creative or mystical experiences. Thomas Mann was right to describe Freud as the direct descendant of Schopenhauer.

The first of Freud's disciples to 'defect' was Alfred Adler. Adler was also Jewish, the son of a well-to-do corn merchant. His father was an easy-going man of strong personality, and Alfred was his favourite. Adler's relationship with his mother was, by comparison, distant. He was a sickly child, who suffered from rickets; but, being naturally cheerful and healthy minded, he fought his illnesses, and ended as a strong and athletic boy. He always enjoyed swimming and mountain climbing. Unlike Freud, he loved Vienna. He was a sociable man who enjoyed café life. His artistic taste was catholic and he was a music-lover. As a conversationalist he was intelligent and charming. As might be supposed from all this, his psychological theories had a very different character from Freud's.

Adler came across Freud's *Interpretation of Dreams* in the year of its publication, 1900; he was thirty at the time, and a successful general practitioner. He became friendly with Freud after defending the book in print. They had a certain amount in common—a cautious scepticism, for example. Unlike Jung, Adler had no time for the occult. Although he dreamed of a ship striking an iceberg and sinking on the night the *Titanic* went down, he insisted this was coincidence. But his outlook on life was naturally more buoyant than Freud's; as Phyllis Bottome puts it in her biography of Adler, he felt that human beings progress from a minus to a plus.

To begin with, the influence was mutual. Adler insisted that sex is by no means the only root cause of neurosis. The most noticeable thing about man, he said, is his inferiority to other animals in the matter of physique; he has turned this disadvantage to an advantage by developing his brain. It seemed clear to Adler that all life is this struggle against 'inferiority', a will to power, and that if sex is one of the commonest causes of mental disturbance, this is because sexual frustration tends to be one of the chief obstacles to the will to power. Freud was at first inclined to agree with this.

With such a basic notion, Adler's psychology might easily have developed into a Nietzschean theory of conflict, such as Sartre later produced. But Adler was also strongly aware of man as a social animal. Freud took from Adler the view stated in *Civilisation and Its Discontents*, that man had to become a social animal to compensate for his inferiority to other animals. This feeling for society was the creative spring at the root of Adler's work; he would have approved of the title of a book by William James's father, *Society, The Redeemed Form of Man*. Together with this view of the fundamentally social nature of man went a powerful desire that his own work should be of use to mankind. This again distinguished him from Freud, who regarded himself as a pure scientist, almost as a mathematician of the human mind. As a psychotherapist, Freud was a perfectionist, willing to devote any amount of time to unravelling the tangled intricacies of the patient's psyche. Adler had a more practical approach. And in this matter he is the direct precursor of Maslow, Frankl and Glasser. Long analysis, he felt, was probably a waste of time, and also encouraged a negative and passive attitude in the patient. A neurotic patient is one who has become subject to discouragement, who finds reality difficult to deal with, and so retreats into fantasy or hysteria or depression. The psychiatrist's problem is to strengthen the patient enough to get him back to grips with reality, to persuade him to snap out of his passivity, to start making plans again, to feel that things are worth doing. This is obviously in line with Adler's view that neurosis springs from feelings of inadequacy, inferiority. But what is more important is that he recognises the vital importance of the human will in mental illness. Freud's psychology is virtually will-less, like Hume's; the human will is very small and unimportant compared to the vast forces of the subconscious; curing a patient consists in somehow reconciling him to these forces, persuading him to stop resisting them, attempting to repress them. Adler's view, in fact, denies the importance of these forces. It is true that Adler accepted the subconscious root of neurosis as completely as Freud did. But he believed far more than Freud in the role of intelligence, will and the sense of purpose as curative agents. But it is in a brilliant chapter on Dostoevsky in *Individual Psychology* that we encounter the essence of Adler. He grasps correctly that the core of Dostoevsky's message is love, an immense redeeming love capable of washing away all evil. (In this, Dostoevsky might be regarded as the prophet of today's hippie generation.) He summarises Dostoevsky's message: Man must look for his formula and he will find it in willingness to help others, in a capacity for sacrificing himself for the people. 'He was in intimate connection with the community feeling', says Adler, 'with the very bases of society.' It is clear from his writing that the symbol, the idea capable of inducing peak experiences in Dostoevsky was this notion of a Christ-like love, the idea of a man suddenly loving all mankind as his brothers, *with no limit of sympathy*. And this is also Adler's ultimate vision. It carries him a long way beyond Freud, whose own analysis of Dostoevsky (1928), while fully acknowledging his genius ('second only to Shakespeare'), centres upon the guilt Dostoevsky is supposed to have felt about his desire to murder his father. But equally important and significant in Adler's essay is another concept: that Mitya Karamazov, labouring in the mines of Siberia for a crime he did not commit, nevertheless feels a secret satisfaction, a *superiority* because of his knowledge of his innocence. Adler also mentions a curious case of a miser who starved himself to death, and was found, after his death, to possess 170,000 roubles. Why did he do it? Because, says Adler, it must have given him an immense feeling of *superiority* to starve himself, pretending to be poor, leaving bills unpaid. Adler also sees this as an act of defiant irrationality, like the suicide of Kirilov in *Devils* (to prove he is free); the spirit of man committing a paradoxical action as an assertion of will. Adler sees Dostoevsky's driving force as the recognition that 'salvation was to lie in submission, as long as submission contained within itself the secret enjoyment of superiority over others'. Here it can be seen that Adler has passed beyond the Freudian sexual theory, into the outer wilderness of the human mind explored by Nietzsche and Dostoevsky. He is aware that the key to human psychology lies in the ideas of will and freedom.

It may seem strange that Freud and Adler ever thought they had anything in common. The answer is that both attached enormous importance to the idea of the family as the foundation of psychological life. At the end of the Dostoevsky chapter, Adler mentions the idea of an 'accidental family', where every member lives for himself and implants in the children a tendency to greater and greater isolation and self-love; he obviously sees this as the ultimately undesirable situation. Studies of criminals seem to indicate that he is right. Hence Adler's emphasis upon the importance of the family unit.

Phyllis Bottome, an anti-Freudian, seems to accept nevertheless that the ten-year association between the two men was entirely to Adler's benefit. This seems to me doubtful. Freud had been deeply impressed by Charcot's tough-minded approach; as Gregory Zilboorg points out of Charcot, 'even one's normal psychological reactions were viewed from the standpoint of brain defects or pathology'.[1]

For Freud, human beings were capable of two mental conditions: normal or sub-normal, and he was inclined to reduce the super-normal—in great artists or mystics—to the subnormal. The reductionist attitude rubbed off on all his chief disciples: Adler, Jung, Stekel, Jones, Rank. In Adler, it meant that he tended to think of human development as an attempt at psychic compensation for inferiority. Even at his most positive, Adler could not quite throw off the Freudian tendency to think in terms of negative compensations. Mitya Karamazov is sustained by a secret feeling of superiority—although Dostoevsky makes it quite clear that he is sustained by his sudden vision of universal brotherhood, and desire to expiate his own sin in wishing his father's death. This is to miss the creative, purposive element in the human personality that sustained many of Frankl's fellow prisoners. In the same way, although Adler's view of man as intimately related to his fellows may be fine and noble, it tends to reduce man to Aristotle's 'social animal'. Certain highly creative men may *need* a sense of isolation from their fellows; Nietzsche described his feeling when he conceived Zarathustra as 'six thousand feet above men and time'. Above *men*. The truly creative man has to learn to gain satisfaction from the work itself rather than from the approval it might

[1] *History of Medical Psychology*, p. 364.

bring him. Camus devoted a novel—*The Fall*—to a man who believes he is driven by the desire to do good to his fellow humans, and one day realises that it was only a form of self-flattery, the hunger to think well of himself.

In spite of this, Adler must be regarded as the father-figure of the new generation in psychology: Frankl, Maslow, Boss. What he called 'the affirmative unfolding of the organism' was, in fact, a recognition of the basic evolutionary drive of human beings, that *man is an evolutionary animal*, and that neurosis is the frustration of this evolutionary drive. In dealing with neurosis, Adler was less concerned to trace its roots in the patient's childhood than to understand its *meaning*, what it was driving towards. The case of Maslow's girl patient—who lost the will to live in a chewing gum factory—would certainly have been within Adler's comprehension, for he recognised that each individual develops a certain 'life style', a basic sense of meaning, and that neurosis arises when this meaning breaks down, when the creative forces encounter a *cul-de-sac*.

Adler's limitations are almost as interesting as his positive insights. His recognition of the problem of the pampered child is a case in point. It is clear that he has an intuition that 'spoiltness' is more universal than one might suppose if one thinks solely in terms of indulgent parents. But he interprets spoiltness in social terms: it causes the individual to think only of his own satisfactions, to become self-willed and lacking in self-control when frustrated. Adler goes on to blame the competitive individualism of the modern world for an increase in 'pampered personalities' who become neurotic because their activities are unrelated to those of their fellows. This is penetrating, but it does not go far enough. What *is* spoiltness, in phenomenological terms? It is the limit beyond which an individual refuses to make an effort without *immediate returns*. The spoilt child demands a very high level of rewards and petting from life. But our limits also depend upon how *far* we can see, upon how far-sighted our purposes are. And this brings us up against the basic evolutionary problem of mankind: our short-sightedness. This is the real significance of spoiltness; it is nothing less than the human condition itself, another name for 'original sin'. Kierkegaard saw that the basic problem is *that all men are bored*. First Adam was bored to be alone, so Eve was created; then

Adam and Eve were bored, so they had Cain and Abel; then all the family were bored, so Cain killed Abel . . . Human history is seen as a flight from boredom, and from the low mental pressures associated with it. But boredom is another expression of spoiltness; it is a refusal to make any mental effort without the reward of an external stimulus. Adler's analysis of spoiltness comes very close to the borders of a truly evolutionary psychology; but he halted there.

Adler 'defected' in 1911; Jung's break with Freud came in 1913, after publication of *Psychology of the Unconscious*. He had hoped—and his wife encouraged the hope—that Freud would be magnanimous and accept some of Jung's differences of opinion; but it was not to be. Freud was deeply upset by the loss of Jung; there had been a time, not long before, when he had even suggested that the care of the psychoanalytic movement should pass into Jung's hands.

Jung had always had a tendency to occultism; he had written upon it as early as 1902. In retrospect, it seems clear that he was attracted to Freud because he felt that Freud had opened up interesting new realms of the spirit, the mysteries of the human psyche. Ira Progoff begins his book on Jung with a typically Jungian sentence: 'The world is rich with many dimensions of reality.' As a young man, Jung was influenced by Hartmann's *Philosophy of the Unconscious*, with its conception of an unconscious drive behind nature. It was Freud's recognition of the unconscious that attracted Jung. And it was Freud's sexual obsession that repelled him, as it repelled Adler. And Freud himself was uneasy about his young disciple's 'occultism'. In the passage already quoted, in which Freud begged Jung never to abandon the sexual theory, Freud went on to explain that it should be defended as a bulwark 'against the black tide of mud —of occultism'. Jung comments (in his autobiography, *Memories, Dreams, Reflections*):

'Freud's attitude towards the spirit seemed to me highly questionable. Wherever, in a person or work of art, an expression of spirituality (in the intellectual, not the supernatural sense) came to light, he suspected it, and insinuated that it was repressed sexuality. Anything that could not be interpreted as sexuality, he referred to as "psycho-sexuality". I protested that this hypothesis, carried to its logical conclusion, would lead to an annihilating judgement upon culture. Culture would then appear a mere farce, the morbid consequence of repressed sexuality. "Yes", he assented, "so it is, and that is just a curse of fate against which we are powerless to contend."' (p. 147)

This is perhaps the most damning paragraph ever written against Freud.

Jung had an extremely active subconscious—even more so than Freud. He describes how, when Freud was inveighing against 'the occult', he suddenly felt as if his diaphragm was becoming red hot, and there was a loud explosion in the book case. Jung declared that this was an example of the subconscious 'exteriorising' itself. Freud said nonsense.

'"It is not," I replied. "You are mistaken, Herr Professor. And to prove my point I now predict that in a moment there will be another loud report!" Sure enough, no sooner had I said these words than the same detonation went off in the bookcase.' Freud, apparently, stared aghast.

Jung's central interest was in the interpretation of dreams and myths. He believed, quite simply, that the symbolism of dreams is by no means entirely sexual, but that it may often be *racial*—that racial memories and emotions may appear in semi-mythical form. He called these 'primordial images' or 'archetypes'. They find expression in a kind of hidden person in the depths of the psyche; in men, this hidden person is a woman and is called the anima: in women, it is a man, the animus.

Jung was, perhaps, a poet rather than a scientist. If he had been born in England instead of Switzerland, he would probably have joined the Order of the Golden Dawn, with W. B. Yeats and Florence Farr, and studied ritual magic. His mind is certainly fundamentally similar to Yeats's. William James once commented of Fechner that it would be a pity 'if even such a dear old man . . . could saddle our science forever with his patient whimsies, and, in a world so full of more nutritious objects of attention, compel all future students to plough through . . . his own works'. James here touches squarely upon the average man's reaction to science or mathematics: the feeling that there are more nutritious objects of attention, objects that fill the stomach of the mind with a warm glow. This was the basis of Jung's reaction to Freud; he had a strong feeling for creativity, for the ideas and images that can touch the source of imaginative excitement. He felt that these had a value in themselves, that places them in a higher class than the fantasies of the neurotic. Freud's psychology recognised no such distinction; fantasy was a negative response to frustration, and all 'culture' is spun out of fantasy. It is surprising that the two men found any basis for friendship for even a single decade; they were cut out to be enemies. The reason that they remained friends for so long is almost certainly that, as in the case of Fliess, Freud was inclined to treat Jung as the superior partner in the relationship; it was yet another version of the relation with his nephew John.

In the practical sense, Jung's objections to Freud were very similar to Adler's. 'Causality is only one principle, and psychology cannot be exhausted by causal methods only, because the mind lives by aims as well.'[1] Man can only be completely understood in terms of his goals.

The immediate result of Jung's break with Freud was to isolate him as a psychologist. 'My book was declared to be rubbish; I was a mystic, and that settled the matter.' In the most fascinating chapter of his autobiography, 'Confrontation with the Unconscious', Jung describes how, in the ensuing years, his subconscious became so active that the theory of archetypes and the 'anima' was virtually forced upon him. In a key passage, he speaks of a fantasy figure whom he called Philemon, with whom he held mental conversations in which 'Philemon said things I had not consciously thought'. This brought the crucial insight that 'there are things in the psyche which I do not produce, but which produce themselves, and have their own life'. And this view goes considerably beyond Freud; for although Freud conceived the subconscious as a kind of mysterious ocean, he thought of it as being full of sub-human monsters, a realm of nightmare. For Jung, it was, on the contrary, a kind of treasure house. One of his most remarkable dreams concerned his descent through a series of underground chambers, each one of which represented an earlier period of history. This was Jung's conception of the subconscious: an archaeologist's dream of buried civilisations, one below the other. Moreover, at its deeper levels, it was not an

[1] Quoted by Progoff: *The Death and Rebirth of Psychology*, Chap. IV.

individual unconscious, but an unconscious common to the whole race, a 'collective unconscious'. One can understand why Freud thought that Jung had become too metaphysical.

But the years with Freud left as much a mark upon Jung as upon Adler. The most obviously striking thing about Freud's type of thinking is its desire to systematise and explain—and some of his explanations sound rather far-fetched. He seems to be driven by a desire to fit everything into a rational framework, so that it is safely labelled, and can be put into a drawer of the mind. Maslow's approach, as can be seen from the introductory chapter of this book, is more casual and easygoing. He approaches problems intuitively, and tries to turn intuitions into words. If they won't turn into words, he leaves them alone and turns to something else, prepared to try again later. There is no compulsion to impose an explanation upon everything. Jung seems to have inherited from Freud the rationalistic approach, the desire to get everything explained and integrated into a system. In the chapter on his 'confrontation with the subconscious', he decribes a dream in which he and a small brown-skinned savage killed Siegfried. His interpretation is that the savage was his 'primitive shadow', while Siegfried was the embodiment of his own will to power, the heroic idealism of the ego, which had to be killed. To the average reader, this in itself sounds like a rationalisation, with no more objective validity than finding ciphers of Francis Bacon in Shakespeare's plays. Jung never lost this tendency to play intellectual games, to work out mythological systems of cross reference as complex —and arbitrary—as the cross references in Joyce's *Ulysses*. He describes, for example, his study of alchemy, and tells how he found increasingly deep significances in old alchemical documents, and came to the conclusion that alchemy symbolises the transformations of the spirit. No one who has actually read Paracelsus or Cornelius Agrippa can entirely accept this. Alchemy was a false direction in man's search for knowledge, based upon the mistaken assumption that metals can be concocted out of other elements like batter pudding; no amount of mythologising can resurrect alchemy as we might resurrect a piece of medieval music. It is true that the greatest alchemists enriched the subject with spiritual significance, using the transmutation of metals as a symbol of the soul's attempt to purge itself of baseness; but even that does not give alchemy profound psychological significance.

Jung thought of himself as a phenomenologist. He says, for example, in *Modern Man in Search of a Soul* (1933): 'A further difference [between myself and Freud] seems to me to consist in this, that I try to free myself from all unconscious and therefore uncriticised assumptions as to the world in general.' That is an exact definition of phenomenology. But the impression one gains from a general study of his work is of a huge *system*, almost as complex as Hegel's, and one can sense his delight in building this system, like some Gothic cathedral. But he is not a rationalist in the ordinary sense of the word, for the complexities upon which he is trying to impose order are psychological and personal, not abstract. So it is not surprising if his work often brings to mind books on astrology or the Tarot pack. His exposition of the theory of types in *Psychological Types* sounds occasionally like a fortune teller's manual. There are two basic types: the extraverted and introverted. The introverted are shy; when confronted with situations or problems, they seem to draw back for a moment, as if uttering a silent 'No'. The extravert goes forward eagerly, says Jung. But apart from these types, man possesses four 'functions' through which he deals with the world: sensations, thinking, feeling and intuition. Imagine I wake out of a deep sleep. First comes mere sensation of the room. If it is a strange room, I then have to recall where I am. This is thinking. Next comes my reaction to the room: is it pleasant or unpleasant? This act of judgement is 'feeling'. As to intuition, this is a subtler version of feeling, a kind of unconscious assessment of things, and it would tend to operate more with people than things: I might feel intuitively that so and so is lying . . .

Jung groups these functions into two. Thinking and feeling are rational and belong together, says Jung: feeling is rational because our feelings about things tend to be as stable as our thoughts about them, not to change from moment to moment. (This will strike many people as a dubious proposition.) Sensation and intuition are grouped as irrational, for obvious reasons. Jung now goes on to describe eight types of people, by applying the adjective 'introverted' or 'extraverted' to the four functions. Briefly, extraverted thinkers tend to be rational, logical and insensitive to fine shades: Professor A. J. Ayer, or any other logical positivist, would fit this classification. Introverted thinkers are interested in inner realities; Jung himself would be a good example; so would Schopenhauer and Nietzsche. Extraverted 'feelers' are more often female than male; any highly successful political hostess fits this type. Introverted feelers would tend to be shy women who feel strongly but do not show it; they are loyal, home loving, and so on. The extraverted sensation type could be a racing driver or pop singer; the introvert sensation type may be a certain type of artist: a painter like Picasso, a composer like Richard Strauss. The extraverted intuitive type would be a highly intuitive person whose flashes of intuition are mainly about people and situations; he might, for example, make a highly successful antique dealer. The introverted intuitional type may be a mystic or visionary, or perhaps a crank.

Jung explains neurosis as follows. Human beings tend to develop one of the four faculties above the others. Since the faculties run in opposites, a person who develops the thinking faculty to a high degree will tend to suppress the feeling faculty. (The other two hover somewhere in between.) A person who develops sensation to a high degree will tend to repress intuition. And so on. Under pressure of a competitive society, individual faculties tend to get over-developed, since they are the individual's means of dealing with the world and making a living. Their opposite faculty not only becomes enfeebled, but finally loses all strength. Jung borrows the Freudian term 'libido' to refer to *all* psychic energy, and he argues that if a man thinks far too much, his feelings tend to go dead and he experiences a sense of life-failure; if a mystical type over-develops the intuitions, the ability to respond to physical sensation tends to diminish. Neurosis is this psychic unbalance.

It will be at once apparent that, from the point of view of existential psychology, this is subtler than the 'sexual theory'. At the same time, it shares with Freudian psychology a tendency to over-schematisation, the reductionist tendency to make reality fit ideas. It stands at the opposite extreme from the tendency of Dostoevsky or Walt Whitman, to see every human being as somehow splendid and unique. And its chief danger is that its schematic obsession makes it *insensitive* to the factors that

control the 'libido'—the sense of meaning or lack of it, the feeling of 'newness', or boredom; the will to power, or the sense of
defeat. This is always the danger of an over-ponderous theoretical scheme: that it seems to set in motion a kind of destructive tendency, like a runaway juggernaut. Readers of Eric
Berne's highly successful *Games People Play* may have noticed
this: how after reading descriptions of dozens of ways in which
people can be dishonest with themselves, playing certain emotional games as they might play a gramophone record, one
tends to see 'games' everywhere one looks, and sincerity seems
to have evaporated from the world. Similarly, an enthusiastic
Marxian can interpret every work of art so as to entirely miss
the meaning the artist put into it.

Jung's revolt from Freud was a revolt against narrowness. ⌐
'Freud's teaching is definitely one-sided in that it generalises
from facts that are relevant only to neurotic states of mind; its
validity is confined to these states.' This sentence, which sounds
like Maslow, is actually from *Modern Man in Search of a Soul*
(p. 135). Like Maslow, Jung was interested in the psychology of
man's evolutionary faculties: his creativity, his religious and
artistic intuitions, even his 'occult powers'. But it was impossible,
in the Freudian climate, to take the decisive step: to *start* from
the point of view of the artist or mystic, in which the centrally
important fact is the creative energies themselves. This view is
implicit, for example, in the work of D. H. Lawrence: the
feeling that psychological health depends upon putting first
things first, and that the 'first things' are the upsurges of vital
energy from the depths of the subconscious: the feeling a man
may experience as he makes love or holds a baby or smells the
the first touch of spring in the air. Theoretically speaking, Jung
wanted to place 'poetry' at the centre of psychology; practically
speaking, he could never quite bring himself to do it.

The result is that the Jungian system is an endlessly fascinating labyrinth, the 20th-century version of the great philosophical systems—of Kant, Lotze, Hegel, Hartmann. It also
has (as Progoff has pointed out), strong affinities with the
'systems' of Paul Tillich and Arnold Toynbee (and, one might
add, Spengler). At one extreme it touches occultism and
alchemy, at the other, Christian redemption. But even in the
later work, the limitations are apparent. His Eranos Conference

lecture in 1946 tried to explain archetypes in terms of the instincts of animals; a bird is born with a nest-building instinct, a
salmon with the instinct to swim up-river in the mating season,
and so on. These instincts define the very nature of birds and
fish. In that case, what is man's 'nature'—what was he 'born
for'? This is precisely the point where evolutionary thinkers,
from Nietzsche to Teilhard de Chardin, would point out that
man is an 'open ended' creature who may evolve indefinitely.
The interesting thing about him is that he is the only creature
capable of controlling his own evolution, of understanding and
changing his own nature. Sir Julian Huxley has remarked that
'man has become the managing director of evolution in the
universe'—and if this seems rather an excessive claim, we can
at least amend it to 'on this planet'. Teilhard asserts that mind
is literally a new dimension of freedom, and Huxley has
pointed out the immense importance of art in human evolution, man's attempt to 'fix' his flashes of transcendence and
therefore to gain control of the most vital part of his psychic
life. Jung is also deeply interested in art, but his desire to find
'archetypes' leads him to overlook its basic importance as an
attempt to create a 'third world', to build castles in the noösphere,
so to speak.

This is not to belittle Jung's achievement. In asserting the
existence of 'impersonal' levels of consciousness, he took the all-
important step 'beyond reductionism'; he opened new territories for psychology. But his limitation must be stated clearly:
in treating these new territories as wholly objective realities,
somehow independent of individual consciousness, *he overlooked
the central importance of intentionality, of the human will, in all psychological processes*. An interesting example is his definition of introvert and extravert, as given in *Modern Man in Search of a Soul*;
that the introvert is the man who reacts to a situation by
drawing back a little as if with an unvoiced 'No', while the
extraverts are men who 'come forward with an immediate
reaction, apparently confident that their behaviour is obviously
right'. Here Jung has created two 'types' out of a response that
is common to all human beings: and not only is it common, but
it is perhaps the most basic, the most important, of all our
psychological mechanisms. When I draw back from a problem
with an unvoiced 'no', I am saying, 'It is not worth the effort.'

When I press forward, it is with the feeling that some important *gain* lies not far ahead of me, a true *value*. And here we are dealing with what I have called 'the St Neot margin problem'. The question of human freedom is involved. For the most interesting thing is that a man with every reason to be cheerful may feel 'Oh no' about some fairly trivial problem, while men with every reason to be miserable may experience a 'yes'—like Frankl's prisoners, cold and wet, but happy because the camp has no incinerator chimney. In defining the extravert and introvert, Jung has touched upon the most fundamental question in all psychology—not only human, for experiment has shown that laboratory rats, and even the planarion worm (an extremely primitive organism) show this same tendency to *devalue* when bored. This is the great problem: *that consciousness without crisis tends to become negative*: an absurd paradox since our whole civilisation is aimed at producing a danger-free existence. Instead of recognising the universal importance of the 'yes' or 'no' response, Jung used it to buttress a false definition—for it is not true that the extravert is characterised by 'yes' and the introvert by 'no'. When confronted by a page of mathematics, or any other demand for mental activity, the extravert tends to say 'no'; on the other hand, most of the world's great music, poetry and philosophy was created by introverts, and expresses an affirmative forward-movement. The paradox is resolved by a moment's thought. It is a question of what James called 'nutritious objects of attention'. The introvert recoils from mere physical activity because it often strikes him as meaningless; 'as for living, our servants can do that for us'. The extravert recoils from a page of mathematics because it strikes him as meaningless. But their ideas of 'meaningless' are exact opposites. The introvert recoils from mere activity because its meaning-concentration strikes him as too low; the extravert recoils from mathematics or philosophy because its meaning-concentration is too high. His teeth prefer to chew softer food. It is once again a question of *meaning*. Jung came close to creating a meaning-psychology but he turned back at the last moment.

'. . . civilised man does not act only upon the rational guidance of his intellectual ego, nor is he driven blindly by the

mere elemental forces of his instinctual self. Mankind's civilisation . . . has emerged from the perpetual operation of a third
principle, which combines the rational and irrational elements
in a world view based upon the conception of the supernatural.
This not only holds good for primitive group life . . . but is still
borne out in our highly mechanised civilisation by the vital
need for spiritual values.'

These sentences are not, as might be thought, by Jung, but by
Otto Rank, the last of the major Freud disciples to break away
and follow his own path. In Rank's case, the break was not the
result of a long process of chafing under the Freudian yoke, but
almost accidental. Rank had come to Freud in 1905,[1] two years
before Jung. He had written a paper called *The Artist*, which
dealt with his lifelong preoccupation, the psychology of the
artist. It is interesting—and significant—that each of the four
major figures of psychoanalysis—Freud, Adler, Jung, Rank—
brought to the subject his own basic preoccupations—in Freud's
case, sex; in Jung's, occultism; in Adler's, the will to power; in
Rank's, the artist—and evolved a psychology in which these
were made applicable to the human race in general. Freud
showed special favour to Rank, whose range of culture was as
wide as Jung's and after the defection of Jung and Adler, Rank
was regarded as the foremost of Freudian disciples. His books
and papers continued to receive the Freudian 'nihil obstat'
throughout two decades. The possibility that Rank might become the most extreme of the rebels against Freudian doctrine
entered no one's head—least of all Rank's.

Round about 1919, Rank became increasingly preoccupied
with problems relating to birth and the relations between
married couples—the immediate reason being his wife's pregnancy. It seems to have been about then that he became convinced that the earliest and most painful shock human beings
experience is being born, when there is danger of suffocation,
and that it is this early shock that causes all neurosis later in
life. Freud had already spoken about the trauma of birth, but
Rank now made it the most important event in human life; the

---

[1] At least, this is the date given by Progoff. Ernest Jones, who borrowed my
copy of Progoff's *Death and Rebirth of Psychology* and made some notes in it scrawled
'No' beside this date. He gives 1906 as the date in volume 2 of his life of Freud, but
no account of the meeting.

cure, he said, was to compel the patient to re-live the shock—
which ought, according to Freudian doctrine, to effect a cure.
His book *The Trauma of Birth* (1923) was badly written—like all
Rank's work—and Jones says that it has a 'hyperbolical vein
more suitable for the announcement of a new religious gospel'.
Freud, oddly enough, did not mind the book; he always maintained the importance of encouraging his followers to make
their own discoveries. But other members of the psychoanalytic
school, particularly in Berlin, attacked it vigorously, and Karl
Abraham, a close friend of Freud's, called it a 'scientific re-
gression which closely resembled that of Jung and Adler . . .'
Freud defended Rank, and it is difficult to see quite why the
others attacked him so fiercely; the book was Freudian in spirit,
even if it shifted the emphasis from rivalry with the father to the
relation with the mother. (Freud was convinced that this
rivalry is so deep-seated that only the death of the father can
really free a man's subconscious creative forces.) At all events,
Rank suddenly found himself in the same position as Jung in
1913—ostracised by the Freudians. In a series of lectures in
America, Rank explained that his birth theory had superseded
Freud, and reports of all this did nothing to improve his position with the Viennese circle. When he returned to Vienna,
there was a brief period when Rank asked forgiveness on the
grounds that he had passed through a period of severe neurosis;
but he could never again become a whole-hearted Freudian.
For he had suddenly understood the basic fallacy in psychoanalysis: that it treats the will as something fixed and static.
Techniques of Psychoanalysis[1] contains the startling sentence:
'. . . it would not be paradoxical to say that psychoanalysis, in
its therapeutic consequences, is an involuntary proof of the
existence and strength of the will, and that this was and is its
only therapeutic value'. This was defection with a vengeance.
In this book he points out that Freud has overlooked the importance of the will in curing neurotic patients, and makes the
revolutionary assertion that the real benefit a patient derives
from being psychoanalysed is that the clash with the psychoanalyst revives his deflated and passive will. The sick patient
has a will-to-health, says Rank, which he has allowed to

---

[1] A three-volume work written between 1925 and 1930; its second two volumes
were translated as *Will Therapy*.

collapse under the pressure of anxieties; when he goes to the analyst, it has often become a mere spark. Successful therapy, says Rank, consists of carefully blowing this spark back into a bonfire.

This was the most revolutionary assertion that had ever been made in psychology; even James had not penetrated to this amazing and simple truth, although he had come very close. Rank said that his discovery fell midway between Freud's sexual theory of neurosis and Adler's will-to-power theory; but in reality, it went far beyond both.

Of all the Freudians, Rank was the inevitable one to make this discovery, for he had never ceased to be absorbed in the problem of creativity and art. If creativity is not to be construed as some sort of compensation mechanism (Yeats once said he wrote poetry as a sick cat eats valerian), then it must be seen as the will's attempt to do more than merely 'cope' with life: to actually achieve some degree of conquest. Freud saw life as a kind of endless battle, a tangled web of problems, most of them lying treacherously below the surface of consciousness like weed below the surface of a lake; the individual was lucky if he could just more-or-less hold his own with them. His attitude was bound to be defensive. According to Rank, the artist actually takes the offensive, hoping to emerge as some kind of conqueror.

Having achieved this insight, Rank now found himself faced with a further problem. So man possesses a 'will to health'—which means, obviously, a will to increased control over his own life (since illness could be defined as a decreased control). If the will to health has almost ceased to operate in a severely neurotic person, then it ought to increase in strength in direct proportion to the health of the person. The healthiest man ought to possess the strongest will to health—to increased conquest—so that there should, theoretically, *be no upward limit to health*. This is contradicted by experience. When a therapist makes a patient well, he does not expect the patient to go on getting weller and weller. Very occasionally, the disappearance of mental problems might produce a burst of creativity—as when Rachmaninov wrote his fine second piano concerto after being psychoanalysed. But usually, all that happens is that the personality reaches a certain kind of integration, and remains more-or-less stable at that level. Freud's negative theory fitted the facts of experience better than Rank's new kind of optimism. It was incumbent on Rank to explain why man appears to be oddly fixed and limited if the will is so important.

He faced the task, but it was an immense one. It involved the study of history, since his task was to outline human develop-ment—how man reached his present stage on the evolutionary ladder. It was also inevitable that he should take account of religious or spiritual values. His long study of art provided him with the key; (he was, as Progoff remarks, a frustrated artist). What is the root of man's most basic striving? It is not really the desire to return to the womb or lose the sense of identity in sexual intensity. The force that drives all intelligent human beings, from the most primitive to the most civilised, is the desire *to be immortal*. Like the Russian philosopher Fedorov, he recognised that the basic aim of mankind is the ultimate con-quest of death. This is why we climb mountains and irrigate deserts and send up moon rockets: the great challenge tenses the will, produces concentration, pushes back the sluggishness of the flesh, unites the mind's diffuseness. Underlying it all is the drive to more life—what Shaw calls the appetite for fruitful activity and a high quality of life.

Rank's next step was the most crucial. For he saw that an aim like this is fundamentally a drive *beyond the personal*. Man longs to slake an immense thirst in the cool waters of the impersonal, of objective meaning. And this longing is on the deepest level of man's being, says Rank. Art and culture are not, as Freud asserted, by-products of the libido's striving for satisfaction, but material testimony of man's craving for the impersonal. One might say that all human beings possess a personality, but the greatest men also possess a 'non-personality', an 'impersonality'. This impersonality (my term, not Rank's) exists in embryo in all human beings; artists and saints strive systematically to de-velop it. 'I would be cold and passionate as the dawn', says Yeats. It is not a desire to be indifferent to life, but to see it from a mountain top, so to speak. The artist may be intensely subjective; but that is only the first stage; he obeys a need to get his personal problems out of his system in order to be free to devote himself to something bigger.

Rank places the hero and the artist at the centre of his system.

Primitive man, he says, lived in a world of intuition; he did not see the world through rationalistic spectacles; his sense of impersonal realities was direct. The hero performed his heroic feats as a kind of assertion of the reality of this super-personal world, an act of commitment, like a pilgrim setting out with his staff and bundle. The hero is driven by the urge for the impersonal, for victory over death. But as the 'era of the soul' gives way to the psychological era, self-division enters; straightforward heroism is no longer the natural outlet of the highest type of man. Caught in a kind of invisible net, the heroic personality is fated to tragedy, a high-powered car trying to drive with the brakes on. Hence the artistic tragedies of the 19th century. Freudian psychology took an important step beyond rational materialism by recognising the unconscious mind, thus taking the artist one step further along his road to salvation. But since psychoanalysis was negative and oriented towards neurosis, it was bound to disappoint expectations. The artist must learn to go 'beyond psychology', to stop chaining himself with a false rationalism, to learn to trust and express the subconscious, to *live* it. A parallel might make this clearer. Negroes, on the whole, dance better than whites because they are closer to primitive self-expression through the body. After several thousand years of civilisation, dancing has ceased to be natural to the Caucasian races. Isadora Duncan and Nijinsky revolutionised dancing by teaching that it must become once again the spontaneous expression of subconscious impulses; when he was mentally sick, Nijinsky terrified an audience by 'dancing the war'. Dancing had become as natural a mode of self-expression to him as speaking is to the rest of us. This is roughly equivalent to what Rank believed the artist would have to do: to live with the subconscious, to learn to become its expression . . .

As a 'solution', this raises an obvious problem. Man developed rational consciousness in order to cope with the world, to create civilisation. Learning to express irrationality may be all very well for a dancer, or even a painter or poet, but it would not do for someone who has to go to work every Monday morning. It is true that anyone can benefit from a deliberate attempt to throw off inhibitions. Instead of examining a new fur rug with critical detachment, I might take off all my clothes and roll on it. This would be an example of the kind of 'mental act' that can reduce conscious tension: to make a continuous attempt to experience things freshly. (This is the aim of the 'gestalt therapy' developed by Frederick Perls; it consists basically in *noticing* everything more, ceasing to do things automatically.[1]) But even this is only a partial answer.

Tragically, Rank died in 1939, before he had even finished his definitive book, *Beyond Psychology*. His major work had been, in a sense, negative: a criticism of Freudian psychology rather than an attempt to create new foundations. His own work and Maslow's were so close that it is a pity they never collaborated. Maslow had to create his own 'will psychology' instinctively, on a basis of experimental psychology in the laboratory; Rank's historical approach might have been a revelation. On the other hand, it might only have destroyed the directness and naivety that were Maslow's chief strength.

And what, in the last analysis, was missing from the new psychology developed by Adler, Jung and Rank? This can be seen clearly by considering one of Jung's unsuccessful cases[2]. A successful business man was able to retire and settle in the country; he had looked forward to peace and leisure. But he had always been a highly energetic man, and the sudden change of routine was too much for him. It led to total nervous collapse, the 'condition of a peevish child'. A doctor pointed out to him that he needed to go back to work. The patient took the advice, but found that he had lost interest in business, and that no amount of persistence helped. The anxiety state increased, a general feeling of inner tension and worry. Jung recognised that business was no answer, that it was 'un-nutritive' to his mind. 'The energy of life demands a channel congenial to itself; otherwise it is simply dammed up and becomes destructive.' But he could not think of any purpose to 'allure the energy', and so the patient had to remain uncured.

The first thing one observes here is the similarity of the case to that of Maslow's girl in the chewing gum factory. The business man has plunged into a state of total boredom with his own existence, and the anxieties are an attempt of his vital forces to compensate in some way for the boredom. It also resembles the

---

[1] *Gestalt Therapy* by Perls, Hefferline, Goodman, Delta Books 1951.
[2] Cited by Progoff: *Jung's Psychology and Its Social Meaning*, p. 116.

cases James mentions in *The Energies of Man,* of neurasthenics to whom every molehill has become a mountain. James points out that such patients respond to 'bullying treatment' in which they are forced to make an effort. 'First comes the very extremity of distress, then follows unexpected relief.'

Let us consider the phenomenology of Jung's case. The patient is a business man. He has devoted his life to self-chosen objectives and meanings, building up a large business, presumably with the aim of providing himself and his family with security. He tells himself that before he is too old to appreciate it, he will retire and spend the rest of his days doing the things he enjoys on Sundays—boating, walking in the woods, playing croquet on the lawn with his grandchildren. A point comes where this becomes the aim that lies beyond his business; he is no longer working solely for money, but for *what it means,* retirement, and some kind of life of the mind or spirit, as it were. He retires. And the St Neot margin problem arises. He has over-anticipated, like a child looking forward to Christmas, so it is bound to be a disappointment. Above all, he fails to grasp the phenomenology of the will: that if you stop making efforts for long enough, the will-batteries go flat, and 'life loses its savour'. He *tries* to relax, as his right; but true relaxation comes only after intense effort. For in effect, the subconscious mind is still poised for effort; the attention is fully awake; the vital energies continue to flow, prepared for further effort. Above all, *the sense of meaning must be left switched-on.* True relaxation—such as is described in many of Wordsworth's poems—is an influx of meaning, as if the brain was a battery 'on charge'. In other words, only the 'surface' of the mind is relaxed. The kind of relaxation that comes just before we fall asleep is quite different; we are deliberately switching-off the sense of meaning. This is precisely what Jung's business man did. The inevitable result followed. To use James's image: the dam moved up-river, turning his lake of freedom into a duck pond. At this point, his doctor sent him back to work; but this is like advising a man who is shivering with cold to take off his clothes and swim in the river. What was needed was 'bullying treatment'; the doctor should have advised him to do something hard and dangerous; try and climb Mount Everest or row a boat across the Channel. The business man would have replied, 'I don't want to'. And the doctor, if he possessed insight, would have said: 'Good. Go and do it all the same, and take a pride in not wanting to. The more you hate it, the quicker you'll be cured . . .' The effort, even undertaken with reluctance, would have restored the circulation of the vital energies.

By the time Jung saw him, the stagnating energies had complicated the case by producing cross currents of revulsion, tension, anxiety. At this point, it was necessary to grasp that the basic problem was a problem of *meaning*. If the man was at all intelligent—as presumably he must have been to be successful in business—then an approach similar to Maslow's—in the case of the girl patient—would have been successful. The psychologist's job was to investigate the man's sense of meaning, and then apply himself—or persuade the patient to apply himself—to re-stimulating it. In the case of the alcoholics, Hoffer used mescalin as a means of stimulating the aesthetic sense of meaning. Psychedelics were (presumably) not available to Jung, but some other drug might have served. It is, of course, quite impossible to state categorically what Jung *ought* to have done. Only one thing is certain; his statement. 'A case so far advanced can only be cared for till death' indicates a defeatist approach. If the patient was intelligent, and interested enough to consult Jung, then he was still curable. The only incurable patients are those who do not want to be cured, like a drunk who refuses to stand on his feet.

Rank would have recognised that the key to this case was the patient's recognition that something was wrong, and his desire to be cured: the will to health. He might also have known enough about 'the bullying treatment' to be able to explain to the patient that the problem was that he had allowed his energies to sink too low, and that any determined effort to contract the will-muscle would eventually cure him, whether or not it was accompanied by pleasure. (Jung made the mistake of thinking that the man needed a *congenial* channel for his energy.) But Rank's 'artist psychology' would have been neither here nor there. All his insight into the cultural dilemma would have made no difference; what he needed was a recognition that the human mind needs meaning to keep it healthy.

It can also be seen that Freud's sexual theory or Adler's will-to-power approach would have been totally irrelevant here.

Psychoanalysis might have helped the patient, by giving him something to think about and arousing the will-to-health; but this would have been accidental.

Let me, at this point, anticipate the final section of this book, and attempt to be more specific about the aetiology of this type of illness. Man possesses a more highly developed 'robot' than any other animal, and the robot is capable of taking over most of his vital functions, particularly those that do not require an acute *sense of meaning*. Most of our everyday acts are partly 'robotic'. This is demonstrated, for example, by the party game in which questions are fired at a victim who is told not to answer yes or no, and not to shake or nod his head; he must find various circumlocutions for yes and no. With the utmost vigilance, most people shake or nod their heads within seconds.

The robot tends to take over when I am tired or when my energies are low. When my sense of meaning is acute, it is the 'real me' who does things; when it is low, the robot does things for me, and I pay for it by lack of sense of meaning, a general wandering of attention. In this state I 'run down'; my batteries do not recharge, for recharging is a function of the sense of meaning, of willed effort.

Jung's business man relaxed and switched off his sense of meaning. The robot took over. So instead of the man enjoying his retirement, it failed to stimulate him. If he wants to enjoy retirement, he must snatch it out of the hands of the robot. He must deliberately awaken his sense of meaning. Instead, he becomes bewildered and alarmed at his state of boredom: a sense of defeat creeps over him. His energies sink, and the robot takes over more than ever. When he wakes up in the morning, it is not *he* who hears the birds outside the window, it is the robot.

When the mind is static, and able to contemplate its own boredom, the trouble begins. Oblomov, sitting on his stove, takes no harm from boredom because he doesn't really mind being bored; you might say he expects to be bored. Jung's businessman allowed it to hurl him into alarmed depression. And once the mind's terrifying negative tendencies have been given the blessing of the ego, as it were, the real devastation begins. The destructive powers of the mind are as extraordinary as its creative powers. It is possible that Jung's patient had gone too far into self-destruction to be cured (although this is rarer than might be supposed, since both body and mind are built to stand immense strains). All this can be avoided only by intimate understanding of the processes involved.

And at this point, let me again emphasise that the robot is not an enemy. None of man's higher creative processes would be possible without the robot. Every kind of skill depends upon him. For example: at the side of our house, there is a narrow space into which I back our jeep to protect it from the winter gales. When I first tried it, it took several clumsy attempts. Now I back it in quickly and easily. But it would be a mistake to say that the robot does the work. On the contrary; 'I' still have to concentrate fairly carefully: the robot *collaborates* with the 'essential me' to do the job smoothly. And it is so in all man's creative functions. When a great pianist sounds inspired, when a great conductor gets the best out of the orchestra, when a great actor seems to become the part he is playing, the 'ego' is working at top pressure, and the robot is *collaborating* superbly; it is a perfect *partnership*. This is when the robot demonstrates his real powers, and shows why he was created. And when man learns to break away from his present thoroughly unsatisfactory state of consciousness, and to achieve something altogether more creative and positive, it will be through the collaboration of the robot.

Before we turn to Maslow's contribution, it is necessary to speak briefly of the school of gestalt psychology; for although its methods are of no concern here—since this book is only incidentally concerned with experimental psychology—its ideas had considerable influence on Maslow.

Gestalt psychology came into being as a revolt against the experimental psychology of the 19th century, Wundt in particular. This type of psychology accepted the basic notion of Locke and Hume that if we could take human experience to pieces, we would end up with small 'atoms', tiny individual sensations like the individual brush strokes in a pointiliste painting. J. B. Watson's behaviourism was based upon the same principle—that the mind could be treated as if it were a complicated machine that worked on stimulus and response.

I have already mentioned (p. 56) Whitehead's view that we

have two types of perception, 'immediacy perception' and 'meaning perception'. This contradicts the 'experimental' position by asserting that we perceive meaning intuitively and directly, in one big leap, as it were. Gestalt psychology came to the same conclusion. What the mind grasps is not a series of bits and pieces, *but the relation between the bits and pieces.* This is what interests it.

What bothered the behaviourists about the gestalt position was that it seemed only one step away from the occultism that Freud was so alarmed about. How does a baby recognise its mother's face? The Wundtian explanation would involve a series of small acts of learning: recognition of human faces in general, the fact that they have eyes, noses, mouths; then recognition of the characteristic features of its mother's face. The gestalt (or 'form') psychologists asserted that the baby simply grasps the *totality* of her face instantly, recognising it by a special faculty whose purpose is to grasp 'meanings'. This seemed to be only one step away from asserting the existence of some telepathic faculty for recognising mothers.

The argument between the two schools might be illustrated in this way. Suppose I am cycling past a fence which has small cracks between the boards. I can see a blurry outline of what lies on the other side—a partly-built house, let us say. The Wundtian school would say: clearly your eyes had a series of brief flashes of the house, but they came so quickly, one after another, that the mind had no problem in *adding them together* to get an impression of the total shape. What is more, the same would be true even if the fence had not been there, so you could see the house directly: perception is an act of addition which has been learned by experience. The gestaltists would declare that no 'adding' process was necessary: the speed of the glimpses enabled 'meaning perception' to work directly. They would point out that if you stood in front of the fence and peered through each crack separately, obtaining a series of partial views, this would not be the same thing at all, although it ought to be, according to the bits-and-pieces school.

Husserlian phenomenology enables us to see that neither view is entirely correct. We *do* perceive things in bits and pieces. This seems to be conclusively proved by Donald Hebb's experiments with congenitally blind people whose sight was suddenly restored. In order to distinguish a square from a hexagram, they had to count the sides, which would seem to prove that our 'instantaneous perception' of the shape of a square is actually very quick counting (or adding). On the other hand, Husserl points out that in order to 'see' anything, I have to do half the work; I have to reach out and switch-on my meaning perception. This meaning-perception is a kind of muscle which can become weaker or stronger. If it becomes very weak, the result is the sensation that Sartre calls 'nausea', in which the world appears to be meaningless. If it becomes very strong, the result is mystical intensity. Grasping meaning is a powerful mental act, like running or making a long leap. William James's experience—in which meaning seemed to expand outwards, until he was aware of distant horizons of reality—shows this faculty performing with an efficiency that is *natural to it*.

The gestaltists are right in their assertion that we possess a 'meaning faculty'; wrong in supposing that it works 'spontaneously'. The act of grasping meaning is intentional—it is *willed*. But the meaning is already there to be grasped. It is not an arbitrary addition by the mind, as Hume believed.

The importance of this conclusion can be seen when we consider the psychology of creation. In *The Psychology of Invention in the Mathematical Field*, Jacques Hadamard cites examples of discoveries occurring suddenly, in a 'flash of inspiration'. In many cases, the facts may have been staring the scientist in the face for years, yet recognition of their meaning comes in a flash. What happens is analogous to James's experience—the meaning faculty makes a leap outward, suddenly 'pays attention' where it had been inclined to take-for-granted. It closes upon the meaning like a hand picking up a small animal by the scruff of the neck. It is as if certain chemicals had been lying side by side for years, and then the meaning faculty acts as a catalyst, and they suddenly combine.

Artistic creation is no different. The actual creative faculty is a muscle for grasping meanings. In the case of most great artists, the material remains unchanged. The Tolstoy of *War and Peace* is using basically the same materials as in *The Cossacks* and *Sebastopol*. But that faculty for grasping distant horizons of reality is more active; like the scientist, he can make the materials enter into chemical combinations. It is the same faculty that I exercise when I look at my watch to see the time. But in order to notice the time, I only have to observe the relation between two hands; in a work of art, a far wider network of relations is involved.

And so we are able to justify phenomenologically Rank's assertion that the meaning in a work of art is fundamentally impersonal, objective, like a law of physics. It may be intermixed with the subjective and personal—particularly in an immature artist—but it reaches out towards the impersonal. It is only one step beyond this to recognizing that the basic evolutionary drive in human beings is towards the impersonal, and that psychological health is simply a measure of the strength of this drive.

PART TWO

I

Maslow: A Biographical Sketch

IN CONTRAST TO Freud, Maslow seems to have landed in psychology almost by accident. There was no obsessive interest in mentally sick people, developing slowly into a theory of neurosis. In fact, the pattern of his development was the reverse of Freud's. He began as a kind of lab. assistant, working in the field of behavioural psychology, studying the reactions of apes, dogs and rats. His creative faculties seem to have been prodded into activity by the dreariness of much of this research; the problem of freedom emerged by way of contrast to the controlled behaviour of laboratory rats. Neither did he see himself as a rebel against Freudian theory, as can be seen from the following letter to a colleague (who shall be nameless), written in November 1960:

'I am very disappointed with your paper on early memory, just as I was somewhat disappointed with your previous mimeographed work on psychological health. What I am afraid of for you is the complete parochialism that is so common in medically trained psychoanalysts, and which I had hoped the academically trained psychologists could avoid. You have completely overlooked the rich Adlerian literature on early memory; for instance, I remember one excellent paper by Heinz Ansbacher. Your footnote on p. 500 is not only inadequate but also snotty and shows the usual contempt with which an orthodox analytic group treats all outsiders and strangers. I may agree with you that Adler's explanatory concepts were limited, and I may agree with you that Freud was easily the greatest psychologist who ever lived, and yet a science is not made up of one leader and a lot of stooges or loyal devotees.

'I urge you to think of the young psychoanalysts as your colleagues, collaborators and partners and not as spies, traitors and wayward children. You can never develop a science that way, only an orthodox church.

Your colleague,
A. H. Maslow.

P.S. It occurs to me that a good way of saying what I want to say is that I consider myself as Freudian as you but not as *exclusively* Freudian.'

The paradox about Maslow is not simply that he was a reluctant rebel, but that he was unwilling to regard himself as any kind of a rebel at all. I have seen a copy of a letter written to him by Mike Murphy, director of the Esalen Institute in California; with infectious enthusiasm, Murphy describes a seminar in which 'the boom was lowered on psychoanalysis and behaviourism', and goes on, 'Unfortunately, none of the enemy were there to punch back . . . You were remembered many times as the father of the revolution.' Alongside this paragraph, Maslow has scrawled in block capitals: 'No, wrong!' He saw himself as a psychoanalyst and a behaviourist, not as the father of a revolution against them. He was a creative synthesiser, not in the least interested in dissension; this was his own way of making the best of his creative energies.

Abraham Maslow was born April 1, 1908, in a slum district of Brooklyn, N.Y. His father, a Russian Jew, had moved to America from Kiev; he was a cooper by trade. After an unhappy love affair, he wrote to a female cousin in Kiev, and asked her to come to the States and marry him. She did, and young Abe was the first of the seven children she bore. The family was 'upwardly mobile'—as Maslow put it—that is, his father's business slowly improved, so that they were able to move from cold water flats and unheated apartments into a series of lower middle-class homes, each one a shade more comfortable than the last.

Maslow also differed from Freud in his feeling about his mother. Their relation was not close, partly because the children came in fairly quick succession (every two years), and when a new one arrived, the previous one lost her interest. Although she was a good childbearer—and rearer (she apparently felt that having children was good for her)—her maternal feelings were not highly developed. Maslow says briefly: 'She was a pretty woman—but not a nice one.' Neither was his relationship to his father any compensation: 'by that time, he was disgusted with the whole business, and stayed away from home as much as possible.' Abe was fond of his father—'a very vigorous man, who loved whiskey and women and fighting'—but was scared of him.

'Since my mother is[1] the type that's called schizophrenogenic in the literature—she's the one who makes crazy people, crazy children—I was awfully curious to find out why I didn't go insane. I was certainly neurotic, extremely neurotic, during all my first twenty years—depressed, terribly unhappy, lonely, isolated, self-rejecting, and so on—but in theory it should have been much worse. And so I traced it back and found that my mother's brother—my maternal uncle—who's a very kind and good man to this day, and who lived nearby—took care of me, and then of my next younger brother, and the one after that. He liked babies and children, and simply took care of us whenever my mother got herself a new baby. He may have saved my life, psychically . . .'

Abe attended New York City schools through eight grades. He was nine when the family moved out of slums into their first lower middle-class home. But this was not entirely an advantage. The slum districts were Jewish; after this, they were usually the first Jews to move into non-Jewish neighbourhoods, and Abe suddenly discovered anti-semitism. He was not subjected to actual physical violence, although he was chased by gangs of Italian and Irish kids (Jewish boys were not supposed to fight). He was skinny, shy, and also, he says, 'looked peculiar', apart from looking very Jewish. He was so underweight that the family doctor was afraid he would get T.B. And although he was a good scholar and loved reading—'I practically lived in the library'—he remained isolated, even at school. 'The atmosphere of anti-semitism was very thick and very obvious and unmistakeable', and his unprepossessing appearance

[1] She has died since this tape was made in early 1970.

tended to prejudice even the more fair-minded among the teachers. He remembers particularly a Miss Doyle—'horrible bitch'—who went out of her way to be unpleasant; since he was top of the class in spelling, she made him stand up, and kept throwing spelling-words at him until he got one wrong (it was 'parallel')—upon which she bawled him out and said, 'I knew you were a fake'. 'Fortunately', he adds, 'there were always some angels around—and there have been through my whole life.' A Miss Griffin treated him with scrupulous fairness, although without warmth, and his response was instantaneous. ('I was just ready to love anybody, I guess.') But it was a lonely time, more so since he had little or no home life; he found the atmosphere uncomfortable, and didn't like his mother's food, so stayed away as much as possible, spending his time in libraries.

There followed four years of high school, the Brooklyn Borough High School, a journey of one and a half hours from his home. Since Brooklyn was then the fifth largest city in the United States, the school was excellent. He had always enjoyed school 'in a funny sort of way', but here he began to feel happy for the first time. One day in the Latin class, he answered a question so quickly that the teacher—a Mr Mann—praised him, and the rest of the class showed their admiration. It was a kind of milestone—the first time he had ever been admired for being a good student—and he describes it as 'the beginning of the happy time'.

It was at the Brooklyn High School that he became friendly with his cousin Will Maslow, who remained his only close friend for many years. They looked so much alike that they were generally taken for brothers. Will Maslow was as bright as Abe, academically speaking, but far more out-going and extroverted. It was through Will that Abe's social life began to open up, and he slowly ceased to be 'the stranger, the outsider'. He became editor of the Latin magazine, and edited *Principia*, the physics magazine, for a year. It was in the latter that, at the age of 15, he published a leader on the future of atomic energy, and predicted atomic submarines and ships. (This was about 1923!) His orientation was definitely scientific; Niels Bohr's *ABC of Atoms* triggered this enthusiasm. He was also in the chess team, and a member of the honorary society Arista. Altogether, Brooklyn High School seems to have been for

Maslow what Cambridge had been for Bertrand Russell a few decades earlier. Although it would not be true to say that he 'found himself'—he remained shy, nervous and introverted—he at least stopped being depressed and unhappy.

At 18, he went to New York City College—which was free—and found the atmosphere less congenial; the place was big and impersonal, and there were many required courses, so that he could no longer follow his own nose. His father, encouraged by these signs of a quick brain, decided that Abe ought to be a lawyer—a good, sensible choice under the circumstances; the only trouble was that Abe couldn't stand the law. But he was too timid to say so, and did a semester of law studies at night school. N.Y.C.C. was a dampening experience in other ways; he lacked 'discipline'—that is to say, he was totally unable to apply his mind to any subject that failed to interest him (a comment he repeated to me on many occasions—'my mind would simply go blank'.) The first semester, he flunked the course in trigonometry—'which I loathed'; he had been relying on his high I.Q., and on his usual method—applied to many other subjects—of cramming for a few days before the exam. In fact, this worked with the trigonometry; he passed; but the instructor, who had been holding his frequent absences against him, decided to fail him to teach him a lesson. ('There was nothing malicious about it . . . but all my begging and wheedling and whining and fast-talk didn't do any good—he just failed me.') Since all his other grades were mere passes—most of the subjects were unexciting—he was put on probation for the second semester, which meant studying only half-time. Again, he did badly—although he was enthusiastically studying-up on subjects he *did* like in every moment of spare time. At about this time—18½—a kind of artistic awakening occurred. He had discovered music, 'and just went wild with it'. (He told me, when we talked at Brandeis, that music had been an unfailing source of 'peak experiences' throughout his life, but that in recent years he felt he had become so familiar with all the repertoire that it ceased to be so.) He also discovered the American theatre, then entering an exciting stage, with the emergence of O'Neill, Maxwell Anderson, Elmer Rice, Robert Sherwood; having no money to spare for theatre tickets, he got in by selling peanuts. All this meant that his studies went from bad to worse. One day, in the law class, he felt that he couldn't stand it for a minute longer, and walked out, leaving his books behind. 'The cases seemed to deal only with evil men, and with the sins of mankind.' The moment of decision seems to have been precipitated by a discussion of 'spite fences', which offended him both as a socialist and as a human being. Still in the grip of his indignation, he went home and told his father that he didn't want to become a lawyer. 'He was terribly disappointed and depressed, but was nice about it.' He asked Abe what he wanted to do, and Abe said he wanted to go on studying. His father asked 'What?' and when Abe said 'Everything', 'he heaved a big sigh . . .' But he decided to back up his son— 'sadly'—and Abe was sent to Cornell for his fourth semester, where he was reunited with cousin Will.

There was another reason for wanting to escape New York city; for some time now, he had been in love with his cousin Bertha, and the strain was considerable. 'For several years, I just sort of looked hopelessly at her and tagged along. I never dared to touch her—didn't even dream of touching a girl, and I'd assumed that never would I have a girl . . . So I made excuses of all sorts to hang around, because she was my first cousin, and I liked her mother anyhow . . . If she had not been my cousin, I don't think I'd ever have dared go. So I hung around her. They, of course, later told me they all knew what was going on, but I hear I was making elaborate excuses for 'casually' dropping in. I was a fixture there, but I had not yet touched Bertha, or ever kissed her, or anything like that . . . And this was getting kind of rough on me—sexually, because I was very powerfully sexed—was thinking about it all the time.' So the move to Cornell was partly a flight from Bertha, 'because we were so young, and I couldn't get close to her anyhow, and it was half blissful, half painful.'

He stayed at Cornell for a semester, and again found himself burdened with required courses that he didn't want. 'But it was very beautiful. It was my first time away from home, from the sidewalks of New York.' There were new friends—through Will—and a feeling of romantic college-life, 'as I'd seen it in the movies'. But the required courses were too much, and 'I was lonesome for Bertha', so he returned to New York at the end of the semester, and went back to City College. Bertha's elder sister Anna gave the romance a shove—literally—by one day pushing Abe into her arms. 'I kissed her, and nothing terrible happened—the heavens didn't fall, and Bertha accepted it, and that was the beginning of a new life.' He was nineteen, and it was the first time he'd ever kissed a girl. The result was an enormous accession of self-belief. 'I was accepted by a female. I was just deliriously happy with her. It was a tremendous and profound and total love affair.' In a letter to me, he described this kiss as one of the major peak experiences of his life. It was now possible to give full rein to his tremendous capacity for affection, and Bertha may have found it overwhelming. 'She accepted it, rather than initiating it, but this was enough for me, and I was very happy.' There was a sense of intellectual as well as emotional liberation. He was becoming aware of just how lucky he was to be a New Yorker. 'It was a great intellectual metropolis', and Abe's heroes were lecturers and writers, who could often be heard at the Cooper Union. (He heard a debate between Bertrand Russell and Reinhold Niebuhr there.) His socialism was reinforced by lectures at the Labor Temple and the Rand School, and he learned about the history of philosophy in a series of free lectures by Will Durant. He attended two concerts a week at Carnegie Hall—the New York Symphony Orchestra was conducted by Walter Damrosch. (A few years later, he attended Toscanini concerts with the same enthusiasm and regularity.) He even took a course in music. 'I was like a dipsomaniac—I just went crazy about music.'

He and Bertha spent every free moment together, although he also mentions that 'I practically lived at the 42nd Street library.' However, the path of true love was not quite smooth. Bertha was an immigrant, and 'among Jews of the time, these were called greenhorns'. It was a matter of status; having been born in America, Abe was socially a step above her; or so his parents thought. 'Since my own feeling of self-worth was so shaky, this all shook me.' As a consequence, he made the extraordinary decision to run away from Bertha a second time—this time to go to the University of Wisconsin. Anybody could have told him that this wouldn't work. 'I thought about her all the time, and a few months later I sent her a telegram and said we were going to get married—I don't think I asked her to marry me. I just announced we were going to get married.' And at

Christmas that year—1928—they were married in New York. Bertha returned with him to Wisconsin, and enrolled as a student.

Having Bertha with him was an important step in adjustment to academic life. Cornell had been a lonely experience; he had waited at table there, to earn his keep, and later recalled that during the whole semester, no one said either 'hello' or 'goodbye'. Wisconsin was a liberal university—which was one of the main reasons why he had chosen it—but there was 'a pervasive atmosphere of anti-semitism', which later on outweighed the pleasant memories to such an extent that he could never bear to join their alumni association, in spite of repeated requests.

It was at Wisconsin that Maslow's interest swung definitely into psychology. To the detached observer, this looks almost inevitable. Although science had captured his imagination at high school, he lacked the temperament for experimental physics. (His endless struggles with the tapes he sent me demonstrate a certain awkwardness in the practical or mechanical realm.) Politically, he was an idealistic socialist; his heroes were Upton Sinclair, Eugene Debs and Norman Thomas. He speaks about his Utopianism, 'yearning for the good world' which is a Jewish tradition. What he needed, then, was a scientific discipline, practical in the sense of having an application to society, but not too practical in the mechanical sense. At Cornell he had attended lectures in psychology; but the psychology department there was dominated by the Titchener-Wundt method known as structuralism (or sometimes as existentialism), which was literally an attempt to turn psychology into a kind of chemistry, in which various 'elemental' sensations or perceptions united to form the compound we call consciousness. The method was dreary—introspection focused upon processes of perception or memory—and was unlikely to appeal to a youth who had just discovered the music of Beethoven and the plays of O'Neill. Fortunately, a philosophy professor at N.Y.C.C. suggested that Maslow look into *Psychologies of 1925* edited by Carl Murchison. He found this altogether more absorbing, particularly the chapter by John B. Watson, an American psychologist who had been profoundly influenced by the work of Ivan Pavlov with dogs. In effect,

Watson's behaviourism was a new form of James Mill's associationism, with the idea of the 'conditioned reflex' adding an element of scientific precision.

It may sound insane that a youth who had rejected Titchener as too dry and materialistic should be bowled over by Watson. But it should be remembered first of all that behaviourism seems to offer a philosophy of human existence: a pessimistic philosophy, perhaps; but then, the young are attracted to pessimism, as the continuing popularity of Schopenhauer among college students demonstrates. Besides, the view that man is a machine suggests that he can be improved scientifically,[1] and it was this aspect of behaviourism that touched Maslow's imagination. Philosophy was all talk, but this seemed a practical way of improving society. 'My goals were very definitely utopian and messianic and world-improving and people-improving . . . and here it looked to me as if I'd got the secret by the tail.' (B. F. Skinner, a Watsonian disciple, later attempted to sketch a behaviourist Utopia in *Walden Two* (1948), a book that has maintained an enormous popularity with American students.)

And so Maslow went to Wisconsin with the aim of majoring in psychology—with minors in biology and philosophy. At last, he was entirely absorbed in subjects that interested him. This made all the difference to his general feeling of well-being, and outweighed the perpetual irritation of anti-semitism.

This was a profoundly satisfying period. The psychology department was small, and at this time—in the depression— there were not many students, usually about ten of them to four professors. So the atmosphere was pleasant, comfortable, 'gemütlich', Maslow says. His lack of ability to concentrate on anything that bored him was counterbalanced by an ability to work fanatically at anything he enjoyed—to such an extent that he quickly ran through all the courses, leaving his whole graduate period free for research and reading.

His chief characteristic was still shyness; but in an obviously brilliant student, this was endearing rather than otherwise. He formed two close friendships with fellow students—Rod Menzies and Paul Settlage, both of whom unfortunately died young. But the most pleasant surprise was the friendliness of the

---

[1] Maslow entitled a seminar in the 1960s 'I was a teenage Mechanist', echoing the title of the movie, 'I Was a Teenage Werewolf'.

faculty. 'I had never talked with a professor before—I'd never been that close.' But now a number of them proved to be 'angels'. William H. Sheldon—later famous as the author of *Varieties of Temperament*—took Abe out for meals, helped him buy his clothes, and became fond of him. He wanted Maslow to work on his theory of constitutional types, which later made him famous; but Maslow, typically, preferred to go his own way. He liked his professors, but didn't regard them as intellectual giants. ('I was looking for Platos and Aristotles.') Even so, he regarded them as members of a kind of social or professional olympus; he has an amusing account of his mixed feelings on standing at the side of his philosophy professor, Eliseo Vivas, at the urinal, and having to go off by himself to assimilate this amazing experience. 'How did I think that pro- fessors urinated? Didn't I know they had kidneys? Yet the fact remains that when I saw a professor urinating just next to me like any normal mortal, it stunned me so that it took hours, or even weeks, for me to assimilate the fact that a professor was a human being and that he was constructed with the same plumbing that anybody else had.' Vivas, like Harry Harlow and Ernest Marchand, treated Maslow as a friend and an equal, and he admits that this was as important for his self-confidence as his acceptance by Bertha had been. Although he does not say so, it sounds as though what developed was a series of father-son relationships; Maslow, with his shyness, brilliance and hero worship must have seemed ideal son-material. The 'outsider' (as he repeatedly refers to himself) was coming inside. This was emphasised at his first meeting of the American Psychological Association in 1931; he was driven there by his professors, who also fed him. He was introduced to the men who wrote his college textbooks, and 'I was taken very seriously by everybody, as a young member of the tribe.' The phrasing here also suggests that it may have been his sense of at last 'be- longing' to a group—satisfying the strong Jewish feeling for community—that influenced his decision to make a career of psychology whether there was money in it or not (and at this time, he had no reason to think there was).

His training under these professors was, as he says, in 'classical laboratory research' i.e. Pavlovian rats and dogs. This was admirable training, even though his heart was not entirely in it. 'Somehow there were inner-voices that made me do some things but not others'—so that although he became Sheldon's research assistant, he instinctively shied away from the 'varieties of temperament' theories. In spite of such differences of opinion, he remained popular with his professors, and graduated in 1934, at the age of twenty-six. The year before graduation he had written his first paper on *Psychoanalysis as a Status-Quo Social Philosophy* for the Wisconsin Academy of Science, which had been accepted for publication; but when the time came to read it aloud, he was overcome with panic. 'I just couldn't face them. I fled . . .' So the paper never appeared. But the mere title of the paper reveals the direction of his thought: that psychoanalysis, with its concept of 'normality' as a kind of passive, neurosis-free condition, is suitable to a static rather than an evolving society. It was the question that Otto Rank was attacking in his studies of the role of the artist in society.

This tendency to timidity—even to panic—was to persist many years; (on one tape, he mentions 1960 as the year when it finally disappeared). For days, even weeks, before he was due to deliver a paper, there would be an increasing tension, so that the paper was sometimes delivered in a state of total exhaustion. (I am inclined to wonder whether this constant hypertension had anything to do with his heart ailment.[1]) As late as 1959, when reading his paper on *The Cognition of Being in Peak Experiences*, he went through all the usual strains and tensions before the address, and then (according to Bertha Maslow) 'delivered the paper as if throwing it at them', after which he had to retire to bed for several days to recover.

Maslow produced some half-dozen papers while he was an undergraduate, one on the emotion of disgust in dogs—verifying that dogs had an instinctive distaste for cannibalism—and the others on the learning process in monkeys. (I shall speak more fully of these later.) It was good, plodding work in the behaviourist tradition. The odd thing is that during these years, he had no expectation of actually becoming a psychologist; it was all done for the sheer love of it. The depression meant that

---

[1] Although after his removal to California in 1969, a doctor made the discovery that his chronic fatigue—that had plagued him all his life—was a form of hypoglycaemia, producing too much insulin; it had never been discovered because it arose several hours after the glucose tolerance test.

it was practically impossible to find work as an experimental psychologist, and if there were jobs available, it was unlikely they would be given to a Jew. He made an attempt at hedging his bets by studying medicine for a year, but his constitutional inability to concentrate on anything that bored him was a disadvantage, and he gave it up when he came to the anatomy course.

After graduation, there arose the problem of a job. Again, he stumbled on an 'angel'—E. L. Thorndike, the Watsonian disciple, who was at Teacher's College, Columbia University (in Manhattan). Maslow remarks that Thorndike took him on solely on the strength of his intelligence; but it was, in any case, logical that Thorndike should find Maslow sympathetic. Thorndike himself had concentrated on work with animals earlier in his career (he was born in 1874). He was an eminent representative of a school known as functionalism, which derived from James and Dewey, and opposed Titchener's structuralism. Functionalism was interested in how and why people do things, and rejected the structuralist notion that behaviour can be broken down into basic 'units'—stimulus and response, individual perceptions, etc. Behaviour, said the functionalists, is a *totality* of responses, all dependent on one another, and you cannot split it up into separate units. They chose to study psychological acts—rather in the manner of the Husserlians. Thorndike was more of a Watsonian than most functionalists; his chief contribution is a form of 'association of ideas' (on the James Mill model) which he called connectionism. But Thorndike had made one important observation that might be regarded as the basis of Maslow's later work. In his experiments with cats in mazes (in the late 1890s), he had observed the *reinforcing* effect of success or failure on the animal's learning—adding, so to speak, an element of *purpose* to the mechanical learning situation. And in the early thirties, after studying human learning, he concluded that success and reward has a far more powerful effect than failure or punishment. Logically speaking—in terms of Pavlov dogs and Watsonian rats—this should not be so: you would expect a negative stimulus to be an equal and opposite balance to a positive stimulus. Thorndike tried to explain his curious observation in terms of a brain mechanism which he called a confirming reaction.

Thorndike wanted Maslow to work as his research assistant on a major project called Human Nature in the Social Order. His first assignment was to work out what percentage of behaviour was determined by genes, and what percentage of behaviour was determined by culture, in various cultures. (He had made a study of anthropology—probably the only American psychologist who had.) 'This was rather silly', says Maslow, 'because everything was determined by both.' The inability to work at anything that bored him made him procrastinate for as long as possible; and when that could no longer be done, he took a deep breath and wrote Thorndike a memorandum explaining that he couldn't do it because he didn't think it was worth doing. ('Gosh, I don't know if I'd stand that if anybody did it to me now', says Maslow, laughing.) It was a risky thing to do, since if he lost this job, the possibilities of another were minimal. Thorndike was a remarkable man; he called Maslow into his office, and said: 'Well, if I can't trust my own intelligence tests, I don't know who can'—and gave him permission to do whatever he pleased, and come and collect his cheque once a month. This was braver and more broad-minded than it sounds; Thorndike told Maslow frankly that he didn't like the work he was doing—at this time on sex and dominance. 'I was interviewing females in his office, and everybody was scandalised.' He even went so far as to promise to support Maslow indefinitely—to the end of his life, if necessary—until he could get him a job. Fortunately, this was not necessary; Maslow found a job at Brooklyn College after only eighteen months with Thorndike,[1] and he remained there for fourteen years, until the move to Brandeis in 1951.

If Thorndike's intelligence tests were important to their inventor, they were even more so for his shy research assistant, who was amazed when he achieved the second highest score ever (195). It suddenly struck him, he said, that if somebody disagreed with him, his own chances of being in the right were pretty high—higher, in fact, than the other man's.

[1] This was by no means easy, again because of anti-semitism. The principal was an Irish Catholic who had been appointed by City Hall—run by Irish Catholics—and he impressed on Maslow how grateful he ought to feel at being accepted, and how he ought to show it by working hard. Maslow said: 'I took anti-semitism so much for granted that I didn't even feel secretly resentful.'

From the job point of view, teaching at Brooklyn College was hardly a great advance on being Thorndike's research assistant. Fortunately, he was not consumed by ambition. (I have already mentioned his comment that he knew he was faced by a choice: either to go all-out for professional success, or to settle for a job he found emotionally satisfying. He was never the kind of person to care about success for its own sake.) He was too glad to be in New York. 'It was like coming out of the dark into the light. It was like a farm boy coming to Athens.' Although the interest in music (and, to a lesser extent, literature) remained, Maslow was now a psychologist through and through, soaked in it, eager to learn everything there was to be learned. He could hardly have been in a better place. Every psychologist who escaped to America from the Nazis landed in New York, and Maslow was in an excellent position for learning from everybody. He sought out Max Wertheimer—the founder member of the gestalt school—Erich Fromm, Karen Horney, Kurt Goldstein, and Ruth Benedict, the anthropologist.

The influences of these various friends and teachers will be seen when I deal with Maslow's development, but something should be said briefly about their various approaches. Wertheimer was the man who had observed the apparent motion of two slits through which lights are shone in succession. The gestalt theory—that psychological phenomena *start off as* '*wholes*', and do not have to be 'built up' from small separate sensations—was a flat contradiction of the whole Wundt-Titchener approach which dominated psychology. Maslow regarded Wertheimer as one of the great psychologists—as great as Freud, except that his writings are less voluminous and influential. Maslow was also much influenced by Wertheimer's colleague, Kurt Koffka. However, the German gestalt school was mostly concerned with experiments in perception—such as the problem of why a square, drawn on a series of concentric circles, looks as if its sides are bent. Kurt Lewin (1890–1947) tried to extend this approach into a 'field theory' of personality and motivation—why human beings do what they do, and how they go about it. One of Lewin's most interesting contributions is the idea of an individual's life-space, meaning all the mental factors which are present at any given moment to influence his actions and choices. (It is closely related to Husserl's life-world.) Lewin attempted to create geometrical models for the typical situations encountered by human beings in the pursuit of their goals. Kurt Goldstein (born 1878) carried this gestalt tendency still further into what he called an organismic theory. His study of brain-injured soldiers during the First World War, convinced him that simple stimulus-response theory is inadequate. The stimulus-response (S-R) theory would assert that since a certain part of the brain has been destroyed, certain stimuli cannot be received, and that therefore certain responses will be ruled out: it ought to be as simple as talking about the damaged engine of a car. In fact, Goldstein discovered that the only way to understand the behaviour of a brain-injured patient is to take into account his whole personality and his whole life-pattern. (The chief characteristic of brain-injured patients is their inability to think in abstract terms; they stick to the concrete.) Eventually, Goldstein stumbled upon his key concept: the notion that the key factor in all human behaviour is what he called 'self actualisation', which might be defined as the human being's attempt to *grow into what he could be, potentially.* Ordinary S-R theory would regard such a notion as almost meaningless. It is true that an individual has certain predispositions and personality-patterns (all created by earlier responses to stimuli), but what he *becomes* surely depends completely upon what stimuli fate thrusts upon him? It may be true that every caterpillar is potentially a butterfly, but that is genetic; are there mental genes that determine whether a man will be a garbage collector or a university president? But since Maslow's own life had been an instinctive seeking-out of the things he needed, from Brooklyn Borough High School to Thorndike's laboratory, the whole notion of self-actualisation was bound to have a profound attraction for him.

Karen Horney (1885–1952) and Erich Fromm (born 1900) were both basically Freudians, but with a difference. Both were concerned with the problem of personal development and of freedom. Karen Horney, like Adler, placed enormous importance on the family background; the child who is affection-starved develops 'basic anxiety', and all neurotic trends are attempts to compensate, usually by various forms of unrealistic behaviour. There are three basic personality trends or types:

compliant ('people who need people'), aggressive, and detached; most individuals tend to have a mixture of all three, with one predominating. Karen Horney's emphasis on the happy home background was bound to appeal to Maslow, as well as her relatively optimistic outlook (as contrasted with Freud's black pessimism). The relation he developed with her was filially tender.

Fromm was more concerned with the problem of an increasingly mechanised and impersonal society, and the political orientation of his work was bound to appeal to Maslow. In an impersonal society, man is bound to feel alienated, an 'outsider'. Human beings need 'belongingness', security, but in order to survive in a competitive, mechanised society, they have to develop the power to stand alone, to repress their basic needs. Man's chief tool of superiority is his power to reason: but again, its development runs counter to his natural instincts, and increases the alienation. Fromm sees modern authoritarian systems—Nazism, communism and so on—as a simple response to this alienation; it also explains 'religious' movements like the Jehovah's Witnesses. The correct response, Fromm believes, is 'humanism', and all that implies: liberalism, non-dogmatic religion, human sympathy and co-operation. (In recent years, Marcuse has developed and popularised many of Fromm's ideas.)

Maslow attended a lecture of Fromm's, then introduced himself; once again, a father-son relation developed, and Fromm's influence is clearly apparent in Maslow's papers on such questions as authoritarianism and anti-semitism.

Ruth Benedict's (1887–1948) central interest was in the comparative study of social groups, with a view to determining the reasons for their inner-harmony (or lack of it). Like Fromm, she was a humanist, and her approach to anthropology was 'gestalt' —a recognition of basic patterns and attitudes—even before she read Koffka and Kohler. The gestalt view, in anthropology, might be defined as the feeling that societies or nations have 'character' or a 'national genius' that cannot be explained as a sum of the individual parts. Ruth Benedict saw cultures as 'configurations', patterns woven of many strands, and she borrowed Nietzsche's terms 'Apollonian' and 'Dionysian' (the first calm and ordered, the second, violent and orgiastic) to describe the overall tendencies of different Indian tribes. (She persuaded Maslow to spend a summer among the Northern Indians.) In 1937 there appeared *Cooperation and Competition Among Primitive Peoples*, edited by Margaret Mead, the central concept strongly influenced by Ruth Benedict: that in co-operative societies, the individuals help one another, and create a sense of belonging for all their members, while competitive societies emphasise status, property, violence. In a series of lectures delivered at Bryn Mawr in 1941, Ruth Benedict developed the idea of the co-operative society, coining the word 'synergic' to describe it. This concept had immense influence on Maslow—the notion of a society in which the alienation described by Fromm is not the inevitable status quo; in which there is co-operation between members, not because they happen to be naturally saintly, but because common sense tells them that this is the way for everybody to achieve some kind of self-actualisation. And here it can be seen clearly that what *basically* distinguishes Maslow from Freud or Adler or the Watsonians is not a disagreement about the nature of perceptions or the correct procedure for an exact science so much as his irrepressible *optimism*. As with Karen Horney, he felt that a sane, healthy society should not be a utopian dream—that the *nature of things as they are* means that it is perfectly possible under present circumstances. And he would defend his view—against Freud's, for example—by saying that it is more accurate, more true to the facts, than cultural pessimism. Maslow's basic position is that when things are seen *as a whole*—either human nature or human society—the prospects are far more cheering than they look at first sight. Pessimism is the outcome of 'partialism', seeing the trees but not the wood. Since he was only trying to see the whole wood, it follows that he had nothing against behaviourism or psychoanalysis—except their 'partialism'—and in a letter written in 1968, he described his aim, over the past couple of decades, as to synthesise and integrate Goldstein and Freud.[1]

It might be added that scientists have always formed a kind of artificial 'synergic society', with a free co-operation based upon the understanding that this is the path of mutual advantage. This is not true of all scientists; in fact, according to Maslow, psychologists tend to be an unfortunate exception,

[1] Letter to Dr Calvin Hall, Nov. 18, 1968.

behaving in the manner of a 'low synergy' society, with a highly developed competitiveness and the bitchiness that goes with it. In the last decade of his life, he made a list which comprised what he called the 'eupsychian network'—a network of men— or organisations—of goodwill; scientists, writers, psychologists, sociologists, whose basic outlook was non-reductionist and optimistic.

To conclude—but not necessarily complete—this list of thinkers who influenced Maslow during his New York period, the name of Adler must be mentioned. Maslow sought him out —as he did most of the others—and was a regular visitor at Adler's Friday evening groups. Adler's influence must be discussed in the next section.

But what all these figures had in common was an intuitive rejection of crude S-R theory and its assumptions. They share the recognition that creative human behaviour is a function of the higher nervous system, and cannot be explained in terms of laboratory rats or Pavlov dogs. Maslow himself remarks that the experience of becoming a father was an important factor in changing his mind from the old behaviourism. 'All the behaviouristic psychology that I'd learnt simply didn't prepare me for having a child. A baby was so miraculous and so wonderful and so . . . er, aesthetic . . . and all the work with rats and with nonsense syllables[1] and so on just didn't help at all.' He was also struck by another thing that has been observed by millions of parents—the totally different personalities of his two children, which seems to contradict the behaviourist notion that human personality is a series of responses created by conditioning. This brings to mind William MacDougall's challenge to the behaviourists to explain what happens at a symphony concert, when 'a man . . . scraping the guts of a cat with hairs from the tail of a horse' can produce rapt attention followed by wild applause. Scientists may find S-R theory adequate to explain laboratory observations, but it is immediately contradicted by experiences shared by every human being.

The fourteen years at Brooklyn College were a satisfying ex-

[1] Syllables used by Hermann Ebbinghaus (1850–1909), an early associationist in his study of the powers of memory.

perience for Maslow, although they may well have struck his wife as something of a dead end. To a large extent he was working with underprivileged kids; they appreciated the loving care he devoted to them, and his classes were always jammed. If it *was* a dead end, then it was all right with him; he was at least doing something worthwhile. By now he was securely established in his field—*Principles of Abnormal Psychology* (1941), written in collaboration with Bela Mittelmann,[1] had made his reputation, and his paper 'A Theory of Human Motivation' (1943), in which he formulated his theory of the 'hierarchy of needs' (that as lower needs are satisfied, higher ones emerge), immediately became a classic, and was reprinted dozens of times in symposia on psychology. But it was towards the end of his time at Brooklyn that his more revolutionary work on peak experiences and self-actualising people began to appear, arousing definite hostility among psychologists of the older schools. Many psychologists felt that his work had become purely philosophical—and therefore self-indulgent—and that his real contribution to psychology had been made during his behaviourist period.

It was at this time—in 1951—that he moved to Brandeis University at Waltham, Mass., a Jewish university. He remained there until 1969, a year before his death, and it was an altogether less satisfying experience. Larry Fross remarks in his study of Maslow:[2] 'Another generation of students, less eager to apprentice themselves than the depression day students of Brooklyn, have been more interested in spoon feeding, uninvolved learning process, which has not been satisfying or stimulating for the most part.' Maslow scrawled in the margin the comment: 'And more recently, rebellious and elder-rejecting, including me. If I had the money, I'd stop teaching tomorrow.' (And a year later, he added in the margin: 'Still feel this way, only more so.') 'I have been isolating myself more and more, trying to get detached, leaving the world. Partly because I am disappointed with Brandeis; especially in the last six months, I've sort of given up.' But the isolation was natural, not the fault of Brandeis. His own form of creativity, depending as it

[1] Most of the actual writing in the first edition, was done by Maslow, but the bulk of revision for the second edition (1955) was carried out by Mittelmann.

[2] Biographical Project, 1967. Unprinted.

did on intuition, made him a born outsider. 'I have nobody in the whole world to talk with about my own work . . . I am a lonely worker.' Fross comments: 'As an established psychologist he finds audiences and colleagues to whom he talks. But a peer relation of equality and common interest he has not been able to find.' ('Except at a distance. Nobody nearby', adds Maslow.) And Maslow's fundamental humility comes through in his remark: 'The closest approximation [to a peer], in that real sense of argument, is Frank Manuel, and he thinks all my work is a lot of shit. Our talks are very good debates.' It is difficult to imagine Freud having 'good debates' with a man who thought his work was a lot of shit.

The release from academic routine came in 1969; he wrote to me: 'My address has changed and also my life. I have accepted a Fellowship for some years that will permit me full time for my writing.' This was at the Laughlin Foundation in Menlo Park, California. But the change came too late; he died in June 1970, aged sixty-two, of a heart attack.

II

Higher Ceilings for Human Nature

'My story begins in 1932 when I was working with Harry Harlow on delayed reactions in monkeys', says Maslow, in his paper on 'The Need to Know and the Fear of Knowing'. 'Why did they work at this boring problem? It soon became clear that it wasn't just the bit of food that they got as a reward for their patience. They would work almost as successfully for a bit of bread that they didn't much care for . . . Furthermore, often they would successfully solve the problem and then casually throw away the food reward, which, according to the motivation theory of that time, was the *only* reason for working at the problem and seeing it through. From conversations about these puzzling happenings emerged Dr Harlow's suggestion that I try little blocks of wood as a lure instead of food. When I did this it was found that the monkeys worked almost as well, though for a shorter period of time. Apparently we could count on the animals to work at these problems and solve them for reasons that had little to do with hunger and food . . . Later on Harlow and various of his students [performed] a brilliant series of experiments which showed that monkeys would work hard and persistently to solve simple puzzles without any external reward; that is, just for whatever satisfactions are inherent in the puzzle-solving itself.'

This was not only counter to the various motivation theories of the time: it seems to contradict our ordinary human common sense. The sort of people who enjoy solving mathematical problems, or even doing *The Times* crossword puzzle, are of a certain type—intellectuals you might call them. The majority of human beings find this kind of problem-solving a bore. As to animals, their major interest seems to be in food and other such physical matters. Says Grey Walter in his book *The Living Brain* (1953), 'The nearest creature to us, the chimpanzee, cannot retain an image long enough to reflect on it, however clever it may be at learning tricks or getting food . . .' And the same assumption is inherent in Sir Julian Huxley's distinction between three levels of existence: first, dead matter, which possesses no freedom or capacity to change itself: next, living matter, from amoebas to chimpanzees, which possesses a certain degree of freedom, but which is trapped by its environment, completely dependent upon it for stimuli; third, the human level, which possesses a *new dimension of freedom*, the ability to think, to imagine, to plan. 'Unable to rehearse the possible consequences of different responses to a stimulus, without any faculty of planning, the apes and other animals cannot learn to control their feelings, the first step towards independence of environment and eventual control of it', says Grey Walter, underlining Huxley's point. Sartre says about a character in *Nausea*: 'When his café empties, his head empties too.' And that, according to Huxley and Walter, describes the lower animals. How can we reconcile all this with monkeys who will solve problems for the fun of it?

And this trait—consuming curiosity—was not confined to monkeys. Maslow observed that young pigs show similar tendencies. The weaker ones—who had difficulty commandeering a teat at feeding time—hung around the mother and behaved in a generally timid manner. But the stronger and healthier pigs seemed to take pleasure in exploring. If the door of the pen was left open, they would venture outside and poke around. If the door was closed they became alarmed and frantically tried to get back in; but the discouragement never lasted for long; when the door was left open again, they couldn't resist it.

Closely related to this is an observation made by W. F. Dove:[1] that if chickens are allowed to choose their own diet, a small percentage of them prove to be *good choosers*; they instinctively select the food that they need in order to grow. The poor choosers would choose food that looked or smelled good, but which was, in fact, bad for them. If the food chosen by the good choosers is forced on the poor choosers, they also begin to grow large,

[1] Cited by Maslow, *New Knowledge in Human Values*, p. 121. Harper 1959.

healthy and more dominant, although they never reach the same level as the good choosers.

What seems to emerge from these observations about monkeys, pigs and chickens is that there is a fundamental drive in healthy creatures towards knowledge, power, insight. It seems natural for the healthy creature to strive to get healthier, and its choices are, in general, good for the rest of the species. Neurosis must be regarded as a kind of 'stabilising' of these vital impulses, in the worst sense; they reach a state of balance, of stasis.

But although he knew about the curious behaviour of Harlow's monkeys in 1932, his training and outlook prevented him from grasping its significance. Harlow was one of Maslow's professors. 'He hired me to do this very dull and repetitive work'—intelligence-testing various primates, from lemurs to orang-outangs. The method was simple. In front of the apes' cage a table was placed, so the animal could reach it. On this table were two cups, turned upside down. The ape was shown a piece of food—a banana, perhaps—and then it was placed under one of the two cups, which were out of the animal's reach. Then, after a certain time, the cups were pushed within its reach. If the animal lifted the right cup, it was given the banana; if it chose the wrong one, it wasn't. This 'delayed reaction test' was a rough measure of intelligence, and it was tried out on dozens of animals dozens of times. The paper was published in the *Journal of Comparative Psychology* in 1932, with the names of Harlow, Maslow and Harold Uehling on it. The twenty-four-year-old Maslow was delighted to find his name in print. 'This was a great moment, and I think then I got hooked ... The awesome feeling of having contributed to the advancement of knowledge, even if it was the tiniest bit—just one coral in a whole coral reef of knowledge.' It may be that we owe the inception of Maslow's life work to the generosity of Harry Harlow in naming him as co-author of the paper, for before that, he found the work thoroughly boring, and now, with this 'reinforcement stimulus' (as Watson would call it), he went back to New York, and spent the whole summer holiday repeating the experiments—hundreds of them—with every primate in the Bronx Park Zoo. (Bertha, who helped him, must have been surprised by this sudden access of enthusiasm.) He had tasted print, and the sensation was pleasant: he wrote up his findings, and the paper appeared later that year, again with Harlow's name on it (although Harlow did no work on it). Maslow was interested to note that baboons, although anatomically lower than many other forms of ape, showed a surprising level of intelligence; perhaps this ranks as his first original 'discovery'.

His next experiment was to cross-check an observation made by C. S. Sherrington, that dogs would not eat dog meat. Maslow didn't believe it, but it proved to be true—most dogs would eat horse meat or practically any other kind, but not dog meat. When the flavour was disguised in various ways, about 50% would eat it. But Maslow concluded that there was no evidence of an 'emotion of disgust' behind the rejection, and that therefore there was so far no evidence that dogs could experience the emotion of disgust. This conservative conclusion seems to tell us something about Maslow at the time. For the moment, he was in love with science, with its cool, clean, odourless world of objective knowledge, its freedom from the trivialities of human emotion. After the emotional problems of his childhood and teens, it must have seemed to possess the beauty of a religion. What did it matter if the experiment led to no particular conclusion, if it was just an isolated fragment of knowledge that was never fated to join a coral reef? The pleasure lay in the knowledge itself.

I do not wish to labour this point, but it deserves a certain emphasis. The non-scientist tends to feel a total lack of sympathy for the 'purist' type of scientist, the kind who wants knowledge for its own sake, and does not object to being called a materialist. Such a man seems to have more than a touch of the monster about him. But this is a failure to recognise that there is an *emotional* relief in being cool and objective, in leaving behind the messy confusion of everyday life and contemplating the world of facts and ideas; it brings a momentary touch of immortality. Facts ignite the imagination, as the young H. G. Wells discovered. And the facts of psychology fired Maslow's imagination.

The next two papers continued the monkey studies in the same plodding way; one concerned the food primates preferred—oranges, nuts, bananas, etc.—and the other confirmed that primates learned better and more quickly if the reward was one of their favourite foods. This is the kind of experiment that made Bernard Shaw remark scornfully that scientists spend weeks proving in the laboratory what ordinary people know by common sense. But Maslow regarded it as a step forward, since it showed him that a reaction that he had taken for lack of intelligence may actually be indifference to the offered reward.

His next paper was what he called 'a stupid master's dissertation' on memory, the kind of thing that Ebbinghaus did with nonsense words. Maslow had wanted to do something on language—he had been excited by *The Meaning of Meaning*—some kind of study of 'exciting' and 'unexciting' words. His professor—Cason—turned this down flat, because it wasn't 'psychological' enough. He also turned down the idea of a dissertation on the effects of music. Maslow asked *him* to suggest something, and the 'Learning retention' paper was the result. It is interesting solely as illustrating what an academic psychologist considered to be 'good psychology' in 1932; Maslow had to make lists of three-letter words on a hundred cards—nine to a card. His students were shown each card for ten seconds, then a white card for five seconds, then asked to repeat the nine words he had just read. A bell was rung occasionally, to see how far it destroyed concentration. The conclusion drawn from all this was that when students did their learning and repeating under the same conditions, they did better than if conditions varied: another way of saying that students learn better when not distracted. Maslow was understandably sceptical about the value of his paper, but submitted it for publication when Cason nagged him about it. 'I didn't want to publish it because it was too crappy', but to his embarrassment, the editor accepted it, 'which shows how crappy the publications were in those days'. He sneaked into the library one day, extracted his dissertation, and threw it out of the window; he even tore out the file card.

The first really original piece of research arose out of the early monkey experiments. By this time, he had met Adler; but he was by no means sure in his mind whether Adler's dominance theory went deeper than Freud's sexual theory. 'Somehow which one I had read last seemed more convincing.' While testing the monkeys for intelligence, food preferences and so on, he had filled pages with observations of their behaviour. And the two things that struck him most were the dominance behaviour and the non-stop sex: 'the screwing . . . went on all the time.' There was a strict hierarchical structure, with a highly dominant monkey, and then less dominant monkeys, in a descending scale, with the more dominant bullying the less dominant. The sexual behaviour was unusual, in that it seemed so indiscriminate: males mounted females or other males, and females mounted males and other females. And one day, when brooding on the problems of this simian Sodom, the answer burst on him—a perfect example of what Koestler calls 'the Eureka process': the sexual behaviour *was* dominance behaviour. The dominant monkeys mounted the less dominant ones, and the sex made no difference. Maslow concluded that Adler's psychology covered the facts more convincingly than Freud's. When he told Adler about his observations, Adler urged him to publish them. The paper, 'Individual Psychology and the Social Behaviour of Monkeys and Apes' is perhaps the most interesting of all these early papers, and may be regarded as the logical first step in the development of Maslow's own psychology. There had been plenty of minute observation of the behaviour of apes—Kohler's classic *Mentality of Apes* had appeared as early as 1918—but very little on dominance, and still less on sex. In American universities, at any rate, sex was regarded with puritanical distaste, and a professor had been dismissed at Wisconsin not long before, for having sexual questionnaires. In spite of this atmosphere of disapproval, Maslow went ahead. He made some curious observations of the patterns of dominance. If two monkeys were left together, one established dominance, and if food was dropped down a pipe into the cage, it was the dominant monkey who got it. In groups of three, the dominant monkey bullies the next dominant one, who immediately takes it out on the least dominant of the group. If a highly dominant monkey is added to a group of two, the 'middle' monkey becomes far more pugnacious towards his inferior, even if he wasn't so before. Significantly, it is the middle animal who initiates the bullying of the subordinate animal; (parallels with human behaviour immediately suggest themselves.) When a fourth animal is added to the group, the behaviour is even more significant. The first three show a tendency to gang-up on the new arrival, unless he is exceptionally dominant. A normally non-dominant monkey (perhaps a young one) may lead an attack on the new arrival—even though the new arrival may have been previously the dominant one of the two. In the event of the newcomer being beaten-up by the rest of the group, he would then remain subordinate to all the monkeys in the group. In that case, Maslow observed, the previously inferior monkey would behave with extreme ferocity, 'as if making up for all the enforced and irksome dominance to which she had been subjected for the entire length of the experiment'. Altogether, the monkeys seemed to exhibit traits that among human beings would be called 'fascist'. (Although it may be as well to remember that Maslow was observing zoo monkeys, who are inevitably frustrated; monkeys in their natural habitat are a great deal less preoccupied with sex and dominance.) Maslow concluded that, for monkeys at any rate, 'the Adlerian interpretation . . . is much closer to the facts' than Freud's, and suggested that the reason the primates—including man—do not go 'into season' like other animals is that dominance behaviour has gradually superimposed itself on behaviour determined by hormones. (This may explain the high level of homosexuality among men and apes; sexual genes and dominance genes have got mixed up, so to speak.) He also pointed out that homosexuality among monkeys is not to be regarded as a 'perversion' because it has nothing to do with the sex drive, and that what previous observers had thought to be prostitution among monkeys—a female allowing herself to be mounted in exchange for food or other goods—was again merely an example of dominance behaviour: she has made it clear that she is subordinate, and is then permitted to share the food.

The last section of this paper is the most significant for Maslow's future development. He observes that the higher one goes up the monkey scale, the less ferocity is involved in the dominance. Among baboons and monkeys, most of the sex occurs in the usual animal position, with the subordinate animal bent over. In the higher apes—chimpanzees, orang-outangs, gorillas—face-to-face sexual behaviour was more frequent. In chimpanzees, where dominance is of a friendlier type, expressed by teasing rather than violence—the face-to-face position is frequent. Whereas in monkeys the dominant animal uses his position to tyranise, in chimpanzees the dominant animal tends to be a protector.

Maslow had stumbled into a field that fascinated him: what might be called the Nietzschean field—although he thought in terms of Adler rather than Nietzsche. It could be said that 1935 to 1940 were his Adlerian years. This does not imply that he ever turned his back on Adler: fundamentally, he remained an Adlerian; but a point came where he passed beyond the dominance theory, recognising that in 'the upper reaches of human nature', it turns into something else.

During these years, 1935–37, he was in a state of inspired excitement, feeling that he had now discovered what psychology is really about—it is not surprising that he felt no interest in Thorndike's researches on genes and culture. 'I worked my ass off—just working, working, working, day and night.' 'I had all these dreams about being famous, shaking the world and so on. And then just while I was writing up these papers for publication, Solly Zuckerman's book came out in England—*The Social Life of Monkeys and Apes*—and my judgement was right; it *did* make a big splash—it was a famous book, terribly important one. The only thing I can say is my work was a hell of a lot better. Because he did his in that one situation, which has now proven to be quite artificial . . .' Maslow seems to have confused his dates slightly here; his work on monkeys was done between 1931 and 1935; Zuckerman's book appeared in 1932, three years before Maslow's important paper on Individual Psychology and monkeys. But no doubt Maslow is expressing the basic truth of the matter—that Zuckerman had beaten him past the post, and that his own work, in many respects, went deeper than Zuckerman's; this must have been a frustrating feeling for a young psychologist hoping to shake the world. In any case, the knowledge of the value of his own work increased his self-confidence. 'I could hardly talk myself out of the fact that this was the best thing that had been done in that department, and that I was a bright young man.' And in 1969, he still felt that the full significance of his work had not yet been grasped. 'What these data reveal, I think is still not visible . . . for instance, to Bob Ardrey[1] or to the ones who've written about the naked ape and instinct and so on.'

[1] I was responsible for bringing Maslow and Ardrey together in about 1966. They felt a strong liking for one another, and Maslow's influence can be felt in *The Territorial Imperative* and *The Social Contract*. Maslow considered, nevertheless, that

The next major step came around 1936. He had evolved a new theory of evolution from his researches, with dominance playing the central role, rather than sexual selection (although this was never published). Inevitably, he began to speculate on how far there was a close correlation between sexuality and dominance in human beings. In spite of a certain amount of opposition from professors who may have suspected his motives,[1] he began a series of Kinsey-type interviews with college women (although, of course, Kinsey's first investigations were not made until 1938, possibly inspired by Maslow). He chose women rather than men because (a) men tended to boast, and otherwise distort their evidence, and (b) women proved to be capable of greater frankness than men, once they had made up their minds to take the plunge. Besides, 'the whole thing was more fun—illuminating for me, the nature of women, who were certainly, to a shy boy, still mysterious . . .' These results, published as *Dominance-feeling. Personality and Social Behaviour in Women* in the *Journal of Social Psychology* in 1939, and as *Self-esteem and Sexuality in Women* in the same journal in 1942, are certainly among Maslow's most fascinating and original work. What he set out to do was to compare ratings for dominance with ratings for sexuality—the latter including promiscuity, lesbian experience, masturbation and sexual experimentalism (fellatio, etc.) His basic finding can be baldly stated: sexuality was directly related to dominance. Highly dominant women were more likely to masturbate, sleep with different men, have lesbian experience, and so on. There was a closer correlation between these things—promiscuity, masturbation, etc.—and dominance feeling than between these things and sex-drive. A medium-dominance or low-dominance woman might have a high rating for sex drive, but her sexual experience was usually limited. Low-dominance women (who were difficult to get into the study group) tended to think of sex as being mainly for child-bearing; one low-dominance woman who knew she

---

writers like Ardrey and Desmond Morris tended to extrapolate too much from animal to human behaviour; he felt—predictably—that the lessons to be learned about human beings from animals are interesting but strictly limited.

[1] A normal enough reaction to scientific curiosity in the sexual field. Maslow told me that when he first heard about the Masters and Johnson researches—in which copulating couples were filmed—he thought 'it was for bad motives', but changed his mind on closer study of their work.

could not bear children refused sex to her husband, even though she had a strong sex drive. Low-dominance women tend to think of sex as disgusting, or as an unfortunate necessity for producing children, to dislike nudity and to regard the sexual organs as ugly. (High-dominance women usually like seeing, touching and thinking about the penis, and regard it as beautiful.)

The choice of men follows similar patterns. High-dominance women like dominant males, and prefer unsentimental, even violent, lovemaking—to be swept off their feet rather than courted. She wishes to be forced into the subordinate role. One highly dominant woman (whom Maslow admitted to be his most neurotic subject), spent years hunting for a man of superior dominance and married him. Years later, she was as much in love with him as at first. 'She actually picks fights in which he becomes violent and which usually end in virtual rape. These incidents provide her with her most exciting sexual experiences.'

Medium-dominance women tend to be scared of highly dominant males, although some degree of dominance is preferred; they want a husband and father rather than a lover, a 'homey' man, adequate rather than outstanding. The low-dominance women tended to be shy and distrustful about men, while still wanting children; they were found to prefer low-dominance males, 'the gentle, timid, shy man who will adore at a distance for years before daring to speak.' While high-dominance women tend to be realists about sex, middle and low-dominance women want romance, poetry, dim lights and illusions. When these women are driven to promiscuity by high sex-drive, feelings of guilt are tremendous and may lead to thoughts of suicide.

The orgasm also seemed to be directly related to dominance. Here again, the findings are fascinating. One highly dominant nymphomaniac, who could have an orgasm merely by looking at a man, admitted to not having had orgasms with two lovers because they were weak. 'I just couldn't give in to them.' Another high-dominance woman who scorned her husband, tried not to have orgasms with him; when she had one—because her sex-drive was high—she concealed it from him.

The sexual behaviour of a highly dominant lesbian seemed

entirely determined by dominance. She was a female Don Juan, seducing a string of girls, preferring girls who were taller than herself, and who were beautiful and feminine. She was initially attracted to girls who disliked her, or were aloof. 'She systematically, over a long period of time, gets them to tolerate holding hands, embracing, kissing, etc. The climax comes at the moment when she first induces orgasm in her partner. 'At such times I get a feeling of smug power, and of great satisfaction.' Her own orgasms come much later in the history of the relationship and are definitely not the primary goal in the seduction. That is to say, once again, that homosexuality and dominance seem to be closely related. Maslow also observed in dominant males that the real satisfaction came in causing an orgasm rather than in having one, dominance being established by the partner's ecstasy and loss of control.

In medium and low-dominance women, the orgasm tended to depend upon a feeling of being loved, upon security. Medium-dominance women tended not to experience orgasm with less dominant husbands. In two cases, the husband had to be instructed in suitable dominance behaviour—probably throwing her on the bed—after which orgasm became possible.

In general, it seems women need to feel their position to be subordinate to the man's, to ensure sexual satisfaction. High-dominance women reported masturbation fantasies of being possessed by huge negroes, athletic men, even animals—the latter, as it were, imposing humiliation.

Some of Maslow's casual asides, not directly related to his theme, are of equal interest—for example, that among Jewish women, dominance tended to be high, but so did virginity. This was not a matter of religion—few of the subjects were religious—but probably of 'compensatory dominance' for belonging to a cultural sub-group. (I would imagine there is also a purely genetic factor here: the Jewish preoccupation with purity of race appears in the form of puritanism, sexual self-control.)

Of equal interest is the observation that although progressive education or sophisticated parents may instill a more frank and open attitude to sex, it did not seem to affect sexual behaviour much: i.e. it would seem that sexual behaviour is an inherent factor, dependent on place in the dominance hierarchy rather than training or education.

All this tended to increase Maslow's feeling that such matters are 'instinctoid' rather than learned reflexes, conditioned by training. What he was doing, in fact, was to move steadily away from behaviourism, with its assumption that the human being is a kind of machine that can be conditioned to think or behave in any given way, towards a view in which most human behaviour is determined by factors coming from 'inside', so to speak. This was a conclusion that had already been suggested by the totally different personalities of his two children. The view he was increasingly inclined to take was the 'holistic' one: that the human creature begins as a kind of acorn, with all the characteristics of the fully grown tree already inside it, so to speak.

But perhaps the most significant sentence in the whole paper on female sexuality occurs in the section on 'Security and Self-Esteem':

'Since our society tends to general insecurity, the average citizen may be expected to be fairly insecure. Wertheimer has pointed out that any discussion of dominance must be a discussion of insecure people, that is, of slightly sick people. Our data show this to be true. *Study of carefully selected psychologically secure individuals indicates clearly that their sexual lives are little determined by dominance-feeling*'. (My italics.)

And this was the core of the problem that, from now on, would dominate Maslow's thinking. He had rejected the Freudian all-purpose sexual theory of neurosis in favour of Adler. Now Freud, as we have seen, regarded cultural activities as a sublimated form of sexuality, 'psychosexuality' (he might have said pseudo-sexuality), and when Jung protested that this view would lead to an annihilating view of culture, Freud replied: 'And that is just the curse of fate against which we are powerless to contend.' Adler was never such a severe reductionist as Freud, but the struggle for dominance—what might be called a sense of superiority—*does* occupy the central place in his thinking. Should one, then, regard the friendly teasing through which chimpanzees express dominance as a sublimated form of the aggressive urge? And is human culture psycho-aggressiveness? For Freud, neurosis is repressed sexuality, for Adler, repressed will-to-power. But did Adler's view of neurosis cover *all* the facts any better than Freud's did? What about the monkeys who solved problems for fun? Or, to get down to essentials, how about Maslow himself? Socially speaking, his dominance was in the medium bracket. Intellectually, it was high—very high indeed. He kept asking himself—even in his last years: 'If I was so timid and frightened and depressed and unhappy as a young man, how come I was able to have courage enough to stick my neck out so much and to be a revolutionary, and contradict everybody? One would think, to read my stuff, that I was a very courageous man, but not so.' And this problem was as obvious to him in 1942 as in 1969. And his intellectual honesty made him disinclined to accept the simple hypothesis that this was sublimated dominance. Besides, he had always noticed the way that he seemed to possess a kind of instinct for seeking out favourable conditions for his intellectual self-expression—ever since he had 'gravitated' to the Brooklyn High School, the only good college preparatory school in Brooklyn. ('I by-passed all sorts of closer high schools, but in some blind way I just sought this place out.') This same instinct had worked throughout his career. According to any of the current psychologies, it was simply a misnomer to call it an 'instinct'. But if it wasn't an instinct, what was it? The problem, as he recognised later, was of 'criteria for judging needs to be instinctoid'.

By this time—late 1942—the book *Principles of Abnormal Psychology* had put Maslow on the map; it remained a standard textbook for years. And since it aimed at being a standard textbook, in the tradition of MacDougall's *Outline of Abnormal Psychology* (1926), it avoided any startling innovation (although the fact that it contains a chapter on *the normal person* can now be seen to be significant). The sex research had caused remarkably little stir, and the same was true for some absorbing work in 'anthropological psychology'—research into such questions as why Eskimoes stay in the north and appear to actually *prefer* difficult conditions. But in July, 1943, there appeared the first thoroughly and typically 'Maslovian' paper, *A Theory of Human Motivation* (in the *Psychological Review* for July), and its impact was immediate. It was the paper in which he expounded his theory of the 'hierarchy of needs'; it stated on the first page: 'Human needs arrange themselves in hierarchies of prepotency. That is to say, the appearance of one need usually rests on the prior satisfaction of another, more pre-potent need. Man is a perpetually wanting animal . . .'

What Maslow states in this paper is the essence of his life work. First, there are basic needs. In order to be comprehensive, he starts back in the physiological needs, such as the salt content, sugar content, protein content of the blood stream. These physiological needs amount to the need for food. A creature that has never had a full stomach is incapable of conceiving any other need—and conversely, is incapable of realising that the satisfaction of the need for food would not lead to a state of permanent bliss.

When hunger needs are satisfied, 'safety needs' now emerge: the need for freedom from pain or fear, the need for a regular routine that will give a sense of a predictable, orderly world. (And here we come back to Karen Horney, as Maslow points out that injustice or unfairness in the parents make the child feel unsafe.) Although adults can handle their fears better than children can, various safety needs persist into adulthood—the need for regularity of employment, protection from criminals, etc. Maslow points out that compulsive-obsessive neuroses are a result of the persistence of childish fears into adulthood; a woman who cannot bear a speck of dust in her house is a mild example of such a neurosis. The dust is not really a danger or even a nuisance, but the safety need remains at an exaggerated, childish level that demands compulsive regularity and order.

Next on the list come love needs, which include the 'belongingness needs'. A person with a fair degree of security—let us say, with a stable place of abode and a regular income—now begins to feel keenly the need for friends, for a sweetheart or wife or children, for a place in his group. Maslow observes that it is the thwarting of these needs that is the chief cause of maladjustment in our relatively well-fed and well-housed society. Here Maslow seems to be apologising for Freud—for after all, his diagnosis of sex as being at the root of neurosis is 90% accurate in the modern world. Even so, Maslow takes care to add that the need for sex and the need for love are not to be equated; the love-need involves both the giving and receiving of love.

If the love needs are satisfied, there emerge the 'esteem needs', the need for a 'stable, firmly based, high evaluation of themselves, for self respect . . . and for the esteem of others'. Maslow points out that Adler was the first to recognise the importance of these needs.

Finally, at the apex or the pyramid, comes the need for self-actualisation, 'to become everything that one is capable of becoming'. 'In one individual it may take the form of the desire to be an ideal mother, in another it may be expressed athletically, and in still another it may be expressed in painting pictures or inventions'. And the need to know and to understand is included under this heading of self-actualisation.

Maslow's theory, then, is that there are five levels of needs: physiological, safety, love, esteem and self-actualisation, and as one becomes satisfied, another takes over. Towards the end of his life he came to modify this view slightly, and to recognise that the need for self-actualisation does not *necessarily* develop when the others are fulfilled—a belated and rather sad recognition that the world is full of Babbitts, for whom self-esteem represents the summit of their personal development. If he had lived, he would undoubtedly have gone further into this question: what is the difference between the Babbitts and the self-actualisers? Are the Babbitts deficient in some psychological vitamin? It might be said that, in a sense, Maslow's career broke off on the threshold of the most vital question of all.

What was so revolutionary about this theory was that it represented such a huge synthesis. Consider only the two basic levels—physiological and safety needs—and you have a Marxian view of man, a creature who needs food and security in order to be happy. (Insofar as sex is a physical need, this level is also partly Freudian.) The next level is the Freudian one, the next the Adlerian one. Finally comes the Goldstein level. Everyone is right—to some extent. And to some extent, everyone is wrong. Freud goes deeper than Max; Adler goes deeper than Freud; Goldstein goes deeper than Adler. (It is interesting to note that Maslow remained relatively unaware of Jung—perhaps because he was still on the other side of the Atlantic.[1])

[1] For example, the following story would have appealed to Maslow:
'. . . during the Psychoanalytic Congress in Munich in 1912 . . . someone had turned the conversation to Amenophis IV (Ikhnaton). The point was made that as a result of his negative attitude towards his father he had destroyed his father's cartouches on the steles, and that at the back of his great creation of a monotheistic religion there lurked a father complex. This sort of thing irritated me, and

The really revolutionary point here—which Maslow did not state in so many words—was that these 'higher needs' are as instinctoid as the lower, as much a part of man's subconscious drives. If this had been stated clearly, no doubt the paper would have aroused more violent antagonism. As it was, it appeared to be making a useful, pragmatic sort of statement about human needs, and the revolutionary implications were overlooked. It is not impossible that Maslow himself overlooked them—for the moment. He was the sort of person who preferred to think in terms of agreements rather than antagonisms. He was a Freudian —the *Principles of Abnormal Psychology* was a proof of it—because he regarded Freud's great contribution as his insight into the vital mystery of the subconscious; he was a behaviourist because he agreed that human beings are also a mass of conditioning; he was an Adlerian because he saw dominance as a more funda-mental drive than sex. But when he came to the question of whether human culture—the need to know and understand—can be regarded as a sublimated form of the dominance drive, he answered, after due consideration: No. All the indications are that intellectual creativity exists in its own right, beyond the dominance urge . . . This did not strike him as a particularly bold or challenging statement, only as a cautious extension of what Freud and Adler had already said. For Maslow had the peculiar, unconscious courage of the introvert, whose certainty arises from intuition—direct observation of inner states. In a letter to me, he wrote about the eight-year-old daughter of a friend. 'She is a very impressive little girl, probably a little genius, and I got awed by the sudden realisation of her 'poten-tialities', or 'possibilities' for the future. It was as if she were my colleague instead of an eight-year-old girl to whom I was telling stories. And in that moment I felt the same respect for her, and

---

I attempted to argue that Amenophis had been a creative and profoundly religious person whose acts could not be explained by personal resistances to his father. On the contrary, I said, he had held the memory of his father in honour, and his zeal for destruction had been directed only against the name of the god Amon, which he had everywhere annihilated; it was also chiselled on the cartouches on his father Amon-hotep. Moreover, other pharaohs had replaced the names of their actual divine forefathers on monuments and statues by their own, feeling that they had a right to do so since they were incarnations of the same god. Yet they, I pointed out, had inaugurated neither a new style nor a new religion.

'At this moment, Freud slid off his chair in a faint . . .'

Jung. (*Memories, Dreams, Reflections,* p. 153)

even awe and mystery, that I tend always to feel before great intellects or brilliant minds . . . It's as if everything becomes simultaneous. And at the same time, there is some dimension of depths, or perhaps better said, heights, in which one penetrates into a more central reality or essence . . .' Here it is again, expressed with perfect clarity, his central assumption—the little girl not only contained her potentialities in embryo, but also, in some sense, in *present actuality*, so he could sense them right there and then. And it was this sense of inner-meaning, an unfolding purpose, that produced a sense of awe. A reductionist tends to think that the human mind *puts* meaning into nature. He looks at the world critically, with pursed lips, confident of his own superiority to this hurrying, meaningless flow of events. Maslow was a true phenomenologist in the basic sense; he felt that the world *out there* was a damn sight more meaningful than anything *his* mind could add to it. There was a strong, clear sense of a 'central reality or essence' that he was only trying to observe and interpret.

It might be expected that now Maslow had achieved this decisive formulation of his own 'holistic' psychology, his ideas would blossom and expand. But this was not the way his mind worked. 'In science . . . usually what happens is that people don't flit from one thing to another the way I do, but rather they get some idea and stick with it for a lifetime. . . . What I like to do is to break open a new field, turn the sod for the first time, and then move on to something else. Because all the careful and detailed work, the supporting work, is less interesting to me than the bright and innovative idea.' To some extent he is doing himself an injustice; his highly creative personality was driven by inner compulsions, and it was no use trying to bridle them. This tendency was a disadvantage: it meant that some of his most important work—on primates, on dominance in women, on the culture of Eskimoes—got overlooked. But it also meant that he had a sense of an immense field waiting to be explored, and threw off new ideas like sparks. To read straight through Maslow's collected papers (as I have for the writing of this book) is to get an impression of a gun dog or a bloodhound casting around for the scent, moving first one way then another, sniffing, exploring, advancing a few yards at a great speed, then stopping again to cast around. This impression is particularly strong after the 'hierarchy' paper. The next publication was an oddly inconclusive paper on conflict and frustration, pointing out that there seem to be two types of conflict, threatening and non-threatening, and that only the former lead to psychopathological effects. Rats faced with difficult choices in a maze do not break down, neither do rats who are deprived of food for 24 hours. . . . What Maslow was groping towards in this paper was a *psychology of the will*, of the kind that Frankl was beginning to conceptualise in Dachau. Frustrations and conflicts are not dangerous so long as the will is healthy. As Nietzsche pointed out, there is even a type of healthy personality that can contemplate tragedy with a certain cheerfulness. But in the paper on conflict, Maslow seems to be groping in the dark, and no fundamental insight develops. There is this same tentative quality in the remaining two papers he published in 1943, one on the dynamics of personality (which found its way into *Motivation and Personality* as Chapter 3) and one on the authoritarian personality. The first is a statement of an 'organismic' concept of personality, which he himself later conceded to be 'very imperfect'. Although this is by no means a badly written paper, by academic standards, it may be cited as an example of Maslow's chief fault as a writer: that when he strayed too far from his laboratory training, and theorised in the abstract, the result tends to be woolly. Good writing tries to stay concrete, and Maslow at his best is clear, pungent and exciting because he is concrete. The same fault can be seen in the paper on authoritarian character structure, which he described to me as an attempt to understand the Nazis. It is unexceptionable but unexciting. He points out that authoritarians have a drive for power, contempt for women, that they are full of hostility, hatred and prejudice, and identify kindness with weakness. It might have been altogether more interesting if Maslow had asked himself the question how a highly creative man like D. H. Lawrence could hold authoritarian views, and tried to understand their positive root as well as negative manifestations.

During the following year, Maslow published only one paper, on intelligence testing—from the work point of view, one of his worst years ever. This was partly because he was being overworked—academically speaking. Overwork brought on his first heart attack in 1945. After this, he began to suffer from bouts of acute fatigue—a problem that was to be with him for the rest of his life. (He wrote to me in 1968: 'As for us getting together, God knows what will happen with this goddam fatigue. I've just made an appointment with a famous diagnostic clinic here in Boston, and I hope they will discover and cure whatever is wrong with me . . .') As a consequence of the heart attack, he became afraid of sexual excitement—a perfect method for negative conditioning, as he observes wryly—and since his own sex-drive had always been strong, a further cause for frustration. These problems are reflected in both the quantity and the quality of the papers from '45 to '48; many of them are only a few hundred words long. A brief paper on 'Higher and Lower Needs', published in the *Journal of Psychology* early in 1948, says very little that had not already been stated unambiguously in the 'hierarchy' paper of five years earlier. One significant paragraph in this paper reads: 'Living at the higher need level means greater biological efficiency, greater longevity, less disease, better sleep, appetite, etc. The psychosomatic researchers prove again and again that anxiety, fear, lack of love, domination, etc., tend to encourage undesirable physical as well as psychological results.' Which raises the question of whether these physical problems may not have been, to some extent, the outcome of creative frustration. Hypoglycaemia is itself, to some extent, a psychosomatic illness.

Two papers from this period deserve special mention, if only because they show what is to come, 'Problem-centering versus means-centering in science' (1946) was later included in *Motivation and Personality*. It is a kind of trial run for Maslow's book *The Psychology of Science*—which, unfortunately, was preceded by and perhaps rendered superfluous by Michael Polanyi's classic *Personal Knowledge*. Maslow knew there was something wrong with the 'scientific outlook' as epitomised in Freud or the neo-Darwinists, but he hadn't the concepts necessary for making his point clear. If he had known Jacques Hadamard's *Psychology of Invention in the Mathematical Field*, he might have pointed out that even the great mathematicians have made their discoveries by a series of wild, irregular leaps and intuitions, and that the so-called 'scientific method' that academics are always talking about is wishful thinking.

Another paper, 'Cognition of the Particular and the Generic'

(*Psychological Review*, 1948) is of interest chiefly because it is an attempt at creating phenomenology of the attention, to describe the way the attention filters out 90% of our experience and selects the remaining 10%. Again, Maslow was interested in the way the attention 'goes for' what *means* something to us, in the instinctive way that healthy chickens go for the food they need for vitamins. A different kind of psychologist might have pursued this insight and created a massive foundation for a psychology of the will; but Maslow wasn't that type.

The real breakthrough—which ought, logically, to have occurred in 1943, after the 'hierarchy paper'—finally came in 1950, in a bulky paper called *Self-Actualising People, A Study of Psychological Health* (later included in *Motivation and Personality*). He has still not formulated his central concept of the peak experience (which seems to have crystallised out in the late fifties), but this is the first enormous step in the new direction. This paper is the foundation of Maslovian psychology, as Freud's *Interpretation of Dreams* is the foundation of Freudian psychology. And although the title itself is borrowed from Goldstein, the concept of the paper is revolutionary. For the first time since Freud—indeed, since Charcot—psychology ceases to be the study of mental sickness. And the antithesis of sickness ceases to be some hypothetical 'norm' of 'adjustment to society'. To begin with, Maslow recognises that society is sick —or, to put it less pretentiously, that we are living in a low-synergy society (synergy means 'acting together') and that it would be healthier if it was a high-synergy society.

It would be accurate, I think, to say that what Maslow meant by a self-actualising person is what I meant by an Outsider. He says: 'Self-actualising people can all be described as relatively spontaneous in behaviour and far more spontaneous than that in their inner life, thoughts, impulses, etc. Their behaviour is marked by simplicity and naturalness, and by lack of artificiality or straining for effect. This does not mean consistenlty unconventional behaviour. If we were to take an actual count of the number of times that the self-actualising person behaves in an unconventional manner, the tally would not be high. His unconventionality is not superficial but essential or internal.' 'Self-actualising people are not well-adjusted (in the naive sense of approval of and identification with the culture). They get along with the culture in various ways, but of all of them it may be said that in a certain profound and meaningful sense they resist enculturation, and maintain a certain inner detachment . . .' In effect, Maslow had sought out the healthiest people he could find, and studied them with the same statistical methods that he had used in earlier years—for example, to determine whether breast feeding really makes people less liable to neurosis. (He discovered that it didn't.[1]) He also studied typical cases from history—Haydn, Goethe, Franklin, Whitman and others. The resulting description of the characteristics of self-actualisers sounds occasionally as though Maslow is sketching an imaginary ideal, and the reader has to keep reminding himself that these were all real people. This is not wishful thinking. This is a statistical survey, like the Kinsey report.

The following is a rough summary of Maslow's findings on self-actualisers.

One of their most fundamental characteristics is that they tend to be centred on *problems external to themselves* rather than ego-centred. Shaw makes Captain Shotover say, 'Our interest in the world is the overflow of our interest in ourselves'; which is to say that until we have thoroughly satisfied our interest in ourselves (the need for self-esteem), external problems seem irrelevant. It is therefore a fundamental datum—that self-actualisers should be interested in the world rather than themselves. It also follows that the characteristics Maslow describes develop in self-actualisers only when they reach a degree of maturity.

Connected to this problem-centred orientation is Maslow's observation that *all* self-actualisers are creative—sometimes artistically or scientifically, sometimes in more down-to-earth ways: but always creative. This again is obviously connected to another characteristic: their continued freshness of appreciation, their capacity to enjoy things again and again with a sense of 'newness'. (In my own terminology, they have the robot under control better than most people.) There is also a

---

[1] His results—tabulated in the paper 'Security and Breast Feeding' (1946)—showed that wholly bottle-fed babies, and babies who had been breast fed for a year and more, developed into secure adults; but it was babies who had been breast fed for under three months who achieved the highest security score. The lowest security score was for babies whose breast feeding had been broken off between six and nine months.

more efficient perception of reality than usual—for example, ability to detect fakes and phoneys; this same perceptiveness was found to extend to all other fields in which they were tested: art, music, politics, public affairs and so on.

Self-actualisers, says Maslow, are capable of more love than most people, and of deeper relationships. They enjoy solitude more than the average. They are naturally democratic, un-snobbish, friendly without bothering about social status, education or politics. And in spite of occasional flashes of anger or disgust with the human race (more likely to be found in young or immature self-actualisers), they have a strong sense of identity and sympathy with it. They have a clear and pragmatic sense of the difference between good and evil, although they are capable of tolerance about other people's lack of it. They have a definite kind of sense of humour, which Maslow calls philo-sophical—based on a sense of the absurd or grotesque, but they dislike negative humour—jokes based on hostility or superiority or authority-rebellion, presumably because they do not share the insecurity on which such humour is based. (On the whole, self-actualisers are less *often* humorous than most of the popula-tion, Maslow observed.) And in the same way, they dislike having to pay attention to negative things, either in art or life—to situations in which people are hurt, snubbed or made to feel inferior—since their response to such situations is a desire to get something done about it.

All this is not to say self-actualisers are free of faults. 'Our subjects are occasionally capable of an extraordinary and unexpected ruthlessness. It must be remembered that they are very strong people. This makes it possible for them to display a surgical coldness when it is called for, beyond the power of the average man. The man who found that a long-trusted acquaintance was dishonest cut himself off from this friendship sharply and abruptly and without any observable pangs what-soever. Another woman who was married to someone she did not love, when she decided on divorce, did it with a decisive-ness that looked almost like ruthlessness. Some of them recover so quickly from the death of people close to them as to seem heartless.' And their independence of the opinions of others may also produce difficult situations; one woman who was irritated by the stuffiness of some people at a party went out of her way to shock them with her language and opinions, putting her host and hostess into an embarrassing position.

While their absorption in impersonal problems may lead to absent-minded or downright anti-social behaviour, their natural kindness often leads them to get involved with neurotics and bores, or to marry out of pity.

It should also be made clear that self-actualisers are not immune to fears, anxieties, self-division; but these arise from genuine objective problems, not neurotic imagination. *They do not dwell on the negative.*

Finally—and most important from the point of view of Maslow's future development—a great number of self-actualisers have peak experiences, mystical experiences, 'the oceanic feeling', the sense of limitless horizons opening up to the vision. In the first edition of *Motivation and Personality* in 1954, Maslow speaks only of the mystical experience and the oceanic feeling; in the 1970 edition—issued after his death—he uses the term 'peak experience'—also pointing out that *some* self-actualisers are non-peakers. He came to suspect later that this difference was going to be more fundamental than it seemed at first, since the non-peaking self-actualisers tended to be the really influential social workers and world-betterers, while peakers are often more involved in the subjective realm of aesthetics or religion. This was another field he was exploring when he died.

This paper on self-actualisers is probably Maslow's most important single work. Its importance does not lie in its detailed argument; it is not an overwhelming piece of research, backed up by minute detail, like *The Origin of Species*. It is revolutionary because this is the first time a psychologist has ignored the assumption that underlies all Freudian psychology: that psychology, like medicine, is basically a study of the sick. In medicine, this is a reasonable assumption, because although sick human beings may be slightly sick or very sick, healthy human beings are just healthy; a healthy athlete is not all that healthier than a healthy professor or factory worker. And in the Charcot-Freud tradition, psychologically healthy people are called 'normal', and regarded as being of little interest until they get sick. And if a man's vitality and creativity place him well-above the average, like Leonardo or Shaw, then this in itself is regarded as a kind of abnormality—a defect disguising itself as a virtue. And the Freudian takes out his magnifying glass, and sniffs around for diseased tissue. In his usual quiet way, without blowing any trumpets or announcing his disagreements, Maslow had turned his back on this whole tradition. On the surface, there is nothing very innovatory about the paper: it is merely a statistical study of the characteristics of a certain type of person. What is so important is the unstated assumption: that most people *could and should* be like this. What was really needed, to complete Maslow's theory, was the realisation developed by Frankl a decade later—that when human beings are passive, *neurosis tends to feed upon itself*. Creative energy tends to be self-renewing, and to produce its own chain reaction of health and further effort. In the neurotic personality, the creative drive is perverted, and unless something can reverse the trend, and re-awaken the feeling of autonomy, the chain reaction is one of guilt, self-hatred and passivity. (This can be seen clearly in the case of Jung's businessman, and will be discussed more fully in the next chapter.) Once sickness is seen as the *inverted form* of our natural human creativity, Maslow's theory becomes internally consistent, as well as more logically satisfying than Freud's romantic pessimism. The Freudian *thanatos* is replaced with an evolutionary drive, common to all living creatures, but highly developed in man. A certain evolution is natural to human beings, but on the personal level, it requires toughness to push it beyond the average level in the society. And this point underlines the most important difference between Maslow's psychology and the 'pathological tradition'. If a man is faced with a difficult and discouraging problem, what makes the difference between whether he decides to attack it, or allows himself to go into a flat spin of defeat? There could, of course, be various character factors, not to mention the effect of past success or failure (we are back to Thorndike's law of effect); there might also be purely chance factors, like the sun coming out. But when it really comes down to it, the ultimate decider is something you can only call my free will. *I* weigh up all the factors and decide which is important and which isn't. *I* decide to summon my energies for an effort, or whether to relax with the thought: 'It's not worth it.'

What we might call, then, the Maslow-Frankl theory of mental health could be crudely outlined as follows:

All living creatures have to struggle for existence in various ways, and the struggle to live is also a struggle to evolve, to grow up, to gain possession of certain powers. Life is difficult anyway, so this struggle may produce acute strains and tensions. Under difficult circumstances, a creature's survival may depend upon its ability to run away, to slink around challenges rather than meeting them head-on; so courage and fearlessness are not always advantageous.

In human beings, success in meeting these challenges produces health, a higher level of vitality. Ideally speaking, *all* human beings would use their intelligence and persistence to overcome their particular life-challenges, and then be able to proceed to the next level in the 'hierarchy of values'. What happens, in fact, is that many of them suffer a few defeats and then get into a habit of retreat. It becomes a mental pattern; that is to say, they create a kind of philosophy of defeat: not, perhaps, as massive and carefully reasoned as Schopenhauer's pessimism, but much the same in structure and origin. It is a kind of reasoned pattern of decision to do as little as possible, to play it safe. But although the intelligence has played its part in this decision—which gives it the appearance of logic—it runs counter to the compulsion to evolve. Neurosis—as distinct from the strains and tensions of the healthy personality—is essentially a *passive* state. The mind is in neutral gear. If I sit in my stationary car with the engine running, I may make a hell of a noise by revving it, but the car doesn't move. Neurosis is noise without action. And once the personality is in neutral gear, new strains and tensions become possible, because neurosis is essentially self-destructive, and the frustrated life energies turn inward, like hooligans wrecking a train compartment for the fun of it. Frankl observed this self-propagating character of neurosis in the case of the bank clerk whose living depended upon his handwriting, and whose handwriting began to deteriorate as he worried about it. Frankl cured him by advising him to *try* to write as badly as possible. That is to say, the root of the neurosis was a fear that began to reinforce itself, becoming fear-of-fear as well as fear of losing his job, so his feeling of human efficiency was eroded. The suggestion that he should try to write badly reversed his basic attitude, the very cause of the fear.

In the Freudian view, a neurosis may be the result of a life-long build-up of traumas and frustrations, like a festering splinter. Frankl recognised that a neurosis may be almost instantaneous, a hysterical build-up of self-reinforced misery and terror; in fact, if my reading of Frankl is correct, he accepts that this is the essential pattern of all neurosis.

Neurosis, then, differs from healthy activity—and strain—in being essentially passive. Vital energy is supposed to be glowing into activity, and instead it is dammed up inside. The result is like not being allowed to urinate, or like the pain of a mother who suddenly stops breast feeding her baby and has to squeeze her breasts to force out the milk. Neurosis, says Maslow, is a failure of personal growth. Frankl adds that healthy activity demands a goal, a sense of something worth doing, and that mental illness begins when men are deprived of the sense of 'something to look forward to'. Boredom, passivity, stagnation: these are the beginning of mental illness, which propagates itself like the scum on a stagnant pond.

The theory is beautifully simple, beautifully symmetrical. There is something lop-sided about Freudian theory; the *id* is a gigantic underground lake full of sinister squid-like creatures, and up above, in the sunlight, there is an uneasy pretence of rationality and normality, a pathetic attempt to behave as if the squids don't exist. H. G. Wells, in *The Time Machine*, showed a better sense of balance; above ground are the Eloi—child-like, carefree, delightful—and below the ground the Morlocks, the sinister dark creatures who feed on the Eloi; they make a suitable pair of opposites. It was this sense of the lack of symmetry in Freud's theory that led Aldous Huxley to suggest that if the human mind had a cellar, surely it ought to have an attic as well? If there is a subconscious mind that is inaccessible to ordinary inspection, why not a superconscious too? Huxley made this suggestion in his introduction to F. W. H. Myers's book on *Human Personality and Its Survival of Bodily Death*, which contains some interesting examples of the operation of the superconscious. For example, at the age of five Archbishop Whately developed abnormal calculating powers, and could do difficult sums in his head. By the age of nine, this faculty had vanished completely. Professor Safford, as a ten-year-old boy, once did a multiplication sum whose answer involved 36 figures, but also lost the gift in a few years. When Benjamin Franklin was six, he asked his father what time of day he had been born, and then, in a few minutes, did a mental calculation of how many seconds he had been alive—taking into account the extra day of two leap years! Non-mathematicians may object that this is nothing to do with the 'superconscious', but is merely a knack. A moment's thought will show this to be un-true. How do I do a mental calculation? I have to hold several figures in my head at once, and manipulate them like a juggler without letting any of them drop. And if I try to imagine some-one doing the same trick with hundreds of balls, whizzing around his head like a cloud of bees, I can see that certain 'higher circuits' must have been brought into operation in order to handle them. You could say that this is only a matter for a highly complex 'robot', but that would be begging the question. How does a child of six develop such a highly complex robot? To say that he already has it—that we all have it but cannot make use of it—is to admit the existence of some kind of super-conscious. (It must be borne in mind that the subconscious consists largely of robot mechanisms—habits, instincts, and this does reduce the whole subconscious to the status of a machine.)

That is to say, these 'higher circuits' already exist, and Whately and Safford 'accidentally' plugged in to these circuits. Why did they lose their powers later? Obviously, because no-body needs the power to calculate a 36-figure answer in his head—not at this stage of our evolution. As they grew up, they adjusted to the *real* demands of their lives, and Safford, even as a mathematical astronomer, could manage perfectly well with quite ordinary calculating ability. But the possibilities *are* there, for when we have evolved to that stage.

Obviously, this view is of revolutionary importance. Scien-tists are suspicious of what they call 'teleology'—the notion of purpose in natural processes. Evolution is a case in point; Erasmus Darwin believed it was a purposive striving; his grandson showed (apparently) that although the results *look* purposive, they are achieved by the laws of chance. And in this respect, Freud's views are Darwinian. The human mind may have evolved beyond that of the chimpanzee, but it didn't set out to do so. It was driven from behind by the harshness of nature. According to Maslow, the evidence of self-actualising persons shows that this view cannot be maintained. The higher circuits already exist, and in that sense, the evolution of self-actualisers is predetermined.

The importance of this view can be seen if we consider serious mental illness—the field in which Freudian analysis is least successful. A recent newspaper story provides an example: a father murders his wife and four children, then kills himself: a fifth child is only wounded, and escapes. There is obviously a high possibility that the child will develop severe mental illness, and carry the marks of the experience for the rest of her life. What can Freudian analysis do in such a case? There is no question of repressed hostilities to be released from the subconscious. It becomes clear that everything depends on the matter of the *counterbalance*. Problems defeat me insofar as I cannot see beyond them. Everyday consciousness is narrow and its purposes are limited. I don't expect to get too much satisfaction out of the average day, so if the problems begin to pile up, my inclination is to retreat. In dealing with these problems, everything depends on the strength of my motivation—as Frankl discovered in Dachau. And what is my motivation? It is my sense of *meaning*. Frankl uses the term 'provisional existence' to describe consciousness with *limited horizons*, such as prisoners have. Provisional existence is existence with a provisional meaning, a limited, short-term meaning. This is the opposite of the feeling of a man in love, who daydreams about the delights of marriage, and to whom the word 'future' sounds like pure poetry, evoking the same kind of emotion as a fine sunset. The ideal way to cure neurosis is to evoke a powerful sense of meaning—as in Hoffer's cure of alcoholics by means of psychedelic drugs, a perfect example of 'opening up the horizons'. The answer does not, of course, lie in the use of psychedelic drugs; in that sense, there is no simple answer. But it *does* depend upon somehow freeing the patient from 'provisional existence' by opening up a sense of wider horizons of meaning. And the one thing that is quite certain is that Freudianism is not equipped to do this. There are no 'higher meanings', just ordinary, everyday existence that drags on:

'In headache and in worry
Slowly life leaks away,'

says Auden, expressing the prison-camp view of human existence.

The Maslovian view—with its 'higher needs', B-values, peak experiences—provides the basic framework in which a cure becomes possible. And the shift in emphasis—from the 'disreputable subconscious' to the creative subconscious—suddenly opens up new ranges of possibility. And this emphasises the one fundamental similarity between Maslow's psychology and Freud's. Freudian therapy is based upon the notion of 'lifting the lid' off the subconscious and allowing repressions to come into the light of day, where they can be dealt with; as Shaw says, 'psychoanalysis [is] the cure of diseases by explaining to the patient what is the matter with him: an excellent plan if you happen to know what is the matter with him'. In Maslow's psychology, the therapy does not depend on knowing what is the matter with the patient. He says: 'One thing I have already learned is that authoritative approval lifts the lid off these experiences for many people. For instance, when I lecture to my classes or other groups about these peaks, obviously in an approving way, it always happens that many peak-experiences come into consciousness in my audience . . . or emerge out of chaotic, unorganized pre-conscious experience to be given a name, to be paid attention to . . . It's a very close parallel to the emergence of sexual feelings at puberty. But this time, Daddy says it's all right.' That is, the most important effect of Maslow's method is the *bringing to consciousness* of a certain kind of knowledge which had been hidden. He goes on:

'A recent subject has taught me something else that may be relevant here: namely that it is possible to have a peak experience as the woman did in childbirth, without recognising that this is like other peak experiences—that they all have the same structure. Perhaps this is the reason for the lack of therapeutic transfer of peaks, a reason why sometimes they have no generalised effects. For instance, the woman finally realised that her feelings when her husband had once made her feel needed and important to him were very much like her feelings while giving birth, and also like the great gush of motherliness and love when confronted by an orphaned child. Now she can generalise the experiences and use them throughout life, not just in one isolated corner of it.'[1] This last sentence makes clear what Maslow means by the 'therapeutic transfer of peaks'. To grasp that the peak experience is a normal state of conscious-ness, not some throwback to childhood (as Freud maintains) effects the same *change of attitude* that Frankl's prisoners ex-perienced when they saw that Dachau had no chimney. And the change of attitude, the release from 'provisional existence', stimulates the vital powers upon which the cure depends.

This again underlines Maslow's point that there is no sharp distinction between self-actualisers and ordinary people. Everybody is potentially a self-actualiser, and the choice is largely a matter of free-will and courage, not of circumstances. Maslow may have considered himself a Freudian, but there can be no doubt of his rejection of the basic characteristic of Freud's psychology—its determinism.[2]

The 'self-actualisers' paper of 1950 established his main direction for the rest of his life. Sometimes he reverted to older themes—as in the remarkable paper on 'Parallels between the dominance and sexual behaviour of monkeys and fantasies of patients in psychotherapy' (1960), which might be regarded as the culmination of his work on the sub-human primates. But—as might be expected from a man of his temperament—most of his work after 1950 could be described as the lateral exploration of his themes. He liked to poke around and re-state and develop, in the hope of achieving deeper insights. He was the exact reverse of the professor he describes in a paper on 'Emotional Blocks to Creativity'—an obsessive who saved old newspapers and razor blades, and who stuck labels on everything. (Maslow raised the lid of his piano one day and found a label 'piano'.) Maslow worked on the assumption that the subconscious does its best work when you allow it to free-wheel.

This means that there would be no point in trying to discuss the remainder of his work paper by paper. Instead, I must try to indicate the main lines of development.

It might be said that the remainder of Maslow's work is

---

[1] *Lessons from the Peak Experience*, 1962.

[2] He was fascinated by the methods of psychoanalysis, and took every oppor-tunity to get himself psychoanalysed.

philosophical rather than scientific. And this is inevitable; for, like Freud, he had now laid the practical foundations; he had done his laboratory work. A different type of psychologist might have devoted the rest of his life to interviewing thousands of self-actualisers and tabulating the results in the manner of Kinsey. Maslow did not neglect this aspect of his work; but he was more concerned to work out the *logical* consequences of his belief that man possesses higher needs that are as instinctoid as the lower ones. In Freud's view, there was a basic antagonism between man and society, and according to Watson, freedom is an imaginary quantity that has no place in a scientific psychology. Even the existentialists—subject of one of Maslow's papers—took a pessimistic view of man's relation to his fellow man; according to Sartre, it *must* be a hostility relation, because men are like separate stars, eternally out of touch. But then, the Freud-Sartre view is based upon the assumption that man has no higher aims than survival, satisfaction of his 'natural' impulses.[1] Maslow's assertion that when man's basic needs are satisfied, he now enters the realm of 'meta-needs', contradicted this view. It meant, to begin with, that such qualities as decency and kindness are not disguised forms of self-defence or self-interest, but as natural to human nature—on a certain level—as sexual desire. And in that case, there is no *a priori* reason why the anarchist dream of a mutual co-operative society should not be realisable. Ruth Benedict had shown that a 'high-synergy society' *can* work—at least, for certain primitive tribes. Freud would have replied that this is because a tribe is a kind of family, and there can be happy families as well as unhappy ones. An industrial society is not a 'family' by any definition; it is as impersonal as a jungle, and its laws are jungle laws. There is no point in appealing to the higher nature of a tiger, because it doesn't have one; and neither does man. Maslow's assertion that man *does* have a higher nature attacks the very foundation of this argument. And during the last twenty years of his life, Maslow devoted much of his time to studying the social implications of his philosophy of the value-hierarchy. This led him eventually to a position

---

[1] And in *The Critique of Dialectical Reason*, Sartre has shifted his position closer to Freud's; there is no 'metaphysical' reason for man's hostility to man (i.e. natural solipsism)—only the basic shortage of food and raw materials.

that might be described as capitalist anarchism—using anarchism in its original sense of fruitful co-operation between equals.

During the first thirty years of his life, Maslow thought of himself as a socialist—like his father, who read Tom Paine and Robert Ingersoll, and regarded religion as something of a joke (although he went to the synagogue once a year 'for sentimental reasons'). After his bar mitzvah (at 13) Abe became 'a fighting atheist', with a powerful streak of utopian idealism. In Wisconsin, he was actually a member of the Socialist Party. (He describes his socialism as 'Fabian rather than Marxist'.) At Brooklyn College, he played a leading part in an experiment to establish a cooperative society, but although they worked hard, it failed. 'Trying to figure out why it failed . . . I had thought of the grocers as big exploiters, just sucking blood out of everybody, and I learned . . . er . . . different.' That is to say, his actual commercial experience convinced him that it was not simply a question of heartless exploiters and helpless exploitees. 'I think that was the moment I dropped socialism . . . even as a thought. I had dropped it before, in a political sense, because when Roosevelt was elected in 1932 he took over our whole socialist programme and put it into law; and even that didn't make any great miracles occur.' He adds in parenthesis, 'I suppose the English experience is like that too. You had a socialist government . . . and so what? What's changed?' It was the idealistic aspects of socialism that had appealed; but its class-war philosophy was bound to repel him eventually. He could see a similar thing in Germany—where the National Socialists decided that the proletariat must have something to hate as well as to love, and set up the Jews as the scapegoat.[1] It was simply not in Maslow's nature to hate—or even dislike—any class or social group. (Similarly, he was never able to perform brain surgery operations on animals when working with Harlow —he had to leave that part to Harlow; nor was he able to bring himself to deceive people in the course of experiments, although this is often standard experimental procedure in

[1] Maslow would have been confirmed in his view of human nature if he had known the relative failure of this policy. A survey conducted by an independent observer in 1938 showed that only 25% of the Nazi party itself were anti-semitic; the rest did not take this aspect of Nazi philosophy seriously.

experiments involving suggestion.) As his views on the 'higher ceilings of human nature' developed, the whole socialist concept became steadily less acceptable. He became convinced that his old hero, Bertrand Russell, was a fool—'personally as well as philosophically'. And after 1950, the belief that 'goodness' is as much a part of man's essence as the sex-drive or dominance, led him to think in terms of a society in which the boss-worker relation is also 'synergic': that is, based upon mutual respect, mutual aid and mutual need.

The culmination of all this was a remarkable book which may well prove to be his most *influential* contribution: *Eupsychian Management* (1965); this could be regarded as Maslow's reply to *Das Kapital*.

Its thesis, quite simply, is that the very best can be got out of workers if their 'humanness' is given full play. A similar theory had already been advanced by Douglas McGregor in *The Human Side of Enterprise*,[1] where he speaks of 'Theory X'—the authoritarian theory of management (or government), which assumes that most human beings are morons who need to be told what to do—and Theory Y, the humanistic theory which treats them as individuals and respects their human rights. Maslow felt this was important but inadequate. He developed Theory Z—a theory of management (or human group relations) which assumes the existence of higher needs, of potential meta-needs, in all workers, no matter what their I.Q.

The basis of Theory Z was Maslow's powerful feeling that 'people are a helluvalot nicer than you'd give them credit for.' 'Among Americans—I don't know how it is in England—there's an effort to look materialistic and to be very shy about goodness and virtue—so that the United States sells itself very, very short in the world press by talking selfish . . . materialism, and so on, when actually they're not'. He was struck by the 'meta-motivations I found hidden away in the aggridents [alphas, or highly dominant people] that I worked with'. 'Hidden away' is the key phrase here. 'There's much of the transcendent, the altruistic, the idealistic, in many many more people than I had ever suspected. It's part of the American character, but it's hidden, because people blush about it, they're shy over it. I found, for instance, that I am too. Part of my . . .

[1] Which, in turn, had been based on Maslow's ideas.

the need for courage is the need to work myself up to saying something sentimental in public. You know, I have to say, 'There is goodness in people', and I find myself blushing . . . That's what I've found in many people that I've worked with (i.e. studied), they kind of keep this to themselves. The anti-Americans over the world—I don't know how they'd react to that statement, but it's an empirical statement . . . And further-more, I suspect there's more of this in other people. If I went wandering round the world, I could find more of this meta-motivation, more—oh, trust and openness and so on, just covered over, ready to come out.' He is not entirely the idealist; he recognises the need to distinguish between 'the phoney and the O.K'. 'There's plenty of crap too, of course, but I think the balance is somewhat better than I would have thought . . . no, I won't say it for myself, because that's what I thought twenty, thirty years ago . . . but then, let's say, your average psycho-logist. As the data keep rolling in, they make human nature look better and better, put it that way.' 'Human nature has been sold short—throughout history. I think.'

Maslow recognised that this view he was developing was bound to be unpopular—not only because optimism about human nature is unfashionable, but because a large proportion of western intellectuals are leftists, and Maslow had moved steadily away from the left. In fact, he was neither left nor right; the left wingers take the view that the workers are the natural superiors of the bosses, and the right wingers simply take the opposite stand. Maslow's Theory Z asserts that it is as pointless to talk about superiority in this context as to ask whether the father in a family group is superior to the mother or the eldest son. The concept of superiority does not enter into it. The father may be the dominant member of the family, but the happiness of the family is not built upon his dominance, but upon mutual love, respect and cooperation.

Maslow had reason to feel ambiguous about the intellectuals. His position—as he remarked to me—was anomalous. In a certain sense, he was well-known, even famous. His books were in the best-seller class. (I first realised the extent of his popu-larity when I noticed, in several Seattle bookstores, huge piles of *Towards a Psychology of Being* at the side of the cash registers, in the place where you would usually expect to find paperbacks of the latest best-selling novel.) *Eupsychian Management* (a forbidding title if ever there was one) had sold 25,000 copies (hard cover) in three years; the original (hard cover) edition of *Motivation and Personality*, 30,000; *Towards a Psychology of Being*—a paperback—150,000. For non-fiction books, these are huge sales. He was—as he remarks without false modesty—a hero to an enormous number of young people, particularly on the West Coast. But, unlike many heroes of the young, he was respected by fellow workers in his own field; in 1969, for example, he was invited to the White House to form part of a committee on national goals.[1] On the other hand, he was a name that the majority of ordinary Americans, even of the intellectual classes, had never encountered. Any student who tried to do a survey of American intellectual trends in the sixties by studying *The Saturday Review*, *The New York Review of Books*, *The Atlantic Review*, *Harpers*, *The New Yorker*, even *Playboy*, would conclude that he had never existed. His name was never mentioned, his books never reviewed. The left-wing wouldn't have him at any price. There was the occasion when he explained his theory of eupsychian management to Herbert Marcuse, and pointed out that there was a factory in which this could be studied a couple of miles down the road. Marcuse declined to see for himself; his own ideas for a 'synergic society' are uncompromisingly left-wing. 'He's a very *a priori* German professor type,' said Maslow mildly, and with typical lack of resentment. The lack of interest simply puzzled him. 'A new image of man, a new image of society, a new image of nature, a new philosophy of science, a new economics, a new everything, and they just don't notice it.' Or, more precisely, don't want to know about it. Maslow wrote an article on 'The Unnoticed Revolution', but when it had been turned down by two mass-circulation magazines, dropped it in a drawer. 'The announcement of a revolution—and they refuse it . . .'

On the other hand, his ideas *were* having influence where it mattered—in corporation board rooms. One organisation that tried the Theory Z experiment was the Saga Food Corporation in Menlo Park, California, and it was Saga who finally saved Maslow from academic drudgery in the year before his death

[1] But his health prevented him from accepting.

by offering him a fellowship, with no strings attached. He might have escaped sooner if he had been able to bring himself to apply for fellowships; but he had not made any applications since the early forties—when he had been turned down several times because he was a Jew. It was Saga who rang *him* up and offered the fellowship. He described Saga to me: 'You can see it for yourself if you want to. This place in which my office is, the Saga Food Corporation, is run in this way—it's a democratising of the boss-subordinate relationship—an effort to appeal to the very highest in human nature, and to set up a work situation in which self-actualisation and personal growth becomes more possible. And in which, as a kind of a by-product —a synergic by-product—they simply do a good job. It makes a better team. Everybody's both happier and more efficient. If America sweeps the world, *this* is the way it's going to sweep the world.' These comments reminded me of Shaw's description of the American workmen he met at the Edison Telephone Company in the late 1870s: 'They worked with a ferocious energy which was out of all proportion to the result achieved. Indomitably resolved to assert their republican manhood by taking no orders from a tall-hatted Englishman whose stiff politeness covered his conviction that they were, relatively to himself, inferior and common persons, they insisted on being slave-driven with genuine American oaths by a genuine free and equal American foreman. They utterly despised the artfully slow British workman who did as little for his wages as he possibly could; never hurried himself; and had a deep reverence for anyone whose pocket could be tapped by respectful behaviour.' Clearly, the characteristics of the American—and British— workman have hardly changed at all in a century. And Edison's London manager apparently understood instinctively about Theory Z; which argues that Maslow was simply the first to consciously understand a basic part of the American character.

But not only of the American character. If Maslow is correct, there are wide political implications. In a non-affluent society, authoritarianism *will* work because the security needs of the workers are strong. A secure job means a home with food in the larder—and perhaps a refrigerator and a television set; compared to these things, the inconvenience of a little authoritarianism hardly matters. But once the job-security has been

taken for granted, a new set of needs begins to emerge, and a
new set of dissatisfactions arises. (Maslow speaks of 'grumbles,
higher-grumbles and meta-grumbles'—i.e. man will always
find something to grumble about, but as lower levels of need
are satisfied, the grumbles begin to concern higher levels.[1]) This
seems to explain the increasing industrial problem in commu-
nist countries—the immensely high level of absenteeism in
Poland and Czechoslovakia, for example—as well as the English
industrial unrest. According to Theory Z, there is *only* one way
to keep up a high level of production in an affluent society: to
make the assumption that the workers have higher needs, and
to try to satisfy these needs by trying to offer the worker greater
autonomy and responsibility. Maslow saw this as America's
great contribution to the future—a *pax Americana* based upon
new industrial methods rather than on militarism. 'America
may conquer the world—or seduce the world—because American management is going to be more . . . happy and fulfilling.
. . . It's just nicer to work for an American manager than it is
to work for a Spanish or British or any other kind of manager
any place. And secondly the finding is that they're just more
efficient, more capable, so that an American firm can just do
better than anybody else.' A variant of Theory Z had been put
into practice in West Germany and Japan, and accounts for
the 'economic miracle' in those two countries in the fifties and
sixties: 'paternalism' in business, with the workers being
offered shares, and encouraged to feel themselves partners
rather than employees. But this is, in fact, closer to McGregor's
Theory Y—the democratic assumption that people work better
if they feel free, if they feel like human beings instead of numbers. The Russian novelist and poet Valery Bryusov had made
this point in a powerful story, *The Republic of the Southern Cross*,
long before the Revolution of 1917; in his story, the workers in
an 'ideal city' of the future are given every comfort and convenience—provided they forego all sense of individual identity;

---

[1] But this should not be confused with my St Neot Margin concept—as Maslow
himself does on occasion. The old woman in the vinegar bottle, who keeps on
grumbling even when the good fairy changes the bottle into a cottage, then a
house, then a palace, is a victim of a habit of *mental negation*, the opposite of Frankl's
prisoners outside Dachau. Her trouble is that she fails to advance to higher needs
as the lower ones are fulfilled—an example of Maslow's later recognition that
meta-needs do not *necessarily* develop when lower ones are satisfied.

they end by going insane and destroying the city. The English football crowds who smash up trains on the way home from matches may be regarded as a variation of this phenomenon; and they indicate that Maslow's Theory Z is as urgently needed in England as elsewhere in the industrialised world.

At this point, I must describe an important study carried out by Clare W. Graves of Union College, Schenectady, N.Y. on deterioration of work standards. Professor Graves starts from the Maslow-McGregor assumption that work standards deteriorate when people react against work-control systems with boredom, inertia, cynicism . . . A fourteen-year study led to the conclusion that, for practical purposes, we may divide people up into seven groups, seven personality levels, ranging from totally self-preoccupied and selfish to what Nietzsche called 'a self-rolling wheel'—a thoroughly self-determined person, absorbed in an objective task. This important study might be regarded as an expansion of Shotover's remark that our interest in the world is an *overflow* of our interest in ourselves —and that therefore nobody can be genuinely 'objective' until they have fully satiated the subjective cravings. What is interesting—and surprising—is that it should not only be possible to distinguish seven clear personality-types, but that these can be recognised by any competent industrial psychologist. When Professor Graves's theories were applied in a large manufacturing organisation—and people were slotted into their proper 'levels'—the result was a 17% increase in production and an 87% drop in grumbles.

The seven levels are labelled as follows:

(1) Austistic
(2) Animistic
(3) Awakening and fright
(4) Aggressive power seeking
(5) Sociocentric
(6) Aggressive individualistic
(7) Pacifist individualistic.

The first level can be easily understood: people belonging to it are almost babylike, perhaps psychologically run-down and discouraged; there is very little to be done with these people. The animistic level would more probably be encountered in backward countries: primitive, superstitious, preoccupied with totems and taboos, and again poor industrial material. Man at the third level is altogether more wide-awake and objective, but finds the complexity of the real world frightening; the best work is to be got out of him by giving him rules to obey and a sense of hierarchical security. Such people are firm believers in staying in the class in which they were born. They prefer an autocracy. The majority of Russian peasants under the Tsars probably belonged to this level. And a good example of level four would probably be the revolutionaries who threw bombs at the Tsars and preached destruction. In industry, they are likely to be trouble makers, aggressive, angry, and not necessarily intelligent. Management needs a high level of tact to get the best out of these.

Man at level five has achieved a degree of security—psychological and economic—and he becomes seriously preoccupied with making society run smoothly. He is the sort of person who joins rotary clubs and enjoys group activities. As a worker, he is inferior to levels three and four, but the best is to be got out of him by making him part of a group striving for a common purpose.

Level six is a self-confident individualist who likes to do a job his own way, and does it well. Interfered with by authoritarian management, he is hopeless. He needs to be told the goal, and left to work out the best way to achieve it; obstructed, he becomes mulish.

Level seven is much like level six, but without the mulishness; he is pacifistic, and does his best when left to himself. Faced with authoritarian management, he either retreats into himself, or goes on his own way while trying to present a passable front to the management.

Professor Graves describes the method of applying this theory in a large plant where there was a certain amount of unrest. The basic idea was to make sure that each man was placed under the type of supervisor appropriate to his level. A certain amount of transferring brought about the desired result, mentioned above—increased production, immense decrease in grievances, and far less workers leaving the plant (7% as against 21% before the change).

The basic assumption is that all workers, given job-satisfaction and the level of freedom they require, will slowly 'change their psychological spots' (as Graves puts it) and graduate towards level seven.

This also has implications for management. Graves describes the case of an advertising agency where most of the creative staff were level six, while the boss was a level five—sociocentric —inclined to call them in to meetings and brood on their personal welfare. The result was much dissatisfaction, until the boss asked the advice of his creative staff. They told him to give them a boss who would do what they told him and forget their welfare. He was apparently sensible enough to try it, and the result was that 'what had once been a withering part of the organisation now started to flower'.

It is hardly necessary to point out that the consequence of these ideas—in our strike-disrupted society—could be enormous. They may be regarded as a Hegelian synthesis of what is best about communism and capitalism, the end of the notion of class war in which *either* the workers or the bosses are 'top dogs': Maslow has pointed out that, if the full potentialities of human nature are taken into account, the freedom of one need not encroach upon the freedom of the other: there is plenty enough freedom to go round.

The uniqueness of Maslow's 'philosophy' lies in its breadth of application. Marxism is a social philosophy that ignores the individual; existentialism is an individual philosophy that has nothing much to say about society as a whole. Koestler spoke about the fundamental irreconcilableness of the yogi and the commissar; the yogi thinks in terms of personal salvation, the commissar in terms of what is good for society as a whole; and they seem to be unable to find any common ground. Maslow, without making any undue fuss about it, has bridged the gap. He has, in effect, solved an equation that was once thought to be insoluble. In *The Grand Inquisitor,* Dostoevsky pointed out that most people seem to need an authority over them. Jesus told people to seek freedom and to work out their own salvation; but, says the Grand Inquisitor, man doesn't want freedom or salvation: he wants bread. Only a few unique individuals can bear the burden of free-choice, and they must be the leaders . . . And Dostoevsky could see no way out of this position, which might be regarded as the philosophy of political

totalitarianism. With Maslow's hierarchy of values, the problem vanishes. In an underdeveloped society—such as Dostoevsky's Russia—men need bread before anything else. When social
organisation has solved the problem of bread for everybody,
man's need for love and self-esteem becomes paramount. And
this cannot be satisfied without a degree of freedom and responsibility.

But the greatest human problems are not social problems, but
decisions that the individual has to make alone. The most important feelings of which man is capable emphasise his separateness from other people, not his kinship with them. The feelings
of a mountaineer towards a mountain emphasise his kinship
with the mountain rather than with the rest of mankind. The
same goes for the leap of the heart experienced by a sailor when
he smells the sea, or for the astronomer's feeling about the stars,
or for the archaeologist's love of the past. My feeling of love for
my fellow-men makes me aware of my human-ness; but my
feeling about a mountain gives me an oddly non-human sensation. It would be incorrect, perhaps, to call it 'superhuman';
but it nevertheless gives me a sense of transcending my everyday humanity.

Maslow's importance is that he has placed these experiences
of 'transcendence' at the centre of his psychology. He sees them
as the compass by which man gains a sense of the magnetic
north of his existence. They bring a glimpse of 'the source of
power, meaning and purpose' inside himself. This can be seen
with great clarity in the matter of the cure of alcoholics. Alcoholism arises from what I have called 'generalised hypertension', a feeling of strain or anxiety about practically everything.
It might be described as a 'passively negative' attitude towards
existence. The negativity prevents proper relaxation; there is a
perpetual excess of adrenalin in the bloodstream. Alcohol may
produce the necessary relaxation, switch off the anxiety, allow
one to feel like a real human being instead of a bundle of over-
tense nerves. Recurrence of the hypertension makes the alcoholic remedy a habit, but the disadvantages soon begin to out-
weigh the advantage: hangovers, headaches, fatigue, guilt,
general inefficiency. And, above all, *passivity*. The alcoholics
are given mescalin or LSD, and then peak experiences are induced by means of music or poetry or colours blending on a

screen. They are suddenly gripped and shaken by a sense of *meaning*, of just how incredibly interesting life can be for the undefeated. They also become aware of the vicious circle involved in alcoholism: misery and passivity leading to a general running-down of the vital powers, and to the *lower levels of perception* that are the outcome of fatigue.

> 'The spirit world shuts not its gates,
> Your heart is dead, your senses sleep,'

says the Earth Spirit to Faust. And the senses sleep when there is not enough energy to run them efficiently. On the other hand, when the level of will and determination is high, the senses wake up. (Maslow was not particularly literary, or he might have been amused to think that Faust is suffering from *exactly* the same problem as the girl in the chewing gum factory (see p. 22), and that he had, incidentally, solved a problem that had troubled European culture for nearly two centuries). Peak experiences are a by-product of this higher energy-drive. The alcoholic drinks because he is seeking peak experiences; (the same, of course, goes for all addicts, whether of drugs or tobacco.) In fact, he is moving away from them, like a lost traveller walking away from the inn in which he hopes to spend the night. The moment he *sees* with clarity what he needs to do to regain the peak experience, he does an about-face and ceases to be an alcoholic.

What is at issue here is, perhaps greater than Maslow himself ever realised. Apes or rats who learn to stimulate the pleasure-centre of the brain by depressing a certain key quickly develop a habit of pressing the key when they want to be stimulated.[1] Human pleasure-seeking follows the same pattern. A man who has intensely enjoyed his first cigarette in particularly relaxing circumstances is more likely to become a

---

[1] 'One study by Olds . . . discovered by means of implanted electrodes in the septal area of the rhinencephalon that this was in effect a 'pleasure centre'. That is, when the white rat was hooked up in such a fashion as to be able to stimulate his own brain via these implanted electrodes, that he repeated again and again . . . the self stimulation so long as the electrodes were implanted. . . . Stimulation of this pleasure centre was apparently so 'valuable' for the animal . . . that he would give up any other known external pleasure, food, sex, anything. . . .' Maslow, 'Towards a Humanistic Biology', 1968.

confirmed smoker than a man who felt sick after his first cigarette. The relaxing circumstances may have had more to do with the pleasure than his first cigarette; but perhaps he cannot duplicate them, and he *can* duplicate the cigarette. So, like a monkey, he pushes the button . . . Addictive drugs are drugs whose physiological after-effects are so lowering—like the raging thirst that may accompany a hangover—that *life doesn't seem worth living* in such a state of discomfort, and another dose becomes an urgent necessity. Non-addictive drugs are those that have no depressing after-effects. But since all life is a matter of emotional ups and downs, any predictable or controllable pleasure may become an addiction. Sex criminals tend to follow an addictive pattern, committing their offences with increasing frequency—presumably because rape produces a kind of peak experience. Casanova, or the anonymous author of *My Secret Life*, spends his life repeating the same experience over and over again—like the conditioned monkey. Why? Does sex have depressing after-effects? No; post-coital sadness is probably a myth. But if life seems rather boring and pointless, the sight of a pretty girl suggests an immediate way of raising its intensity. Viktor Frankl talks about the existential vacuum—the feeling of meaninglessness—that underlies so much modern neurosis, but this has always been a major determinant of human behaviour. As soon as life becomes boring, man looks around for a button to push. That is why more babies get conceived in midwinter than in midsummer.

Having said this, we must make a clear distinction between two types of 'addiction'. Addictive drugs leave behind negative after-effects; but there are some pleasures whose after-effects are positive. A teenager who becomes addicted to the music of Wagner may develop into a good musician, or at least, an all-round music lover. The youthful science-fiction addict may become a scientist. Flaubert's Bouvard and Pecuchet are knowledge-addicts; any piece of information about anything delights them; but they are comic exaggerations, and a real-life knowledge-addict is more likely to develop into an Anatole France or H. G. Wells.

That is to say that some forms of addiction are purposive—they lead somewhere: others are non-purposive or anti-purposive (i.e. debilitating). And the purposive addictions stimulate a sense of meaning. The delight aroused by a Wagner overture excites a desire to know the whole opera, and that in turn becomes a desire to know all the operas . . .

Hoffer's cure of alcoholics is the cure of a negative addiction. But it can only become a permanent cure if it can be replaced by a positive addiction, an addiction that produces 'positive feedback'.

What it amounts to is this: Thorndike's law of effect, which says that we go back to the source of pleasant stimuli, is a universal law of behaviour. Most creatures obey it blindly, and the puritanical disapproval of pleasure is basically a recognition of our slavery to this law and an attempt to free us from it. That is to say, human beings differ from other creatures in having a power of *choice* when it comes to pleasurable stimuli. The puritan principle is a crude, unthinking response to the problem of choice (i.e. become free by treating all pleasure as undesirable; *but* you may also become narrow and devitalised). But Maslow's psychology suggests an altogether more interesting possibility: a study of the mechanics—the phenomenology of peak experiences—in order to make long-term calculations of creative feedback. Man is an evolutionary animal whose *instinct* is to keep pushing forward and upward; deprived of this forward movement, he becomes mentally ill, and loses the will to live. His main problem so far is that he is so often a bad chooser, and ends in blind alleys. The most intelligent human beings are often the most neurotic, which indicates that their intelligence does not guarantee fruitful choices. Why? Because where important life-choices are concerned, they often mistrust intelligence, and rely on instinct—or pure luck. So they end up with impossible wives, or with frustrating jobs and life-styles. Maslow's study of peak experiences throws light on the whole problem. 'Positive feedback' becomes a matter that can be grasped by the intellect; it ceases to be a hit-and-miss affair.

What, in fact, do we know about the peak experience? Well, to begin with, we know one thing that puts us several steps ahead of the most penetrating thinkers of the 19th century: that P.E's are not a matter of pure good luck or grace. They don't come and go as they please, leaving 'this dim, vast vale of tears vacant and desolate'. Like rainbows, peak experiences are governed by definite laws. They are 'intentional'. And that statement suddenly gains in significance when we remember Thorndike's discovery that the effect of positive stimuli is far more powerful and far reaching than that of negative stimuli. His *first* statement of the law of effect was simply that situations that elicit positive reactions tend to produce continuance of positive reactions, while situations that elicit negative or avoidance reactions tend to produce continuance of these. It was later that he came to realise that positive reactions build-up stronger response patterns than negative ones. In other words, positive responses are *more* intentional than negative ones. Which is another way of saying that if you want a positive reaction (or a peak experience), your best chance of obtaining it is by putting yourself into an active, purposive frame of mind. The opposite of the peak experience—sudden depression, fatigue, even the 'panic fear' that swept William James to the edge of insanity—is the outcome of *passivity*. This cannot be overemphasised. Depression—or neurosis—need not have a positive cause (childhood traumas, etc.). It is the natural outcome of negative passivity.

The peak experience is the outcome of an intentional attitude. 'Feedback' from my activities depends upon the degree of deliberately calculated purpose I put into them, not upon some occult law connected with the activity itself. You might compare this with the situation of a hypochondriac who stays indoors and fills himself with pills and patent medicines. He observes that he is no longer enjoying his dinner, and orders his cook to try to make his food more appetising. It never strikes him that if he wants to enjoy his dinner, he only has to take a ten-mile walk, or any other vigorous exercise. *Because appetite doesn't depend upon the dinner so much as upon his own hunger.*

Obviously, this recognition can be the starting point for a whole life of research. One fascinating possibility is mentioned by Maslow in the paper 'Towards a Humanistic Biology' (1968). J. Kamiya, a gestalt psychologist, was working with the electro-encephalograph, allowed his subjects to study their own alpha wave intensity—presumably by letting them see the dial on which it was registered. (Alpha rhythms are a basic brain rhythm, and they seem to be associated with 'idling'—when the mind is in neutral gear, so to speak. As soon as something arrests the attention, they cease.) The subjects soon developed a degree of control over their own EEG (electro-encephalo-gram), and it was at this point that Kamiya discovered that when the alpha rhythms reached a certain intensity, the subject experienced a mood of serenity, even bliss. That is to say, the subjects learned to generate a certain kind of peak experience in themselves by learning to 'handle' their subjective feelings as they might handle a car, or learn to play a musical instru-ment. Follow-up studies with subjects who had studied Eastern techniques of contemplation showed that their alpha rhythm pattern was similar.

And this is precisely what we might expect. The alpha rhythm is the brain's idling rhythm; when we go 'into gear' it ceases. A healthy, perfectly adjusted human being would slide smoothly into gear, perform whatever has to be done with perfect eco-nomy of energy, then recover lost energy in a state of serene relaxation. Most human beings are not healthy or well adjusted. Their activity is full of strain and nervous tension, and their relaxation hovers on the edge of anxiety. They fail to put enough effort—enough seriousness—into their activity, and they fail to *withdraw* enough effort from their relaxation. Moods of serenity descend upon them—if at all—by chance; perhaps after some crisis, or in peaceful surroundings with pleasant associations. Their main trouble is that they have no idea of what *can* be achieved by a certain kind of mental effort.

And this is perhaps the place to point out that although mys-tical contemplation is as old as religion, it is only in the past two centuries that it has played a major role in European culture. It was the group of writers we call the romantics who discovered that a man contemplating a waterfall or a mountain peak can suddenly feel 'godlike', as if the soul had expanded. The world is seen from a 'bird's eye view' instead of a worm's eye view: there is a sense of power, detachment, serenity. The romantics—Blake, Wordsworth, Byron, Goethe, Schiller—were the first to raise the question of whether there are 'higher ceilings of human nature'. But, lacking the concepts for analys-ing the problem, they left it unsolved. And the romantics in general accepted that the 'godlike moments' cannot be sus-tained, and certainly cannot be re-created at will. This pro-duced the climate of despair that has continued down to our own time. (The major writers of the 20th century—Proust,

Eliot, Joyce, Musil—are direct descendants of the romantics, as Edmund Wilson pointed out in *Axel's Castle*.) Thus it can be seen that Maslow's importance extends far beyond the field of psychology. William James had asserted that 'mystical' experiences are not mystical at all, but are a perfectly normal potential of human consciousness; but theie is no mention of such experiences in *Principles of Psychology* (or only in passing). Maslow made them the basis of all his major work.

At the same time, there is a certain limitation in Maslow's view of the peak experience. He acknowledges (in 'Lessons from the Peak Experience') that his findings conform more closely with Taoism and Zen rather than with other forms of religious mysticism. Taoism and Zen are basically concerned with the 'serenity experience'. But there are (as I have pointed out in *Poetry and Mysticism*) two major types of mystical experience: one of serenity, one of an explosive joy and sense of power. This is what Nijinsky meant when he wrote, 'I am God, I am God.' It is the experience that happened to Nietzsche on the hill called Leutsch, when the crashing of a thunderstorm and the bleatings of a goat being slaughtered combined to produce a sense of enormous zest. 'Pure will, without the confusions of intellect—how happy, how free . . .' Kamiya's method of producing 'peaks' works for only one type of mystical experience. The question of the other type remains.[1] Maslow would undoubtedly have turned his attention to these if he had lived—he defined his programme at the Laughlin Foundation as being 'an investigation of the further reaches of human nature'. One of his later projects was to discover whether peak experiences could prolong the life of old people, using methods similar to the ones Hoffer adopted with the alcoholics; this would have involved study of both types of peak experience.

Let me try to summarise Maslow's achievement, and also to suggest my own sense of its limitation—as a necessary preliminary to the final section of this book.

The first half of the 20th century saw a reaction against the idealism of the age of romanticism. Biology was dominated by a rigid Darwinism, philosophy by various forms of positivism and rationalism, science by determinism. This latter could be

[1] I shall consider this in the final section of this book.

summarised as the notion that if we could build a giant computer, and feed all our present scientific knowledge into it, the
computer could take-over the future of scientific discovery. (It
follows, of course, that a human scientist should do his best to
approximate to a computer.) This tough-minded approach
struck many scientists and philosophers as a little too rigid, but
there seemed to be no way to remedy this *logically*—that is,
without simply taking refuge in 'faith' or emotionalism. Even
literature developed a new tough-mindedness—as when T. E.
Hulme dismissed romanticism as 'spilt religion'. Whitehead—
who was both a scientist and a philosopher—tried to break the
deadlock; but his attempt was so strenuous, and his intellectual
struggles so complicated—reminiscent of Houdini trying to
escape from a strait-jacket—that the final 'system' appealed
only to the kind of people who were natural idealists anyway;
the tough-minded dismissed him with a shrug.

Whitehead may have been handicapped by his intellectual
understanding of the situation; he was something of a cultural
historian as well as a philosopher. By comparison, Maslow
may seem ingenuous. He began as a Watsonian determinist,
then passed on to the Freudian variety, then rejected this in
favour of Adler. The study of dominance led him a step beyond
Adler, when he recognised that the alphas (or aggridents) have
urges that transcend the simple desire to dominate. When he
expressed this observation—in the 'hierarchy of values' theory—
he regarded it as a modest extension of Adlerian psychology,
rather than as a contradiction of the whole trend of modern
psychology. And apparently no one else noticed this either—
until too late.

The developed theory—as it took shape in the fifties and early
sixties—stated that man is driven by evolutionary needs that
transcend the physical or emotional urges—for food, sex,
security, dominance. Stated in this way it has a common sense
ring—after all, man's survival in the universe depends upon
knowledge as well as strength. Knowledge is the extension of
consciousness. And if the need for sex and territory has become
an instinct, why not the need for wider forms of consciousness?
They are equally essential for man's survival in the universe.

It was all remarkably simple, and the total picture had the
same simplicity to recommend it. The early psychologists had

restricted themselves to trying to explain our feelings and responses in terms of brain mechanisms; that is, to constructing
a mechanical picture of the mind. Freud's picture was altogether more 'rich and strange', but it was deeply pessimistic—
what Aldous Huxley calls the 'basement with basement' view
of the mind. (Huxley found Maslow's ideas important and
exciting, and Maslow's influence can be clearly discerned in
the last novel, *Island*.) Maslow was the first person to create a
truly comprehensive psychology stretching, so to speak, from
the basement to the attic. He accepted Freud's clinical method
without accepting his philosophy. Man is driven by sexual
urges, dominance urges, territorial urges; but these are only
the lower part of the picture. Shaw had always asserted that
there are saintly men and women in whom the sex-drive has
been transcended;[1] but in the Freudian era, this was taken for
old-fashioned idealism. But it is a logical consequence of
Maslow's 'hierarchy of values' theory. The 'transcendent'
urges—aesthetic, creative, religious—are as basic and permanent a part of human nature as dominance or sexuality. If
they are less obviously 'universal', this is only because fewer
human beings reach the point at which they take over. (Even
the sexual urge has the power to transcend the personality, to
release it into realms where the satisfaction of the personal ego
becomes unimportant.)

Maslow saw human nature as *naturally* self-transcending.
Healthy, satisfied people seek naturally for wider horizons, for
the 'far' rather than the 'near'. Freud was unable to see beyond ego-satisfaction: it seems plain to him that all urges are
directed to this end. He would have said that for a human being
to perform any action *not* directed at ego-satisfaction would be
as illogical as a hungry man slicing up a steak and then putting
it into the mouth of the man sitting next to him. But—as in the
case of the 'oceanic feeling'—Freud had simply got his phenomenology wrong. The ego is not simply a stomach craving food;
it would be more accurate to compare it to a man's whole
physical organism. *Some* needs will be satisfied by eating and

---

[1] In the last year of his life, Maslow read my recently published book on Shaw,
and wrote to me saying he had forgotten just how important and original Shaw is.
His interest was considerable—he took the trouble to send me all the reviews he
came across. I pointed out the resemblance between Shaw's ideas and Maslow's.

drinking, others by walking or swimming, others by making love, others by playing games of skill, and so on. And the needs of the psychic-organism are as various.

Maslow's 'holistic' model of the psychic organism led him to three major conclusions:

(1) Neurosis may be regarded as the blockage of the channels of self-actualisation.

(2) A synergic society—one in which *all* individuals may reach a high level of self-satisfaction, without restricting anybody else's freedom—should evolve naturally from our present social system.

(3) Business efficiency and the recognition of 'higher ceilings of human nature' are not incompatible; on the contrary, the highest levels of efficiency can *only* be obtained by taking full account of the need for self-actualisation that is present in every human being.

This outlines Maslow's achievement, and it is enormous. Like all original thinkers, he has opened up a new way of *seeing* the universe. His ideas developed slowly and organically, like a tree; there are no breaks, or sudden changes of direction. His instinct was remarkably sound; none of his work has been disproved; none has had to be re-done. When his papers are read in sequence, it can be seen that his guesses and hunches usually proved correct; in fact, I can see no single example in which he was definitely mistaken. He advanced with the faultless precision of a sleepwalker.

A temperament so highly individual was bound to have its limitations. Maslow began as an old-fashioned atheist and rationalist, an admirer of J. B. Watson and Bertrand Russell. His mother was a highly superstitious woman—about such matters as walking under ladders, opening umbrellas in houses, etc.—and no doubt his reaction against her strengthened his rationalistic tendencies; he told me that one of his early dreams was to demolish all religious superstition. And as late as 1963, when writing *Religions, Values and Peak Experiences*, he was still thinking in terms of a devastating attack on the edifice of the priests and rabbis. The emphasis shifted slowly from the negative to the positive side of religion. But because all this was new territory to him, he had to explore it for himself like a beginner.

The consequence is that some of his later papers sound like a mixture of scientific reports (to be read aloud, perhaps, at the A.P.A. congress) and lay sermons. What one feels to be lacking here is precise philosophical training. He may explain in passing that he rejects Sartre's view that the 'self' can be created by a kind of fiat, but he makes no attempt to outline his own position in the kind of phenomenological terms used by Sartre. He states, in the preface to *Religions, Values and Peak Experiences* that the book is in the same tradition as James's *Varieties of Religious Experience;* but what the book lacks is precisely that sense of precision, of logical development, of trying to stick to 'stubborn, irreduceable fact' and case histories. The following passage (from 'A Theory of Metamotivation', 1967) illustrates this tendency to sound like a lay preacher rather than a psychologist: 'It is my (uncertain) impression that any B-value is fully and adequately defined by the total of other B-values. That is, truth, to be fully and completely defined, must be beautiful, good, perfect, just, simple, orderly, lawful, alive, comprehensive, unitary, dichotomy-transcending, effortless and amusing.' This statement sounds more logical and exact in its proper context, but it makes my point: that he often sounds as if he is writing about religion rather than psychology, and risks damaging his own case with the 'tough minded'.

Again, his kindly and generous temperament made him incapable of fully understanding the problems involved in authoritarianism or violence—so that his papers on these subjects are among his least satisfactory. A certain type of dominant human being may be described as a 'Dionysian'—Nietzsche is an example—and his expressions of intolerance, harshness, admiration for strength, are not *necessarily* symptoms of sickness and insecurity. When Nietzsche was a medical orderly during the Franco-Prussian war, he saw his old regiment riding to battle, and wrote in a burst of exaltation: 'the strongest and highest will to life does not lie in the puny struggle to exist, but in the Will to war, the Will to Power . . .' And this is an authentic insight that deserves to be explored *in its own terms*, even if, in this particular form, it has to be rejected. I suspect that Maslow was temperamentally incapable of an over-all, objective view of the 'Dionysian', and his view of the peak experience is conequently one-sided.

Finally, there is the problem that Maslow himself raised many times in the last years of his life: of the 'mechanism' of self-actualisation, 'It is a great mystery to me' (he says in a footnote to the 'Metamotivation' paper) 'why affluence releases some people for growth while permitting other people to stay fixated at a strictly "materialistic" level'. The problem here seems to me to reflect again Maslow's lack of an adequate phenomenology. He accepts that all people have a 'potential higher nature' that ought to develop naturally when lower needs are taken care of; so why does it develop in some people and not in others? But the word 'naturally', as used in the last sentence, could be replaced with 'mechanically', and this in turn shows a failure to grasp what Husserl meant by 'intentionality': its essentially *free* nature. In another sense, he understood this perfectly well. He saw that the way to cure alcoholics—or any other kind of depressive—is to induce somehow enough *vision* to galvanise the will, to give them a *reason* for summoning vital energy. But, it seems to me, he had not grasped the full consequences of this insight. The problem can be seen again in a chapter devoted largely to Maslow in Betty Friedan's *The Feminine Mystique* (which has become the bible of the militant feminist movement in America). The 'feminine mystique' is the idea that women should be contented to be mothers and wives, and sacrifice their personal development to the male—the problem Ibsen wrote about in *A Doll's House*—and the chapter on Maslow quotes his views on self-actualisation and on dominance in women. The implication, naturally, is that women should face up to their potentialities of self-actualisation, and stop behaving like zombies. And it is, of course, an excellent suggestion—so long as we do not take the argument too literally, i.e. 'women can actualise their creative potential, and it is the male-created feminine mystique that is preventing them'—which is simply a version of the Rousseau fallacy that man is born free, and all he needs to do to lose his chains is smash the social system. This is like saying, 'In a truly democratic state, every man would be a Leonardo da Vinci.' Miss Friedan points out that among the 3,000 college students interviewed by Maslow, only about twenty seemed to be moving towards self-actualisation. And these were not 3,000 women. Obviously, then, self-actualisation is not the straightforward, universal possibility that it looks; there are obstacles here *that have to be defined.*[1]

Again, when I discussed the problem of sensory deprivation with Maslow in 1966, I was writing a novel called *The Black Room*, whose central question is: How would you train a spy to withstand brainwashing in a totally black and silent room? Confinement in the black room can produce nervous breakdown in most people in a matter of days, and intelligent people tend to crack more quickly than stupid ones, no doubt because they worry more. Maslow told me that he had solved the problem of the black room. Although it is true that intelligent people break down sooner than the less intelligent, mature self-actualisers could stand it longer than anybody. (I think he said that one self-actualiser had stayed inside the room for fourteen days.)

I agreed that this was a partial solution; but it was not what mathematicians would call the general solution. It is no doubt true that Einstein could stand the black room longer than James Bond, but not indefinitely longer. And yet the black room should not drive human beings insane; there is no actual hardship. They are not threatened with suffocation or starvation. What rises up against them in the black room is their own immaturity, their own weakness. The 'general solution' would be to produce a *type* of human being capable of self-sustaining mental activity, of mental activity so firmly grounded in a sense of objective values that it could not be eroded by the usual fears, daydreams, confusions.

This underlines my own central point about 'self-actualisation': that it is, in a sense, a different *kind* of development, separated from other kinds by a chasm. Ordinary development can take place on a horizontal level; self-actualisation requires a kind of vertical movement. I do not mean, either, that self-actualisers have to sweat blood; it may come easily. But the gap between ordinary human passivity and the active freedom involved in creation is absolute, as different as real activity is from dreaming. The black room destroys men because dreams take over. In order to survive the black room indefinitely, a man would have to develop a peculiar faculty—which I have elsewhere called Faculty X—for exploding dreams like bubbles.

[1] Miss Friedan is not, of course, arguing that it is a simple matter of 'losing chains'.

Maslow *was* aware of this problem. Betty Friedan quotes him as saying: 'Growth has not only rewards and pleasure, but also many intrinsic pains and always will have. Each step forward is a step into the unfamiliar and is thought of as possibly dangerous . . .' As he explored the question of why self-actualisation is so rare, even for people who have satisfied the more basic needs, he would be obliged to study it more closely, and to create a phenomenology of self-actualisation. In fact, in the last work listed in his bibliography—the preface to the new edition of *Motivation and Personality*—he again raises the problem, and ends:

'It is possible already to start *thinking* about the transhuman, a psychology and a philosophy which transcends the human species itself. This is yet to come'.

He knew precisely what had to be done.

PART THREE

Where Now?

MASLOW WAS ALWAYS a loner; he spent his life studying and developing his own intuitions. The major influences—Adler, Goldstein, Horney, Ruth Benedict—came early in his career; after that, his development proceeded by a process of self-unfolding. It is interesting to speculate what would have happened if the Second World War had been followed by a migration of psychologists similar to the migration of the mid-thirties. For an 'existential' reaction against Freudianism had been building up in Europe—especially Vienna and Zurich—since before the war, and by 1946, had many distinguished champions: Ludwig Binswanger, Eugene Minkowski, Medard Boss, Erwin Strauss, V. E. von Gebsattel, Henry Baruk, Igor Caruso; and, of course, Viktor Frankl. Maslow knew little about most of these until 1958, when some of the most important papers of the school were translated in a book called *Existence*, edited by Rollo May. Perhaps it was just as well. The foundations of Maslow's work were in the laboratory, while many of the new European school took Husserl, Kierkegaard and Heidegger as their starting point. Maslow might well have found their approach a little too metaphysical or religious for his taste. For better or worse, he remained unaware of them until his own psychology had crystallised into its final form.

Frankl, like Maslow, had been an Adlerian in the late thirties in Vienna. He spent the war in concentration camps; the rest of his family—wife, parents, brother—died in them. Frankl had taken the manuscript of a book on what he called *Existenz-Analyse* into the prison camp with him, but it was destroyed. He spent much of the war trying to reconstruct it, and later became aware how much his survival had depended upon possessing this purpose. (Similarly, Jakow Trachtenberg had preserved his sanity in Hitler's concentration camps by inventing his revolutionary 'speed system' of basic mathematics— simple rules for calculating enormous sums in the head.) After the war Frankl returned to Vienna and became head of the department of neurology at the Polyclinic; there he wrote his brief but revolutionary book *From Death Camp to Existentialism*. His major insights might be summarised under three headings:

(1) The recognition that physical health is so directly related to the sense of purpose, as illustrated in the story, quoted in the introduction to this book (pp. 38–9) about the composer who dreamed he would be liberated from the camp on March 30, and who died the day after his hopes collapsed. In order to feel fully alive, man needs *goals in the future*. Frankl called the goalless state of 'marking time' in the present 'provisional existence'.

(2) The recognition that purposive consciousness depends upon an *attitude of mind* rather than upon definite goals—as illustrated in the story about the prisoners who were made to stand all night in the rain outside Dachau, but who were immensely happy *because Dachau had no chimney*. You might say that once this attitude of optimism exists, it is like connecting a horse up to a buggy, or a water-skier up to a speedboat; the vital life-line has been established. And when this life-line is dropped, either through boredom or despair, man becomes instantly vulnerable to physical and mental illness.

(3) His discovery of the 'law of reverse effort'—as illustrated by the case of the Mainz schoolboy who stuttered badly, and was asked to act the part of a stutterer in the school play; but he had to be replaced because once he got on stage he couldn't stutter. The same point is made in Frankl's case of the bookkeeper suffering from writer's cramp; when all other therapy had failed, Frankl advised him to practise *writing as badly as possible*, which cured him in forty-eight hours. Here, it can be seen, an undesirable pressure is built up by anxiety, and Frankl is removing the anxiety by creating a change of attitude. Mark Twain's comment that a pessimist is a man who has to live with an optimist shows an intuitive grasp of the law of reversed effort. So does the episode in *Tom Sawyer* where Tom induces his friends to whitewash the fence by whistling loudly and pretending to enjoy it.

Frankl's basic position is identical with Maslow's, as can be seen in his assertion: 'Meaning sets the pace of being. Existence falters unless it is lived in terms of transcendence towards something beyond itself.'[1] And in *The Will to Meaning* (1971) he writes: 'Existence falters unless there is a "strong idea", as Freud puts it, or a strong ideal to hold on to. To quote Albert Einstein, "the man who regards his life as meaningless is not merely unhappy but hardly fit for life."' In Maslow, this 'something beyond itself' can be anything that arouses interest —as in his case of the girl student who became frustrated in the dead-end job (p. 22). Frankl emphasised the importance of religion, the belief in God. A. J. Ungersma, in his study of Frankl *The Search for Meaning* (1961), emphasises this religious aspect, and speaks of 'pastoral psychology'. Understandably, such an approach does not suit the majority of psychologists, even those sympathetic to existential psychology, since it introduces the danger of mixing the dirty bathwater with the clean.

Ludwig Binswanger is generally regarded as the most influential member of the Zurich school of existenz-psychologists. Like Jung, Adler and Rank, he began as a Freudian and a friend of Freud's, and they remained on friendly terms even when Binswanger began to develop in his own direction. Freud wrote to Binswanger: 'I have always confined myself to the ground floor and basement of the edifice [of psychology]. You maintain that by changing one's point of view, one can also see the upper storey in which dwell such distinguished guests as religion, art, etc. . . . I have already found a place for religion by putting it under the category of the neuroses of mankind.'[2] It is interesting that Freud himself should have hit upon the image that was later used against him by Aldous Huxley—and a reminder that Freud is too intelligent and vital to be classified and pigeon-holed.

Binswanger was deeply impressed by the work of Martin Heidegger, whose unfinished *Being and Time* (1927) is mainly concerned to analyse the various forms of 'inauthentic existence'

---

[1] Frankl's article in *Phenomenology, Pure and Applied*, ed. Erwin Straus, Duquesne, 1964.
[2] Quoted by H. M. Ruitenbeek, *Psychoanalysis and Existential Philosophy* (Dutton, New York, 1962), p. xviii.

into which man is trapped by the triviality that is inherent in civilised life. (Eric Berne's *Games People Play* might be regarded as a popularised version of *Being and Time*.) The central point of Binswanger's psychology is his feeling of the complete 'otherness' of the patient's life-world, and the need for the psychologist to try to see this through the patient's eyes. Expressed very simply, the Binswanger approach might be regarded as a warning to psychotherapists not to impose their own preconceived ideas on the patient—an obvious enough maxim, but one that had a revolutionary sound in the Vienna of the twenties. Binswanger attempted to import Husserl's phenomenological method into psychology. Perhaps his chief contribution was to recognise that various 'compulsive neuroses' represent a kind of blockage of the vital system—at a time when most psychologists were thinking in terms of sexual repressions. Binswanger regarded himself as an analytical psychologist[1] rather than as a psychotherapist. Erwin Straus—who came to America in 1938 from Berlin—has continued Binswanger's type of phenomenological analysis, while Medard Boss, another student of Binswanger's, had popularised the term *Daseinsanalysis* in his excellent book *Psychoanalysis and Daseinsanalysis* (1963). He also states explicitly: 'Existential analysis has nothing to do with psychotherapeutic practice.' This emphasises that the approach of the Zurich school is methodological rather than philosophical. I speak of it here for the sake of thoroughness, but it will not be referred to overmuch in the discussion that follows.

A study like this would be incomplete without a brief outline of the work of George Ivanovitch Gurdjieff (1873[2]–1949), although, strictly speaking, he belongs to the history of 'occultism' rather than psychology.[3] Gurdjieff's 'system' was aimed at what he called 'the harmonious development of man'. He begins by stating that man is not one single 'I' but dozens of 'I's', each of which takes-over briefly. The consequence is that man has no *continuity*—he alters from moment to moment. It *is* possible, said Gurdjieff, to develop a 'central I' or 'essence', but

---

[1] Not, of course, in the Jungian sense.

[2] The exact date is not certain; it could be as late as 1877.

[3] See my book *The Occult*, p. 385 et seq. (1971).

it costs enormous effort. It is rather as if every human being was full of tiny fragmentary crystals of glass, like the crystals that a car windscreen dissolves into when it receives a violent blow. Every really intense effort of will or imagination fuses together a few of these crystals, and if man keeps on trying, he could, eventually, become a unity, a solid fused mass of hard crystal instead of a million fragments. One of Gurdjieff's pupils summarised the aim of his system: 'a method for preventing your past from becoming your future'—which is to say that it is a method of evolving instead of remaining the same. Men tend to develop 'personality'—a mere superficial shield against the world—but their essence remains almost non-existent. (This is often true of actors, and of anyone who cares a great deal about the opinions of other people.) Gurdjieff also insists that most people are literally *asleep*, wandering around in a kind of anaesthetised daze, and that only a sudden shock or some extreme effort can awaken them briefly from this dream-state to a state of full awareness of the meaning of their existence. The starting point of his system—his view of 'man as he now exists'— is certainly an extreme pessimism. He would not accept that the ordinary tinkering-about of most psychologists can really make much difference; the psychologist is very nearly as sick and fast-asleep as his patient. But the essence of Gurdjieff's work is a highly developed phenomenology of human consciousness, in many ways akin to that of Husserl and Heidegger. Like Heidegger, he feels that the only thing that could make man snap-out of his permanent 'forgetfulness of existence' is a clear, unwavering vision of the inevitability of his own death.

Gurdjieff was less concerned with the cure of neurotic human beings than with the problem of how to turn normal human beings into super-normal ones, and various books describing his 'Institute for the Harmonious Development of Man' at Prieuré, in France, make it clear that his success was remarkable; his pupils achieved an amazing degree of coordination of body and mind. At the moment, Gurdjieff's importance in the history of psychology is not recognised; but as the 'existential' revolution proceeds, he is bound to become known as one of the greatest originators of the 20th century.

Roberto Assagioli, a friend and colleague of Maslow's (born

in Venice in 1888) is responsible for a remarkable system of psychotherapy which he calls 'Psychosynthesis'; its ideas are closely related to those of Gurdjieff, as well as Maslow and Carl Rogers. Like Rogers, Assagioli starts from the notion that man possesses a central core of being, a 'self'; but for most people, this central 'I' is not the centre of gravity. One might say that it is surrounded by a cloud of emotions and desires that whirl around it like the hot gases of a half-formed planet. Man's first task is to recognise his central core and achieve a balance, a position of command, so to speak. But this is only the beginning; the achievement of the sense of Self is the starting point of real development—and here Assagioli is in total agreement with Maslow's notion of the creative potentialities of consciousness; in fact, he speaks of 'growth towards the Superconscious'. His important book *Psychosynthesis* (1965) outlines the techniques that he has developed towards this end. They are 'exercises' whose function is to awaken the imagination, to stop man from living in a world he takes for granted.

Perhaps one of the most important aspects of psychosynthesis is the central place Assagioli gives to art. For example, he offers three exercises in self-realisation based on the legend of the Grail, on Dante and on the blossoming of a rose—as a symbol of inner-opening. In the Grail exercises, the therapist describes at length the use of the Grail symbol in medieval myth, and in Wagner operas, and extracts of Wagner are played. Members of the group are asked to meditate on each symbol for a week, brood on its significance, write about it: perhaps the symbol of Titurel (father of Amfortas in *Parsifal*) climbing to the mountaintop to feel himself beyond the trivialities of daily life; another week of meditation on Titurel in prayer; another week on the angels appearing in response to the prayer . . . The meditation on Dante's descent into hell, then slow ascent via Purgatory, is treated along the same lines. The poet Yeats insisted that certain symbols possess a power quite independent of the human mind—or at least, of individual minds; Assagioli's experience with his patients seems to confirm this, or something close to it; the symbols become charged with a power which in turn charges the mental batteries.

In effect, the patient is being encouraged to come out of his personal little world of minor problems, and to direct the mind towards objective meaning. When a man is depressed, our tendency to 'a certain blindness' causes a rejection of *other* meanings, 'outside' meanings; he behaves as if his own problems were the most important thing in the whole world, and is correspondingly 'discouraged' by them. Art is encapsulated meaning, a particular meaning captured and 'fixed' by the artist. This applies even to pessimistic art. The poems of Verlaine or Ernest Dowson are full of nostalgic 'remembrance of things past', elegies for lost beauty; but what is moving about the poem is not the poet's defeat, but the strength that enabled him to rise above it and crystallise it in words. All art is, in effect, an assertion of strength, of man's essential detachment from his miseries. Art *is* therapeutic. Wordsworth begins the *Intimations of Immortality* ode by mourning a lost vision, but ends by saying, 'And I again am strong.' The writing of the poem has created the feeling of strength, by giving him detachment and—as Assagioli would say—by emphasising that the 'miserable I' is not the essential Self.

The relation of these ideas to the psychology of Jung will also be immediately apparent; Jung also believes that one can descend into the imagination—while still wide awake—as into a coal mine, and encounter its symbols as objective realities. Assagioli quotes a case history in which the patient was told to imagine that he was descending to the bottom of the ocean. There he had a powerful image of being attacked by an octopus. The psychotherapist (Dr Robert Gerard of Los Angeles) thereupon asked the patient to visualise rising to the surface and taking the octopus with him. He did this, and on reaching the surface, the octopus seemed to change into the face of his mother, revealing the extent to which she was at the back of the neurosis. But in the case of a girl called Maria, cited by Medard Boss,[1] her imminent recovery was announced by a dream in which she stood on a balcony with a handsome man, and the stars arranged themselves into the form of a great Christmas tree, while a huge organ seemed to be playing music of the spheres; here the creative forces of the mind rise in a tide of optimism and express themselves symbolically.

Assagioli's work underlines the major criticism that 'existential psychologists' level against the Freudians; that in leaving

[1] *Psychoanalysis and Daseinsanalysis*, 1963, p. 155.

out of account these immense creative forces of the human mind, they are neglecting the most powerful instrument o. therapy.

I should here refer to two psychologists of a younger generation: the American Rollo May, and the Scotsman R. D. Laing. May was responsible for introducing the Zurich school to Americans (in *Existence*, which he edited). He has also suggested the interesting concept of 'centeredness' (or 'self-centeredness'). 'When a patient comes in and sits down in the chair opposite me in my consulting room, what can I assume about him? . . . *I assume that this person, like all beings, is centered in himself, and an attack on this centeredness is an attack on his existence.*'[1] This is an important concept, provided it is understood correctly, as a man's instinctive self-certainty, freedom from the feeling of being 'contingent' or accident-prone.

R. D. Laing, author of *The Divided Self* (1959), has become a figure of controversy in England in recent years, and has been denounced by the behavioural psychologist Eysenck. He is centrally preoccupied with the notion that it is our society that is sick, and that schizophrenia has a social origin. It might be said that he is obsessed with the forces that prevent people reaching self-actualisation—particularly with the family. He once opened a lecture with the statement: 'The initial act of brutality against the average child is the mother's first kiss . . .' This sounds like the kind of statement that makes anti-Freudians blow raspberries, but it is only an extreme statement of his theme that family pressure often forces the personality into completely unsuitable moulds. 'The condition of alienation, of being asleep, of being unconscious, of being out of one's mind, is the condition of the normal man', he asserts in *The Politics of Experience*. This emphasis upon the madness of society—and the menace of family relationships—has inevitably made him an important figure to rebels of the younger generation. But his pessimistic tendencies relate him more closely to Freud than to Maslow. Reading his work after Maslow, the reader senses the Freudian problem of the 'norm': what is the psychiatrist trying to bring the patient *to*? Maslow's concept of creativity

[1] In *Readings in Existential Phenomenology*, ed. Lawrence and O'Connor, Prentice Hall, New York, 1967.

and self-actualisation provides a notion of a goal, something beyond mere 'social adjustment', while Laing's talk about the sickness of society hints at it but leaves it undefined.

There is one obvious central difference between the new movement in psychology—the trends and theories that can be loosely grouped together as 'existential'—and the older schools of Freud, Jung, Adler and Rank. The existential school adopts a more down-to-earth, empirical approach to mental illness. There is a notable absence of dogmatic underpinning, theories about the subconscious and its hypothetical contents. The psychiatrist tends to approach the patient with an attitude of self-identification: 'How could I myself get into that condition?' And obviously, the answer will be in terms of conscious pressures.

As a starting point for a discussion of this approach, we might consider the case of 'Larry Cassidy', described by the novelist Irving Wallace.[1] Cassidy was a depressive who was finally 'cured' by means of pre-frontal lobotomy, the severing of the tissue between the frontal lobes of the brain and the thalamus. Cassidy was the son of a highly dominant newspaper owner in New York; he had a high I.Q., learned languages easily and loved music. The mother was anything but dominant; Larry loved her and disliked his father. He was one of five brothers. In his late teens, he had developed into a shy, introspective boy with a strong tendency to *weltschmerz*, a feeling of the futility of life. Nevertheless, he graduated at 22 (in 1936), and took a job writing for pulp magazines—the father of his closest friend owned a string of them. He seems to have lived a bohemian existence. In 1939, his mother died; it was a blow to the whole family. The father and five brothers continued to live in the same house, Larry now working—erratically—for his father's small newspaper. He began to sink into a slough of boredom and passivity, spending much of the day at home reading books; he frequently vomited after meals. When America entered the war he tried to join the army but was turned down. He married the girl who had been their housekeeper for several years. Marriage did not improve him; the depression increased. When he was finally accepted into the army six months later, he hated

[1] 'They Cut Away His Conscience', in *The Sunday Gentleman*.

it, and finally managed to get his discharge. Not long after, his father died, but he hardly seemed interested. He spent his days sunk in apathy, doing crossword puzzles. The illness became worse. He could not get up in the mornings; he felt a kind of perpetual foreboding; he would burst into tears; he felt like screaming. He perspired all the time. Psychiatrists did no good at all. The only improvement occurred when his wife, exhausted by nursing him, fell ill. While nursing her, he improved enormously. When she recovered, he became sunk in apathy again. One psychiatrist made things much worse by telling him that the mind was like a telephone switchboard, and that in his own mind, the wires had all got tangled. 'He began to look upon himself as a hopeless mental case.' Insulin and electric shock treatment did no good; occupation therapy was useless. On a trip to Arizona, he had attacks of terror, and kept shouting, 'Kill me, kill me', to the alarm of his fellow passengers. And in 1947, the lobotomy operation was finally performed. It worked—as far as it ever works. Larry became a contented cow, although flashes of the old brilliance kept breaking through. He became boastful about his academic qualifications, and his lack of inhibitions were an embarrassment to his family, but the tensions had gone. Since he was unable to concentrate, he was unable to support himself, and much of the next twenty years was spent in private mental homes—his brother and the old school friend contributing to his support. Some years after writing the original article, Irving Wallace added a postscript, describing how Larry had discharged himself from hospital, and married a second time—a frustrated English spinster, who, like his first wife, found it more difficult than she expected to be married to a five-year-old adult.

I have cited this case—rather than any of the cases recorded by Straus or Medard Boss—because most of the psychiatrists who saw Larry Cassidy assumed the trouble was Freudian: Wallace says: 'The root of this, most likely, was father domination. Too, he had a strong Oedipus complex, as evidenced by his marriage to Harriet, who was older than he and in whom he saw his adored mother . . .'

There may be some truth in this; the domination of his father no doubt played some part in the illness, by making him passive. But what is surely clear, even from this brief account, is that the basic trouble was a *habit of passivity*. The brilliant schoolboy spent all his time reading and listening to music; he became soaked in a romantic-pessimistic view of the world. At Princeton, he wrote a long letter on the futility of life, and his younger brother remarked: 'It was brilliantly written, terribly logical, and at the time seemed practically unanswerable.' Another relative dismissed it with the remark that he had probably just discovered Schopenhauer.

And so it is clear that the pessimistic romanticism was, to some extent, thought out. (His I.Q., Wallace says, was near genius level.) This is not uncommon with unusually intelligent and imaginative young people: Nietzsche absorbed Schopenhauer in his late teens and often thought of suicide; even Chesterton, the sanest of all geniuses, passed through a period of profound depression in his teens. (He adds, significantly: 'What I may call my period of madness coincided with a period of drifting and doing nothing'; *Autobiography*, Chap. 4.) The English composer Peter Warlock soaked himself in the music of Delius—sad, dreamy, enormously sensuous—and wrote: 'I am sure there is no music more beautiful in all the world; it haunts me day and night . . .'; it also made him completely unfitted for the solid actualities of life, and he committed suicide at 36. Americans are as susceptible to this problem as Europeans—as the case of Poe witnesses. Binswanger would say that Larry Cassidy was a clear case of Kierkegaardian *angst*,[1] but it is more straightforward to say that he was a case of romantic world-rejection.

The lack of success in the various jobs he undertook would confirm him in his feeling that 'the world' is a disgusting place for an intelligent man. If, at this point, he had been forced to make his own way, things might have been different; but there was nothing to stop him idling at home—for three or four years. Passivity became a habit; self-disgust, failure to use his remarkable powers. ('Capacities clamour to be used', writes Maslow, 'and cease their clamour only when they are well used . . . Not only is it fun to use our capacities, but it is also necessary. The

---

[1] Binswanger writes, in 'The Case of Ellen West' (printed in full in *Existence*): '[she] suffered from that sickness of the mind which Kierkegaard . . . described and illuminated from all possible aspects under the name of 'Sickness Unto Death'. The case—one of Binswanger's best-known—offers some striking parallels with the case of Larry Cassidy.

unused capacity or organ can become a disease center or else atrophy, thus diminishing the person.'[1]) Significantly, his only brief period of normality was when his wife was ill and he was forced to pull himself together and take the active role. Then she recovered, and he could sink back into the now habitual state of passivity, boredom, frustrations that filled him with self-pity or a desire to scream. The longer a case like this continues unchanged, the less likelihood there is of a cure. Why should psychiatry have failed so totally to affect even a temporary improvement? Why was insulin treatment, shock therapy, occupation therapy, so ineffective? Maslow has answered the question in the title of a paper: 'Neurosis as a failure of personal growth.' The psychiatrists, trying to root out his Oedipus complex, were wasting their time; he was suffering from the same trouble as Maslow's girl in the chewing gum factory: creative blockage. Long after the leucotomy operation, he actually tried writing again, but it was hopelessly bad: he had allowed the essential equipment to be destroyed.

Either Maslow or Frankl might have stood a fair chance of success in curing Larry Cassidy. One of Frankl's cases in Vienna concerned a woman whose obsession with cleanliness had brought her to the edge of suicide, and whose only chance seemed to be a lobotomy operation. Frankl decided first of all to try his reverse-effort therapy. The woman was advised to actively seek contact with bacteria—to clean out chamberpots and toilets in the ward of the hospital. Within weeks, the neurosis had been reduced to manageable proportions; not long afterwards, she was discharged as completely cured. My own belief—for what it is worth—is that Larry Cassidy could have been cured by similar therapy, particularly if the therapist made a strong appeal to his intelligence.

For all compulsive neurosis has a similar pattern, phenomenologically speaking. Man is a many-layered creature, whose highly complex structure is largely 'robotic'. The unconscious mind is an enormous computer, and all instincts are intentional in the sense of being learned habits. Because the subconscious is a huge machine, its circuits need to be 'triggered' by certain definite signals. The 'vital reserves' that

[1] 'Basic propositions of a growth and self-actualising psychology', 1962.

William James speaks of are not normally accessible to ordinary conscious effort. His Indian colonel who lived for weeks on brandy during the mutiny had gained access to his vital reserves by sending the robot a whole series of urgent telegrams. Ordinary civilised life does not provide many such emergencies —only petty bothers that set up a kind of irritable self-division, so the signals keep cancelling themselves out. And the robot begins to acquire the negative habit of *not* releasing vital reserves. The result is that the individual's evolution—in Maslow's sense—comes to a standstill. And then the problem of boredom and self-contempt is increased by a feeling of suffocation which may build up into a panic. The mind, like the body, must be considered as a whole; and in order to stay healthy, the whole thing needs to be exercised. The mentally healthy individual is he who *habitually* calls upon fairly deep levels of vital reserves. An individual whose mind is allowed to become dormant—so that only the surface is disturbed—begins to suffer from 'circulation problems'. Neurosis is the feeling of being cut off from your own powers.

When you are feeling physically sick, anything you think about seems sickening; this is because your vital energies need to be concentrated on not being sick, and therefore anything that distracts them from this purpose causes a feeling of increasing sickness—i.e. seems sickening. And when the vital reserves are blocked by a sense of inactivity, anything can arouse a feeling of nausea. 'He who desires but acts not, breeds pestilence,' says Blake, with a poet's phenomenological insight. When the vital energies are blocked, it is like being stuck on a train in a siding for hours; the view finally becomes sickeningly familiar; you are forced to keep on contemplating the same thing because there is nothing else to contemplate. In *Heartbreak House*, Hector asks Shotover: 'How long dare you concentrate on a feeling without risking having it fixed in your consciousness all the rest of your life?', and Shotover answers: 'Ninety minutes.' This provides all the background we need to understand compulsive neurosis—usually an obsession with something relatively trivial. Even healthy people can experience a mild version of such a neurosis if they happen to sleep badly with a worry on the mind. The worry appears in distorted forms in dreams, and assumes exaggerated proportions during the periods of lying awake. Mentally speaking, you are on a train stuck in a siding.

The more serious forms of the compulsion are due to the law of reversed effort, or paradoxical intention. The phenomenology of reversed effort is worth a brief description. The mind possesses a kind of amplifier, which enables us to concentrate on some impressions to the exclusion of others. A mother can hear her baby crying over the noise of a party; a man expecting an important call hears the phone ringing in spite of other noises. The amplifier is mechanised—the mother doesn't have to sit listening for the baby's cry; the robot picks it up and alerts her. I have already pointed out what happens when the conscious 'self' tries to interfere with the robot's functions—if, for example, I try observing the workings of my fingers as I type: the result is a 'stammer', a jerky flow of 'intention' instead of a smooth one. So when a depressed or over-anxious person tries to turn the amplifier *down*, the reverse is achieved, and the worry becomes deafening. Prefrontal leucotomy severs the amplifier wires, all the disturbing feedback effects cease. And this emphasises something we should keep in mind. The amplifier is intended for other things besides amplifying worries. When Maslow's young housewife looked at her husband and family eating breakfast, the amplifier suddenly worked, and what would normally have been a faint whisper of satisfaction became a blast of sheer happiness. The real job of the amplifier—its positive, useful job—is to aid peak experiences, creative experiences, even mystical experiences. It is intended to work when you listen to music or look at beautiful scenery, or simply enjoy the taste of a good meal.

What *is* this amplifier? It is nothing less than a kind of lake of vital energy. The vital energies need to flow, like a river; but when I am happy, looking forward to the future, I also accumulate a large reserve supply of energy, ready for use. Peak experiences are an *overflow* of this lake. But the lake also forms if the river gets blocked; I become a reservoir of unused vitality, but now my general attitude is negative, and the lake acts as an amplifier of negative emotion. The longer the blockage goes on for, the more difficult it is to release, because the river that carries it away seems so inadequate. In the same way, if you want to urinate badly enough, the discomfort finally becomes so great that the normal method of release seems inadequate, and the discomfort persists even after relief.

The point I am now making is of central importance, perhaps the most important consequence of Maslow's psychology. Man's capacity for worry and anxiety was intended to be a capacity for peak experiences—or at least, for creative forward movement. For various reasons, he has consistently misused it. The tendency to misuse it is so deep-seated that Christian theologians call it Original Sin—meaning man's capacity for making the worst of a good job, for making himself unhappy. There appears to be something fundamentally wrong with the human mechanism; but on closer analysis, it turns out that it is nothing that cannot be put right. The root of the problem proves to be man's generally negative attitude towards himself, all the Darwinian and Freudian and behaviourist assumptions about his slavery to his 'lower nature', his helplessness in the hands of natural forces. There is an interesting parallel here with the science of economics as developed by Adam Smith, Ricardo and Malthus, which seemed to demonstrate with rigorous logic that the 'laws of production' doom our civilisation to final ruin. At this juncture, John Stuart Mill pointed out (in *Principles of Political Economy*) that although we cannot evade the rigid laws of production—which lead to overpopulation and the 'rat race'—there is no *law of distribution*: we can do what we like with the wealth, once it has been created, and use it to build a less self-destructive society. (Unfortunately, Mill was quickly superseded by Marx, whose economics is even more savagely pessimistic.) Maslow's psychology, firmly based upon Freud and Watson, simply points out that the optimistic side of the picture has been overlooked; the deterministic laws of our 'lower nature' hold sway in their own field; but there *are* other laws. Man's freedom is a reality—a reality that makes a difference to his physical, as well as his mental health. When Frankl's prisoners ceased to believe in the possibility of freedom, they grew sick and died. On the other hand, when they saw that Dachau had no chimney, standing out all night in the rain seemed no great hardship; they laughed and joked. The conclusion deserves to be stated in letters ten feet high. In order to realise his possibilities, man must believe in an *open* future; he must have a vision of something worth doing. And this will not be possible until all the determinism and pessimism that we have inherited from the 19th century—and which has infected every department of our culture, from poetry to atomic physics—has been dismissed as fallacious and illogical. Twentieth-century science, philosophy, politics, literature—even music—has been constructed upon a *weltanschauung* that leaves half of human nature out of account.

Man is not naturally static; his mental energy, like his blood, was intended to be kept moving. His mental being must be understood as something essentially dynamic, forward-flowing, like a river. All mental illness is the outcome of damming the river.

That is the basic proposition of all 'existential psychology'. Admittedly, it has never been stated in precisely this way, either by Maslow, Frankl or Binswanger; but once it has been formulated, it can be seen as a basic premise of their psychologies, James, as we have seen, actually used the image of a dam, without fully grasping that it implies a river (as he used the phrase 'stream of consciousness' without recognising that a stream flows *from* somewhere and goes *to* somewhere).

The second proposition of the new psychology is this: what makes the stream flow is not the Freudian libido or the Adlerian will to power, but a *sense of values* which operates rather like radar, by a kind of 'reaching out'. Frankl's prisoners, standing in the rain, were bouncing their radar signals off the future, and receiving back a sense of potentialities, of exciting and worthwhile prospects. A child is probably happier on the eve of a holiday, or on Christmas Eve, than at any other time of the year, for the same reason. *Man is future-orientated*, not sex-orientated or power-orientated. What causes him to look eagerly into the future may be sex or power; it may also be travel or discovery, science or poetry. In a sense, the power hypothesis is the reverse of the truth. He does not read *War and Peace* because it gives him a feeling of power, but because it seems to open the mind wider, to let more reality in ; and as he experiences this sense of reality, he is passive, receptive. What man craves is not power, but objective reality, values beyond himself.

Man is not unique in this; it is true, to some extent, of all animals. In *African Genesis*, Robert Ardrey describes the behaviour of a tribe of baboons threatened by a leopard. The leopard appeared on a rock overlooking the fig tree where the baboons slept and stood watching them, taking its time, knowing they could not escape. Two male baboons climbed the cliff above the leopard, and dropped together on its back. The leopard killed both of them within seconds, but not before one of them had torn open his jugular vein. This sounds like supreme self sacrifice. But Ardrey's tale of Carpenter's monkeys dispels that impression. The zoologist Carpenter took 350 monkeys from India and settled them on an island off Puerto Rico. On the ship, the monkeys were, naturally, unable to establish 'territory'—they all had to be mixed up together. Male monkeys ceased defending their wives and children, while the wives seemed to lose the maternal instinct and would fight their babies for scraps of food. Once on Santiago Island, the monkeys divided into groups, and each group established its territory; then the protective instincts of the males and females returned to normal. The unselfishness that distinguished the baboons ceased to operate as soon as the monkeys were thrust a step down the ladder of values.[1]

In man, the territorial imperative has taken second place, as Shaw points out in *Man and Superman*: 'Why was the Crusader braver than the pirate? Because he fought, not for himself, but for the Cross. What force was it that met him with a valour as reckless as his own? The force of men who fought, not for themselves, but for Islam. They took Spain from us, though we were fighting for our very hearths and homes [i.e. for territory]; but when we, too, fought for that mighty idea, a Catholic Church, we swept them back to Africa.' Shaw had anticipated Maslow by some fifty years; he understood that man's basic drive is for *values*. But Maslow was the first to grasp that values form a hierarchy.

It is now necessary to examine the deeper implications of Frankl's 'law of reversed effort'. Consider the following passage from *Wuthering Heights*:

'While enjoying a month of fine weather at the sea-coast, I was thrown into the company of a most fascinating creature, a real goddess in my eyes, as long as she took no notice of me. I

---

[1] I have pointed out elsewhere that William Golding's *Lord of the Flies* shows the same kind of thing happening to a group of schoolboys; Golding feels that this is a proof of Original Sin; in which case, monkeys also suffer from Original Sin.

"never told my love" vocally; still, if looks have language, the merest idiot might have guessed I was over head and ears: she understood me at last, and looked a return—the sweetest of all imaginable looks. And what did I do? I confess it with shame— shrunk icily into myself, like a snail; at every glance retired colder and further; till finally the poor innocent was led to doubt her own senses, and, overwhelmed with confusion at her supposed mistake, persuaded her mama to decamp.'

What happens here? Why does he want her, and then change his mind? The phenomenology resembles that in the 'Tom Sawyer painting the fence' story—Tom whistles vigorously while doing a job that bores him, and cons his friends into paying him to allow them to take turns at it. Pavlov would have no difficulty in explaining it. By whistling cheerfully and looking as if he is enjoying himself, Tom sets in motion a more-or-less automatic reflex in his friends. Like Pavlov dogs, they salivate. What is more, they *do* enjoy painting the fence, because they have taken a positive attitude towards it. But this is absurd. If painting the fence *can* be enjoyable, then why would they find it boring if ordered to do it? The answer is: the robot. If I am ordered to paint a fence when I think I would rather be playing football, I treat it as a tiresome, *routine* activity, and I leave my robot to get on with it. It is not 'I' who paint the fence, but my robot. Tom's whistling changes my attitude; it makes *me* want to paint the fence, and I remain wide-awake as I do it. And now we can understand the episode from *Wuthering Heights*. He is a rather immature and unstable young man (the authoress thinks him Byronic); while he thinks he cannot have the young girl, he wants her. When she begins to respond, her smile triggers a series of automatic responses: spoilt-child reactions of only wanting the things he can't have, and devaluing the things he can have. Again, his robot takes over the moment her response makes him begin to take her for granted. This is a tendency that is often found in young and imaginative people: the imagination makes for a certain passivity, a shrinking from the real world, a tendency to 'Oblomovism'. The stagnation produces boredom and fatigue, and the robot takes over when the energies are low. The romantic *weltschmerz* of Obermann and Childe Harold has its origin in fatigue. Thomas Mann's first literary effort, a story called *Disillusionment*, illustrates this clearly. The narrator is accosted by a stranger, who asks him: 'Do you know what disillusionment is? Not a miscarriage in small, unimportant matters, but the great and general disappointment which everything, all of life, has in store?' And he goes on to explain how everything that has ever happened to him has produced the same response of disappointment. 'Is that all?' Even when the house caught on fire he asked himself, 'Is that all?' He has travelled the world, looking at all its most famous sights, and always feeling, 'Is that all?' He now dreams, he says, 'of a life where there are no more horizons,' and waits for death—although he is convinced it will be as boring as everything else.

This story could only have been written by a young man (Mann was twenty-one at the time). It describes the condition that finally made Larry Cassidy a hopeless schizophrenic. The everyday world, with its crudeness and stupidity, causes continual revulsion. Passivity and self-contempt cause a certain running-down; the vital batteries go flat. More and more, the everyday business of living is taken over by the robot, until the 'I' becomes little more than a spectator, sitting behind the eyes as if sitting in the passenger seat of a car, watching the world go by. I realise that if I let the fire go out, I shall get cold, but coldness seems as pointless as being warm, and if I summon the energy to go and refill the coal bucket, I feel as though I might be dreaming. In fact, the clear distinction between the world of dreams—or imagination—and the world of reality seems to vanish. Reality is experienced as a dream, and the confused world of dreams frightens me because it is too disturbingly like my everyday reality. The longer my 'I' remains in a state of abdication, the more it sinks into James's 'psychasthenic' state of 'torpor, lethargy, fatigue, insufficiency, impossibility, unreality and powerlessness of will'. A negative circuit has been set up, instead of the usual positive circuit that drives healthy human beings. For when I am in a healthy, active state, unexpected pleasures are always producing minor peak experiences, and the peak experience, with its sense of an *objective standard of meaning, worth striving towards*, releases my vital reserves. That is, it gives me a *reason* for making efforts, and it is through effort that the will stays healthy.

The reason that insulin or electric shock treatment often

works in such cases is that it forces the 'I' to make a painful effort, and starts the flow of vital energy. This is also why the 'bullying treatment', mentioned by James, often works. 'First comes the very extremity of distress, then follows unexpected relief.' Graham Greene's Russian roulette—played with his brother's revolver—had the effect of temporarily relieving his psychasthenic fatigue, and producing a momentary sense of vitality and delight in being alive. And it was obviously the lesson learned from this experience that led him to write the last scene of *The Power and the Glory* where his 'whisky priest', about to be executed by a firing squad, feels suddenly that 'It would have been so easy to be a saint.' Throughout the novel he has been in a near-psychasthenic condition, weak and self-divided. That is to say, the robot has taken-over most of his living activities. When the rifles point at him, he recognises that his weakness and misery are nothing more than hypochondria; they vanish like nightmares. If he had walked across this same courtyard a few hours ago, it would have seemed unreal; he would have been in the passenger seat, with the robot driving. Now, because he is seeing it for the last time, he has suppressed the robot: he sees it direct, through his own eyes. And if, for some reason, his execution were delayed for a few hours, he would walk back to his cell feeling completely alive and wide-awake. A pool of muddy water, that had struck him as depressing a few hours earlier, would now seem strangely real, aloofly *itself*.

The dictionary defines schizophrenia as a disorder characterised by dissociation, a lack of connection between the intellectual processes and the feelings. Camus's Meursault in *L'Etranger* is a good example of mild schizophrenia. It should be apparent, from the above analysis, that schizophrenia is a disorder in which the robot takes over from the 'I' (or what Husserl would have called 'the transcendental ego'). Schizophrenia is the typical mental disorder of our civilisation, because the repetitive but highly complex ritual of civilised life tempts us to hand over most of our functions to the robot. In his book on *Vagrancy*, Philip O'Connor remarks of his own period as a tramp: 'My excursions were motivated by what our social patchers-up, the psychiatrists, would call "neurosis". But in truth it was a sane attempt, hopelessly hopeful, to get out of a positively neurotic convention of living "respectably".' O'Connor has stated Ronald Laing's thesis in two sentences, and underlined the problem of 'automatised' living that produces so much schizophrenia.

Automatised living produces a state of *imprisonment*—what Eliot means when he says, 'We each think of the key, each in his prison.' The kind of freshness, 'newness', that T. E. Lawrence describes on the 'clear dawn that woke up the senses with the sun', becomes more and more infrequent. It is like living in a room in which the door and window are never opened, so the same stale air has to be breathed over and over again, until it becomes poisonous. Eventually, a man who remains trapped in this state for too long falls into a kind of instinctive solipsism, the belief that he is the only person in the universe. People in this state may commit suicide—or murder—because life is self-evidently not worth living. Dostoevsky's novels are full of descriptions of this state. Stavrogin in *The Devils* has been so completely taken-over by his robot that he has ceased to feel spontaneous emotion; he has to commit criminal or masochistic acts to produce some faint vital response. (And the reason for his boredom, Dostoevsky makes clear, is that he has been so thoroughly spoilt by his mother, that he has lost the habit of making efforts.) Ivan Karamazov reaches the stage of schizophrenic hallucination, and holds a conversation with a devil who admits he is a figment of Ivan's imagination. (Here Dostoevsky crystallises the schizophrenic's worst fear—that dream and reality may completely reverse their roles, proving themselves to be interchangeable.) And Svidrigailov, in *Crime and Punishment*, is another bored sensualist who has at some stage raped (or seduced) a little girl; it is he who provides a classic expression of this type of schizophrenia in his account of his dream in which eternity proved to be a small, stuffy room with cobwebs in the corners. It could be said that the basic horror of schizophrenia is a fear of suffocation, of mental suffocation in a world without 'newness', permanent life-failure.

The healthy mind needs 'newness', 'otherness', as healthy lungs need fresh air. It is part of what we might call the natural ecology of the mind. Man is so constructed that he needs a certain healthy interaction with the environment; the more high-powered his intellect, the stronger the need for this interaction

—just as a powerful two-stroke engine needs to be driven above a certain speed if its plugs are not to oil-up. This might seem to prove that the black room problem is totally insoluble, but this is not so. When man runs or swims, his body interacts with physical reality; when he thinks creatively, his mind interacts with another form of reality—mathematical, for example. (It is worth bearing in mind that Husserl began as a mathematician, and that his 'realism' was originally an assertion of mathematical reality.) At this point in evolution, man's power to interact with 'mental reality' is embryonic compared to his power to control the physical world; but it *could* be increased to the point where the black room would no longer be an insoluble problem.

For it is important to realise that man's mental powers are potentially far stronger than his physical powers. Why were the Moors able to conquer the Spaniards, when the Spaniards were fighting for their territory? Why, to put the question another way, can we be more inspired by an idea or belief than by the need for physical security? Because our physical desires tend to be *short sighted*, while our mental ideals and aspirations lead us to look into the distance. And a distant objective—provided it seems attainable—inspires greater determination and enterprise than any immediate physical need. It is man's 'distance vision' that makes him potentially superhuman, that gives promise of an entirely new range of powers.

In America, an increasing amount of therapy is being based upon the recognition of the mind's need for 'reality'. The Los Angeles psychiatrist, William Glasser, actually calls his own approach 'reality therapy', and has written a book of that title (1965). Dr Hobart Mowrer—himself the creator of a system called 'responsibility therapy'—explains in a foreword the difference between Freud's approach and Glasser's. In Freud, all kinds of disagreeable things get repressed by the over-active conscience (super-ego), and the task of the psychiatrist is to persuade the patient to face up to his incest desires (or whatever they are) and forgive himself for them. 'The purview of Reality Therapy is . . . that human beings get into emotional binds, not because their standards are too high, but because their performance has been, and is, too low.' Glasser's argument, briefly, goes like this. People get psychiatric problems as a result of an inability to fulfil their needs. They have one common characteristic: They deny the reality of the world around them.

If a cure is to be effected, the patient must be involved with other people, or at least, with one other person. Because obviously, so long as he acknowledges the real existence of another person, and treats that other person as someone who deserves deference (or concern), he cannot get completely locked up in the prison of solipsism. '. . . an involvement with someone you care for, and who you are convinced cares for you is the key to fulfilling the basic needs . . .' 'Psychiatry must be concerned with two basic psychological needs: *the need to love and be loved and the need to feel that we are worthwhile to ourselves and to others*'. Glasser is here close to Maslow, except that he leaves out of account the self-actualisation level of the hierarchy of values. The problem, as Glasser sees it, is to get people to address themselves realistically to the fulfilment of their needs; and this, in turn, means persuading them to take-on an attitude of responsibility. He instances a child who wants to watch television instead of doing his homework and who cajoles his parents in an effort to evade responsibility. If this is successful, and he finds himself in class the next morning without the homework, he may direct his feeling of annoyance at his parents, retreating further into an attitude of irresponsibility. A habit of evasion of responsibility may lead to a complete inability to fulfil needs. (To begin with, such a person chops and changes so much that he never sees anything through to the end and gets the benefit—in self-congratulation—of a successful effort.)

In practice, Glasser is disinclined to allow the patient to enter into long explanations of his problems. He prefers to ask: What do you intend to *do*? Reality therapy, like Binswanger's existential psychology, demands a deep involvement with the patient—a position from which the therapist can propel the patient into responsible activity. 'The therapist must be able to become emotionally involved with each patient', a demand that psychiatrists of the older school may find disconcerting, perhaps even disgusting. Once involved, the therapist must try to steer the patient in the direction of self-actualisation. 'We must open up his life, talk about new horizons, make him aware of life beyond his difficulties.'

The actual description of cases makes it clear that Glasser's approach is kindly but firm. For example, in the case of a delinquent girl named Jeri, who threatened suicide, Glasser declined to take the threat seriously, and told the staff of the institution to pay no attention to her desire to be recognised as mentally ill. Shortly afterwards, the girl promised to 'give up acting crazy', and the real therapy could begin. Even so, there were continual efforts to evade responsibility, to lie, to put the blame on others, and so on, and it became necessary to send her to the 'discipline unit'. Glasser emphasises that there must be a clear distinction between discipline and punishment; punishment would mean that the psychiatrist was 'getting his own back', and this would destroy the relation of sympathetic involvement on which everything depends. In the discipline unit, the girl did some heart-searching and eventually faced up to her evasions—clearly because evasions had ceased to be the path of least resistance. When the girl left—several months before the normal end of the programme—her personality had changed considerably; for example, she now loved her housemother, whom she had formerly denounced as prejudiced, unfair and so on. This in itself is significant, for it proves not only that her adjustment to reality had made her capable of warm human relations, but that she had also recognised that loving may be a better method of getting your own way than lying on the floor and kicking.

Students of the 19th century will note the similarity of Glasser's method to Dr Arnold's 'moral force'. It is an interesting thought—that Freudian psychology is a total rejection of Victorian attitudes, that the existential approach should involve a return to them. Perhaps there is one major difference: Victorian moral force was often applied in a detached, authoritarian way. What comes over most strongly from Glasser's book is that the psychiatrist must have almost heroic personal qualities of decency and self-control—for example, never getting angry or alarmed, no matter how violent or irrational the patient's behaviour may seem. Glasser's methods seem to be a school of moral training for the psychiatrist as well as the patients.

It may be noted that methods similar to Glasser's have been

tried successfully in English mental institutions, although without the same emphasis on involvement; 'incorrigible' patients
who behave in a thoroughly irrational way are ignored until
it dawns on them that this is not the way to get results. Millen
Brand remarks, in his psychiatric novel *Savage Sleep*, that even
in the most violently psychotic patient, there is a small, sane
observer watching from some corner of the brain. This is the
assumption behind reality therapy: mental illness is recognised
as a kind of abdication of responsibility. The same attitude
underlies the remarkable Synanon experiment, that Maslow
has written about.[1] Synanon is a community of former drug
addicts on Staten Island, N.Y., with an offshoot at Daytop
Village, which Maslow visited. 'The assumption in your group',
said Maslow, 'seems to be that people are very tough, and not
brittle. They can take an awful lot.' He called it 'no crap
therapy'. The ex-drug addicts had group therapy sessions in
which they were brutally frank with one another—the result
being re-establishment of contact with reality, with other
people. The drug addict retreats into his ivory tower of subjectivity; he probably becomes basically afraid of other people, as
a threat to his way of life. Maslow mentioned an ex-addict who,
'for the first time in his life, had experienced real intimacy, real
friendship, real respect. This was his first experience of honesty
and directness, and he felt for the first time in his life that he
could be himself, and that people wouldn't kill him for it.' This
is, in effect, Frankl's reverse-action therapy; the woman who
was terrified of bacteria was persuaded to wash out chamberpots, and the drug-addicts who had become alienated from
other people were encouraged to face up to the toughest criti-
cisms. The Synanon visit led Maslow to express again his feeling
that modern society is sick. He speaks of his stay among the
northern Blackfoot Indians: 'I had a funny experience. I came
into the reservation with the notion that the Indians are over
there on a shelf, like a butterfly collection . . . Then slowly I
shifted and changed my mind. Those Indians on the reservation were decent people; and the more I got to know the whites
in the village, who were the worst bunch of creeps and bastards
I've ever run across in my life, the more it got paradoxical.
Which was the asylum?'

[1] *Synanon and Eupsychia, Journal of Humanistic Psychology*, 1967.

In the same paper, Maslow reformulates his basic idea:

'It seems to me that there is a fair amount of evidence that the things that people need as basic human beings are few in number . . . They need a feeling of protection and safety: to be taken care of when they are young, so that they feel safe. Second they need a feeling of belongingness, some kind of a family, clan or group . . . Thirdly, they have to have a feeling that people have affection for them, that they are worth being loved. And fourth, they must experience respect and esteem. And that's about it. You can talk about psychological health, about being mature and strong, adult and creative, mostly as a consequence of this psychological medicine—like vitamins. Now if this is true, then most of the American population suffers from lack of these vitamins. There are all sorts of games cooked up to cover the truth, but the truth is that the average American citizen does not have a real friend in the world. Very few people have what a psychologist would call real friendships. The marriages are mostly no good in that ideal sense as well. You could say that the kinds of problems we have, the open troubles—not being able to resist alcohol, not being able to resist drugs, not being able to resist crime, not being able to resist anything—that these are due to the lack of these basic psychological gratifications.'

Perhaps the most difficult concept for Freudians to grasp is this: that a person's attitude—which ultimately determines his mental health—may act as a barrier which prevents him from reaching the 'vitamins' which are there for the asking. All phenomenologists know that our senses are *filters*, whose main function is to *keep out* experience rather than letting it in. When a man walks through the streets of a large town, his senses are being bombarded by impressions that would drive him insane if he 'noticed' them all. The healthier a man is, the more he can ignore; it is the unhealthy man whose nerves are torn to shreds every time a baby cries or a door slams. Our senses are *selective*; one neurologist estimated that they 'cut out' about 95% of our possible experience. This explains why human beings find it so easy to distort reality. If I begin to get depressed, it is quite easy for me to see the whole world in a negative light. Maslow performed experiments that make the same point. He writes:

'The deprivation of beauty can cause illness. People who, are aesthetically very sensitive become depressed and uncomfortable in ugly surroundings. It probably affects their menstruation, gives them headaches, etc.

'I performed a series of experiments on beautiful and ugly surroundings to prove this point. When subjects saw pictures of faces to be judged in an ugly room, they viewed the people as being psychotic, paranoid or dangerous, indicating that faces and presumably human beings look bad in ugly surroundings.'[1]

The experiment could be dismissed as proving nothing except that people are suggestible; but that would be missing its real significance: which is that the senses select what they wish to notice. This was proved conclusively in a series of experiments by Hadley Cantril, Adelbert Ames, F. P. Kilpatrick and others —the most famous of which is the 'distorted room'. For the sake of completeness, this must be described here. The subject of the experiment is taken to a small hole in a wall. When he looks through it (with one eye) he sees an apparently normal room. In a wall facing him, there are two windows, and under each window there is an ordinary wooden chair. In one corner of the room there stands a boy; in the other corner a man. Now the man and the boy walk towards one another, and as they do so, they change size. The boy gets larger, the man gets smaller. When they have each arrived at the opposite corner, the boy is very tall, the man very short.

The trick is that it is not a normal rectangular room. The wall with the two windows is actually shaped like a parallelogram, with one end shorter than the other. It looks like an ordinary wall because it is sloping *away* from the observer, and the normal effect of diminution-by-distance (which would warn the observer that it is sloping away from him) is counteracted by the widening of the parallelogram. The windows and the chairs also have to be distorted to the same scale, of course. The boy appears to grow larger because he is walking towards the observer; the man gets smaller because he is walking away. The observer is made to use only one eye because we need two eyes to judge distance or depth.

It follows, from the above description, that one of the parallelogram-shaped windows is actually larger than the other, and

[1] *Goals of Humanistic Education*, 1968.

this suggested another experiment. If someone's face appears first at the far window, then at the near one, it appears to have suddenly increased in size.

In 1949, this experiment was tried with a married woman as the observer; two men were used as the 'face at the window'—one, her husband, the other a stranger. She reported the usual distortion in the case of the stranger—his head appeared to have blown up to twice its size at the second window—but saw no alteration in her husband. Warren J. Wittreich, in his paper on this,[1] mentions that both husband and wife were over sixty years of age, and the husband was an extremely distinguished man who was greatly admired and loved by his wife. And her perceptions refused to distort his head. This became known as 'the Honi phenomenon'—her husband called her Honi. The same thing was observed when the experiment was tried with service personnel. If ordinary recruits were used to look in through the window and the hole in the wall, the usual distortion was observed. But if officers looked in through the window, *their* heads were not distorted; the recruits felt too much awe of them to distort them.

The basic assertion of 'transactional psychology'—the school founded by Cantril and Ames—is that a large part of our 'perception' is made up of assumptions about what we ought to see. These assumptions are so taken for granted that they have become a part of the perception. What is 'seen' depends on *how much I put into the seeing*; perception is a transaction with the environment, like buying a pound of butter. This is, of course, only another way of stating Husserl's conclusion that perception is intentional; but the experiments devised by the transactionalists demonstrate it in a striking and memorable way. We see that the senses are not the faithful, unimaginative servants we had assumed them to be; that they are, on the contrary, a kind of intelligence network that sifts information and decides what can be allowed to reach conscious awareness.

This same principle has been utilised in recent years in a new approach to rehabilitation called attitude therapy, developed by Dan MacDougald, president of the Yonan Codex Founda-

[1] 'The Honi Phenomenon', in *Explorations in Transactional Psychology* (1961), ed. F. P. Kilpatrick. New York University Press.

tion. In his pamphlet 'Attitude Therapy', Mr MacDougald, a lawyer, cites William James's statement: 'Human beings can alter their lives by altering their attitudes of mind.' He mentions an interesting experiment described by Dr Jerome Bruner of Harvard. An electric wire was attached to the aural nerve of a cat—the nerve that conducts sounds from the ear to the brain; the other end of the wire was connected to an oscilloscope, so that when a loud noise was made in the cat's ear, the nerve impulse was registered on the oscilloscope. Then a jar containing white mice was placed in front of the cat, which instantly directed its full attention to them. The same noises now failed to register on the oscilloscope—which means, in effect, that the cat was somehow 'cutting out' the nerve impulse; not merely ignoring an impulse, as a mother might ignore an importunate child who tugs at her sleeve, but somehow preventing the tug itself.

Dr John Eccles, an Australian, has apparently located the part of the nervous system which he calls the 'inhibitory system'. He showed that this inhibitory system works by stepping up the resistance of the nerve as the resistance of an electric circuit can be stepped up by means of a rheostat. Nerve impulses are transmitted by neurons (nerve cells), and a signal must exceed the 'neural threshold' of a nerve cell before it can be transmitted. When the cat concentrated on the white mice, it somehow raised the resistance of each nerve cell. Similarly, we could think of a safe-breaker who listens intently for the clicks coming from the combination lock, and see that he has lowered the neural threshold. I.e. if his criminal associate drops the bag of tools, he will jump two feet in the air. But human beings can also lower their neural threshold selectively, so a mother can hear the sound of her baby crying above the noise of conversation (as I have already pointed out).

This leads Mr MacDougald to formulate the notion of mental illness as the result of 'faulty blocking' by the inhibitory system. We are flooded with information; *we* have to decide which to disregard. This means we could be wrong. So a person suffering from over-anxiety decides to pay full attention to all kinds of negative signs and to disregard all the nice things. The mental illness that develops—if this goes on too long—depends upon what kind of information is being disregarded and what kind is being given too much weight. A person suffering from hysterical deafness or blindness would be blocking physical channels. A person suffering from paranoia has become obsessed by unpleasant facts: hostility, catastrophe, and so on. Neurosis, says Mr MacDougald, is the opposite of a blockage; it is a lowering of the resistance of the neurons, so they admit too much. Schizophrenia he defines as 'the blocking of the operation of the source of the true self'.

In the light of what has been said above, it can be seen that some of these definitions are adequate, others less so. It is surely a mistake to make this distinction between neurosis and psychosis? The neurotic may have a lower neural threshold, but this has led him to blocking off large areas of his experience. The neurotic lives in a self-enclosed universe, and suffers from a reality-starvation that leads to various kinds of over-reaction to problems. Reality-starvation is due to faulty blocking. But faulty blocking is only half the problem, as we have seen. Blocking leads to a general cut-back in vitality, and to a drop in the charge on the vital batteries. Schizophrenia—loss of emotional contact with reality[1]—may develop if the anxiety builds up to a point where it becomes self-propagating. So schizophrenia may also be defined as blockage of the sense channels rather than as blocking of the operation of the true self.

The phenomenology of Attitude Psychology may be only half-developed, but its practical success has been remarkable. Dr C. D. Warren, former medical director of the Georgia Department of Corrections, describes in a pamphlet[2] his scepticism when two men from the Yonan Codex Foundation visited the maximum security prison near Reidsville and explained that they believed hard-core psychopathic deviates could be cured in two or three months by instructions that would last an hour or two each day. But the results were spectacular. Two inmates were trained as instructors—this took only two weeks. Then the four instructed 22 men for eight weeks, in a two-hour session each week. Four of these 22 were appointed instructors,

[1] MacDougald writes: 'All psychosis, except schizophrenia, is usually described as a loss of contact with reality.' But so, of course, is schizophrenia.

[2] 'A promising new approach to rehabilitation', published by the Thomas Jefferson Research Center, Pasadena, Cal. I am indebted to Frank Goble, of the Thomas Jefferson Center, for providing me with both papers on Attitude Psychology.

and the six prisoner-instructors took on a group of 150 men. 63% of these were completely rehabilitated; eighteen months later, a check showed that all the 63% were still unchanged; there had been no backsliding. The instructors had confidently asserted that the rehabilitation would be permanent.

The Yonan Codex approach is apparently, to some extent, religious. Dr Warren writes that, having checked with many inmates, 'I have not found one who comprehends the meaning of the word 'law', the word 'love', the word 'neighbour', the word 'forgive', the word 'God', or the word 'self', as these words are comprehended in the teachings of Jesus'. He adds: 'When the key words and concepts are taught to an anti-social personality, it will become a social personality if they are used and applied in life situations.' And this makes sense, whether we happen to be conventionally religious or not. The outlook of the criminal tends to be negative and narrow. He is *locked into* a series of set responses to the world. One could make a good analogy here with a gramophone that has a 'filter' control; you can play a record with a lot of surface noise, and 'tune-out' the hissing by turning down the filter control. Unfortunately, you also tune-out the quality of the music—the strings, etc. The criminal mind has simply tuned-out all the higher frequencies of life. The job of the psychologist is to demonstrate how to tune them in again. Dickens' *Christmas Carol* offers a precise parallel. Scrooge has 'tuned out' all the higher frequencies; the acquisitive urge has made him deaf to everything except the clink of money. The task of the three spirits is to persuade him to 'open up' by *reminding* him of the things he has chosen to forget, by showing him that he has fallen into a completely unrewarding way of life. The effect is exactly the same as the effect of mescalin and P.E's on Hoffer's alcoholics: an 'opening up'. In this context it is also worth taking note of the episode in which Scrooge sees himself as a child in the schoolroom, reading *The Arabian Nights*. That is to say, there *was* a time when Scrooge possessed imagination. This is important because we might otherwise fall into the error of supposing that what is wrong with Scrooge is the force of his *will drive*, and that what he needs to put him right is the equivalent of a psychedelic trip. It is not his will that is the trouble; it is the way that he has allowed his imagination to go dead.

As far as one can gather from Dan MacDougald's account, the practical method of his rehabilitation therapy consists in concentrating on the meanings of certain words connected with moral attitudes. He points out that the Hebrew word 'kosher' (proper) is derived from the Aramaic word 'koodsha'. Aramaic 'is the language of Adam and Eve, Abraham of Chaldea from Ur, most of the prophets of the Old Testament', of Jesus, Mahomet, and so on. 'Referring back to this lingua franca of the prophets and the Garden of Eden, we found considerable instruction on *koodsha* attitudes, good attitudes'—and he points out that the word 'beatitude' means precisely that. The meaning of such words as 'God', love', 'neighbour' is considered in Aramaic, and 'with these meanings in mind, all we had to do was substitute them for our customary word meanings . . .'

How does one account for the extraordinary success of the Yonan method? I would suggest that we must take into account certain factors of which its practitioners themselves may not be fully aware. A large number of criminals belong to the 'dominant 5%' of the human race. This 5% seems to be something of a biological constant. When Shaw asked the explorer Stanley how many of his men could lead the party if he himself fell ill, Stanley replied, 'One in twenty.' When Shaw asked if that was approximate or exact, Stanley replied, 'Exact.' During the Korean war, the Chinese found they could economise on guards if they split American prisoners into the dominant ones and the non-dominant ones, and set a heavy guard on the dominant ones. Deprived of their natural leaders, the non-dominant group needed almost no guard at all. The dominant soldiers were always 5% of the total number.

Dr John Calhoun, performing experiments on overcrowding with albino rats, discovered that when overcrowding causes a breakdown of rat 'mores', the dominant 5% becomes a criminal 5%.[1] We know that an enormous proportion of human criminality is the result of overcrowding, and it is a fair inference that many criminals, perhaps the majority, are members of the dominant 5%. (It must be understood that the dominant minority —Maslow's alphas or aggridents—are not a minority of 'geniuses' or even especially talented people; it includes *every-*

[1] See *Mysterious Senses* by Vitus B. Droscher and *The Doomsday Book*, by G. Rattray Taylor.

one who holds a dominant position in society, from pop-singers to army N.C.O's, from politicians to clergymen.)

If we consider Harlow's experiments that revealed that monkeys could be made to take an intellectual interest in problems, it becomes apparent that there can be very few human beings who are totally incapable of deriving pleasure from mental effort—provided 'Tom Sawyer' methods are used to persuade them. Modern prisons must be regarded as enormous cess-pits, full of stagnating human potential, and it is the 'alphas' who are bound to suffer most. If Maslow is correct in believing that the need for evolution is a basic human characteristic, it follows that prisons must be full of alphas who urgently need any kind of opportunity for development.

If we allow these assumptions—and I agree that they are, at present, unproved—the success of the Yonan Codex approach at once ceases to be baffling. Prisoners are treated as human beings with a full human potential—the possibility of some form of self-actualisation—and drawn into a discussion of Aramaic words. The result is bound to be the widening of horizons that Maslow regarded as the key to psychotherapy, the sense of new possibilities. If human beings are deprived of all sense of purpose, they follow the path of least resistance. But this is not natural to them; their human potential leads them to prefer the path of greatest profit, greatest advantage. Man is a purposive animal. He is at his best with a purpose—and a long-distance purpose produces better results than a short-distance purpose. When the path of least resistance—the essentially criminal characteristic—is replaced with the path of greatest satisfaction, man becomes aware of himself as a social being. Criminality could be regarded as a form of boredom, lack of purpose, which leads to a kind of aimless destructiveness and acquisitiveness. Such a man is alienated from society because he feels society to be simply an obstacle to the fulfilment of his desires. His attitude towards society is bound to be one of dislike, fear, guilt; society is the judge, he is the judged. As soon as he becomes possessed by any real purpose of his own—apart from satisfaction of immediate desires—he ceases to feel guilty. At the worst, society is irrelevant; he is 'minding his own business', and at last he *has* a business to mind. But any disinterested purpose is ultimately to the benefit of society; even collecting stamps or beer-bottle labels draws a man closer to other men. When a man has a feeling of autonomy, of 'doing his own thing', he ceases to be anti-social. It may also be noted in passing that this view provides an acceptable alternative to Freud's *thanatos*—the basic urge to death and destruction, which Freud professed to discover in the depths of the subconscious. [According to Freud, crime and war are expressions of *thanatos*. When the existence of the dominant 5% is recognised, violence is seen as the outcome of frustrated creativity, the need for excitement and adventure. Socially privileged members of the dominant minority can work off their energies in mountain climbing or travel. For the underprivileged, there are less outlets, and frustration builds up like the lava inside a volcano, until it explodes, either in individual violence or mass violence. (I have explored this theme at length in *Order of Assassins* (1972).)

An important contribution to the study of paranoid attitudes has been made by the science fiction writer A. E. Van Vogt, and embodied in the novel *The Violent Man*,[1] as well as in an unpublished paper, 'A report on the violent male' (1962).[2] In this paper, Van Vogt describes how he spent years accumulating data on 'the violent male' or 'the right man'. The 'right man' is a man whose sense of self-esteem depends upon feeling himself to be always in the right: he cannot bear to be thought in the wrong, and will go to any length to deny that he is ever mistaken. (Dan MacDougald says accurately: 'All paranoid symptoms can be derived from the fact of blocking this or that fact or memory . . . which would tend to evidence personal error.') People like this, says Van Vogt, are usually pretty intolerable in their relations with women, since they demand to be absolute master, and the relationships are apt to be one-sided. In one case he cites, the husband had divorced his wife and set her up in a suburban home, on condition that she remained unmarried and devoted herself to the welfare of their son. The husband was promiscuous—and always had been; but because his wife had confessed that she had not been a virgin

---

[1] Although this is not a science fiction novel.
[2] Which I have also discussed in the preface to my novel *Lingard* (1970), (in England, *The Killer*).

when she met him, he treated her as a whore who had to be re-
formed at all costs. During their marriage he was violently
jealous and often knocked her down. It was obviously essential
to his self-esteem to feel himself her absolute master.

But perhaps the most curious thing about the violent male,
says Van Vogt, is that he is so basically dependent on the
woman that if she leaves *him*, he experiences total moral collapse
that sometimes ends in suicide. The reason should be clear,
from what has been said above. She is the foundation stone of a
tower of fantasy. The sexual needs, as Maslow points out, are
pretty basic in the hierarchy of values. His self-esteem is built
upon this notion of himself as a sultan flourishing a whip, with a
submissive and adoring girl at his feet. If she leaves him, the
whole fantasy world collapses, and he is faced with the prospect
of an unliveable life. Van Vogt suggests that many dictator
figures were 'right men'—Hitler, Stalin, Khrushchev—and that
their urge to dominate was based upon this need to make the
world conform to their fantasy of infallibility.

The 'right man' theory may be regarded as the essential link
between Glasser's reality therapy and MacDougald's Attitude
Therapy; it certainly throws some important light on both.
Glasser's case of the juvenile delinquent 'Jeri' shows the same
process of retreat from reality—power fantasies (her boasts
about her influence over Glasser) and a complex pattern of self-
justification: hatred of the house-mother for her unfairness, etc.
This involves a kind of wilful 'blocking' of what she must know,
in some corner of her mind, to be the truth about herself. Why
does she prefer to retreat further into a labyrinth of self-justi-
fication? Because she feels that her own method *may work*, and
therefore pass the pragmatic test; she may outwit them all . . .
In fact, she is *miscalculating*, like a liar who determines to stick
by a lie, unaware that it will cost a hundred times as much
energy and effort as telling the truth. *All* human beings have a
natural dislike of retracing their steps; it is part of the evolutionary drive in us, to keep on going in a straight line. Sensible
people try to guide their decisions by logic; when a course of
action shows no result, they think about cutting their losses.
Immature or undisciplined people are dominated by emotion,
which is as difficult to control as a runaway horse; for them, the
path of least resistance is to let the horse keep going until it

gets tired, rather than wrestling it to a stop and making it turn round. In the case of Jeri, Glasser steered her gently into conflict with reality—the discipline unit—and waited for her commonsense to weigh up the odds. What was important was that while this happened, he continued to treat her as a sensible human being, capable of making up her own mind—which is also the principle of the Yonan Codex instructors.

Another basic recognition emerges from all this: that there is no clear dividing line between the criminal and the non-criminal. Criminality is lack of contact with reality, and we are all, to some extent, out of contact with reality. Criminality is also the outcome of self-division, and we are all more or less self-divided. If I pass a lighted window and see a girl undressing, I become aware of the extent of this self-division: that part of me is a hungry animal, and the other half has to hold it in check. It is important to grasp that there are certain general deficiencies in human consciousness, and that the criminal is only an extreme example of these. 'Belief in the abnormality of the murderer is a part of the delusion of normality on which society is based', I have written elsewhere.[1] Glasser's reality therapy, MacDougald's Attitude Psychology, Van Vogt's 'violent man' theory, can only be fully understood in the light of Maslow's recognition that man is capable of an extremely high level of self-actualisation, and that most human beings are still a very long way from it.

All the existential psychologies I have described in the last thirty pages have one thing in common: an attempt to approach the problem of mental illness in a practical rather than a theoretical way, to understand it by saying, 'There but for the grace of God go I', and then asking: 'In that case, why am I not ill?' A Freudian would not approach the problem in the same way, because he assumes that he is dealing with 'hidden factors' that he can only discover by poking into the patient's subconscious. Existential psychology would not deny the existence of the hidden factors, but it assumes that the most important part of the problem is connected with the conscious mind and the will. There is the story of the psychoanalyst who asked Frankl to define logotherapy in a sentence. Frankl countered by

[1] Preface to *An Encyclopedia of Murder* (1961).

asking him to define psychoanalysis in a sentence, and the analyst said, 'In psychoanalysis, the patient lies on a couch and tells things that he finds unpleasant to tell'. 'In logotherapy', said Frankl, 'the patient sits on a chair, and hears things that he finds unpleasant to hear.' The same description could obviously be applied to Glasser's reality therapy and to 'encounter group' therapy like the Synanon experiment; it also plays an important part in MacDougald's Attitude Psychology. The idea is to cure the neurosis by jarring the mind into a more active and responsible attitude—producing what I have called 'promotion'. Everyone has experienced this. After a hard day at work you may feel tired and low, and the tiredness seems genuine; then a house down the street catches on fire, and your tiredness vanishes instantly. It is a question of 'vital reserves'. Mental illness is losing contact with your vital reserves, and then getting into a vicious circle of fatigue and depression.

All existential psychologies would accept this. Where they differ most is in their *phenomenology* of the neurotic process. We have seen, for example, that Rollo May's major assumption about a neurotic is that an attack on his 'centeredness' has been made, and this seems at first a perfectly adequate description. When Larry Cassidy went into the army, we can see that it was an attack on his 'centeredness', his feeling of identity, which had so far been associated with books, music, ideas . . . The same with Maslow's sociology student forced to work in a chewing gum factory. One is reminded of Pound's lines from the *Pisan Cantos*:

'What thou lovest well remains, the rest is dross
What thou lov'st well shall not be reft from thee.'

Unfortunately, what we love well *is* occasionally wrested from us, and the result is a loss of 'centeredness', mental strain. But how does this notion fit the case of Jung's businessman (p. 120) who gave up his work, became depressed and neurotic, then went back to work but found it unsatisfying? You might say that when the businessman decided to retire, he retreated from the business which had given him centeredness, and therefore from himself. (Carl Rogers defines the 'self' as a structure compounded of experiences of which a man feels himself the centre.) But in that case, his return to the business should have been a return to 'centeredness'; and it wasn't. And in the same way, one can see that Maslow's girl patient needed a *creative* outlet that would allow her to move towards self-actualisation. Jung's businessman found that the business had ceased to interest him because he was returning to an earlier stage of his life instead of *moving forward*.

In the same way, Attitude Psychology and 'no crap therapy' only make sense when we think in terms of creative purpose, of evolution. Frankl's prisoners outside Dachau were happy because it had no chimney—which proves that happiness depends on an attitude; but when we look closer, we realise that the absence of a chimney meant that their *future* was no longer in immediate danger.

The conclusion is that the notion of self-actualisation must lie at the centre of all existential psychologies. It is the indispensable common factor. To make other factors more important—centeredness, faulty blocking, will to power, the sex urge—is to misplace the emphasis.

Having said this, one must admit that Maslow, preoccupied with humanistic values and peak experiences, failed to grasp the importance of 'attitude', the mind's transaction with the environment. He went straight to the heart of the matter, but his phenomenology tended to be shaky and inadequate.

On the whole, this is probably the major complaint to be laid at the door of the various forms of humanistic psychology. Freud offered a comprehensive system; so did Jung. On the other hand, Medard Boss, Frankl, Rogers, MacDougald, Cantril, Glasser, Mowrer, are full of brilliant and obviously basic insights, but the various pieces of the jigsaw fail to fit together. Nobody has yet written the *Principles of Psychology* of the new movement. In the course of this book, I have tried to show that existential psychology *is* a single, comprehensive system, without glaring inner-contradictions. But the connections, the unifying principles, may not be easily apparent.

Let me, in these final pages, attempt a sketch of my own general phenomenology of mental health.

The major problem of modern man is the *fragmentariness* of his experience. The present demands so much of his attention that he seldom has a chance to take stock, to see things as a whole. A great deal of his everyday living is done for him by the robot; the consequence is that everyday consciousness consists of what Eliot called 'partial observation of one's own automatism'. Heidegger says that the crisis of modern life is caused by 'forgetfulness of existence' and the 'triviality of everyday-ness'. The blame can be laid largely on the robot. In *The Outsider* I quoted Hemingway's story 'Soldier's Home' in which Krebs, the soldier back from the war, finds himself completely bored and devitalised in his home town:

'All the times that had been able to make him feel cool and clear inside him when he thought about them; the times when he had done the one thing, the only thing for a man to do, easily and naturally, when he might have done something else, now lost their cool, valuable quality, and then were lost themselves.'

He is suffering from Frankl's 'existential vacuum'. The times when he had done 'the one thing, the only thing' were times of crisis, when there had been perfect collaboration between the 'self' and the robot. Now, in this anticlimactic situation, the robot simply robs him of direct experience.

Yeats described the same thing in 'Under Ben Bulben':

You that Mitchell's prayer have heard
'Send war in our time, O Lord!'
Know that when all words are said
And a man is fighting mad,
Something drops from eyes long blind,
He completes his partial mind,
For an instant stands at ease,
Laughs aloud, his heart at peace.
Even the wisest man grows tense
With some sort of violence
Before he can accomplish fate,
Know his work or choose his mate.

The most important line here is 'he completes his partial mind'. When a man is bored, his mind is three-quarters eclipsed, like the moon in its last quarter. When galvanised by some crisis or ecstasy, the full moon suddenly appears, and he feels completely in control of his real powers, in contact with the 'source of power, meaning and purpose' inside himself. If he could remain in this state all the time, there would be no question of mental illness.

Neurosis is a consequence of contemplating problems with the 'partial mind'. When the full moon appears, I feel strong enough to conquer anything:

> What were all the world's alarms
> To mighty Paris when he found
> Sleep upon a golden bed
> That first dawn in Helen's arms?

But when Paris is thoroughly bored from a long period of inactivity, the world's alarms terrify him. This is why problems always seem worse when you wake up in the middle of the night. A person who gets too bogged down in the triviality of everydayness ends in the neurasthenic state described by James, with a feeling of being completely cut off from his vital resources.

This recognition carries us immediately beyond Maslow's position. For what is the peak experience but a glimpse of the full moon? 'He completes his partial mind . . .' That is to say, the peak experience is a glimpse of an objective truth about the mind and about your own vital powers; the full moon really exists. The central human problem is that when you are back in a state of 'partialness' and depression, you can stare as hard as you like, and you *can't* see the rest of the moon. And this is the problem that destroyed so many of the romantics of the last century. The moods of intensity and ecstasy seemed so reasonable and normal while they lasted; so why *did* they go away and leave 'this dim vast vale of tears vacant and desolate?' Perhaps, concluded Shelley, because they are an illusion, a mirage . . . They are not, as the above analysis has shown. 'Bullying treatment' can, as James pointed out, drive away the neurasthenic state and bring a feeling of relief. Why should this be so? And how is it that neurasthenia can encroach so cunningly, creeping like a shadow across the moon?

We return to the question of our 'controls'. I possess a boat that has an outboard engine; this engine is connected to the steering wheel by a wire cable that runs back along both sides of the boat. Occasionally the cable gets slack, so that when I turn the steering wheel, there is no immediate response; there is a jerk, as the cable tightens up, *then* a response. Human beings also possess the equivalent of control-cables. And they sometimes allow these to get so slack that an ordinary movement of the steering wheel has no effect at all, except to produce that slight jerk of panic in the heart. The slack steering induces a sense of helplessness and contingency; my efforts of will produce no effect. Crisis—'when a man is fighting mad'—instantly tightens the steering, and gives me a sudden amazed glimpse of my own potentialities. Neurosis is basically a slack steering cable; the problem is to tighten it up.

This in turn leads to what I would identify as the central insight of this 'control psychology'. When the controls tighten, the world appears to become *more real*. New meanings appear. And it is the act of concentration *itself* that causes this intensification of consciousness.

What is so difficult for us to grasp is that there is a *basic fallacy* in our instinctive assumptions about consciousness. We think of meaning as coming from 'out there'. And to a large extent, this is obviously true. Babies have to learn how to live and act from other people and from experience. A child staring out of the window of a train as he sets out on holiday feels that new meanings are being *offered* to him like a bag of sweets. But what is equally important is that he is looking at the passing scenery with eager attention. And in a sense, this eager attention is more important than the scenery.

An exact analogy would be this. A man suffering from cramps in the arms is given two heavy bronze weights by the doctor, and told to exercise with them for half an hour each morning. As soon as he lifts them from the floor he experiences a delightful rippling sensation in his muscles, which turns into a pleasant, warm glow as he continues to use them. When he next sees the doctor he says: 'I wonder if you'd consider selling those weights? Their metal obviously has some strange virtue that produces a kind of electric shock of delight when I lift them.' The doctor replies: 'Nonsense. The feeling of delight comes from *using your muscles*. Any heavy object would serve just as well. I gave you the weights only because they are more convenient to hold. You could get the same sensation by *tensing* the muscles of your arm.'

Where the peak experience is concerned, human beings are totally convinced that it depends upon an *object* that gives pleasure just as sugar gives a sensation of sweetness to the tongue. But the truth is that the schoolboy enjoys the train journey because he has been looking forward to it eagerly; he has aroused himself to a state of expectation which has had the effect of 'tightening the steering cable', so that everything he looks at causes instant response. But it must be added that the 'steering cable' is actually a muscle, which becomes stronger with use. This also explains why human beings cannot stand a great deal of intense delight; it soon tires us. The muscle begins to ache with the unaccustomed tension . . .

Every peak experience, every orgasm of pleasure, brings this realisation in a flash of insight; but we cannot grasp it, and the insight fades. And we remain trapped in the 'passive fallacy'. A slight depression produces a feeling of defeat and a slackening of attention. We feel 'discouraged'; it no longer seems worth putting so much effort into problem-solving. And the world actually *appears* to be a duller and nastier place: that is what our eyes seem to tell us. And unless 'something interesting' happens and rescues us from this vicious circle of boredom and passivity, the eventual result would be nervous collapse. But if something *does* arouse our interest and start the 'vital reserves' flowing, we once again fall into the old error of supposing that it is the 'bronze weight' that produces the tingle of delight.

Throughout human history this has been true, and it has been the cause of all our troubles. Man is at his best when he is 'up against it'. When a battle is won, the enemy defeated, he experiences the sense of 'fruitful existence and a high quality of life'. In peace time he is bored, so he begins to brood on war again . . . Casanova experiences a sense of supreme wellbeing as he makes love to a woman for the first time; so he spends his life in pursuit of 'first times'.

In our relatively brainless ancestors this was understandable and excusable. But any intelligent modern man knows that he can experience a wider range of sensation as he sits in his arm-chair and reads *War and Peace* than in six months' fighting. He knows that Beethoven and Van Gogh and Newton were heroes in the same sense as Julius Caesar and Alexander the Great. But he fails to draw the conclusion: that the future of the human race lies in increasing our power over the mental world, over our *mental processes*. When an experience is intense and memorable, this is due to the element we put in to the experience. We do not have to accept boredom, dullness, low mental pressure; a steady effort of willed concentration can remove the slackness from the controls and produce an expanding sense of meaning.

Since we habitually live in a state of more-or-less slack controls, it would not be inaccurate to say that *we are mentally ill all the time we are not having peak experiences*—or at least, capable of having them.

The basic human problem is to maintain continually the state in which peak experiences are possible. This means, in practical terms, a certain forward-drive, and a deep-seated refusal to accept depression, discouragement, all the various shades of defeat. We have got to recognise that the 'pressure' we live at is too low to allow the development of our evolutionary potentialities. The steering cable is permanently slack. Imagine a city in which the gas supply is so inadequate that all its inhabitants take it for granted that it takes an hour to boil a kettle and a whole day to cook a joint. And then someone tries lighting the gas stove at three in the morning, and realises with astonishment that there is no reason why a kettle should not boil in five minutes. The next problem would be to work out how the gas pressure might be permanently raised, and this would involve a consideration of the whole city's gas supply. And the problem of permanently increasing the pressure of consciousness demands a similar consideration of all our vital mechanisms.

This is not a new problem. For thousands of years, saints have gone into the wilderness so that they might spend their days in undistracted concentration; others wore chains or lashed themselves with whips to strengthen the concentration muscle. The American traveller Catlin describes Indian ceremonies of initiation that involve bearing intense pain for days, or even weeks: for example, being suspended from a beam by cords that are sewn into the skin of the chest. What is actually being tested here is the ability to maintain continuous tension of will. The human drive towards adventure and exploration, the 'outward urge', is an attempt to create challenges that will force the explorer to 'get the best out of himself'; it could be compared to building a gymnasium to maintain a high level of physical fitness.

On the other hand, a gymnasium is not a necessity for the

athlete; he could do exercises locked in an empty room; in fact, there are isometric exercises that can be performed sitting at a desk. And the human mind does not need physical adventure or discomfort as an aid to concentration. We already possess the greatest of all aids to concentration: imagination, the sense of reality: what I have elsewhere called Faculty X. The main thing that prevents us from making use of these powers is our ignorance of their nature; we are like savages confronting a motor car. Understanding of them comes in flashes—in the peak experience, the orgasm, the response to a moment of crisis, 'when a man is fighting mad'; and this insight must be somehow fixed, consolidated, expressed in terms of concepts and ordinary language. This is the central aim of the 'new psychology'.

I must digress slightly at this point to outline a further important consequence of this theory—one that, to some extent, contradicts text-book definitions of neurosis and psychosis. For it follows that the difference is again quantitative. We are misled into thinking there is a qualitative difference between neurosis and, say, schizophrenia, because neurotics do not often develop into schizophrenics, and schizophrenia usually develops without an intervening stage of neurosis. But the case of Larry Cassidy shows a process of continuous development: boredom and world-rejection leading to neurosis, and the neurosis slowly changing into schizophrenia (with intense depression forming the no-man's-land between them).

The difference between neurosis and schizophrenia can be seen in a case I have cited elsewhere.[1] The novelist Margaret Lane described to me her own experience of mild schizophrenia, which lasted a year or more. Shortly after the war, she had had a baby—a difficult birth, that left her exhausted, but very happy. But her low state of physical energy made her emotionally over-sensitive, so that when the cat hurt its paw, it seemed a major tragedy. She was in this state of over-sensitivity, when she read John Hersey's account of the dropping of the atom bomb on Hiroshima, printed complete in *The New Yorker*. The horror of it seemed to blow some mental fuse; she became acutely depressed, and ceased to have emotional responses. She felt nothing, even towards the new baby. She continued to be

[1] *Beyond the Outsider*, Appendix 1.

a good wife and mother in a mechanical way, but felt burnt out. She had various schizophrenic symptoms: for example, grass looked to her like blue paper, while leaves seemed to be made of green tin.

This lasted a long time, although her way of life—as a member of a secure and affectionate family unit—kept it from developing into anything worse. It came to an end in the following way. She and her husband went to look at a country cottage that she had wanted to rent. She was feeling slightly more cheerful and involved than usual. She walked up the back garden, and the grass looked like blue paper as usual. Suddenly she was struck by the sight of a bluebell in the grass; its blue seemed very intense and vivid. As she stared at it, the inner-greyness vanished. The grass looked like real grass and the leaves looked like real leaves. She burst into tears as she realised that the long emotional freeze-up was over. It took a day or two more for it to disappear completely.

The phenomenology of the attack could hardly be clearer. She had been in a physically low state; but if nothing had upset her, she would have made a recovery in a few days or weeks. Fatigued people feel unusually vulnerable. They are in a state of 'partial mind'—more so than usual; which means that, like Ivan Karamazov, they are likely to be more aware of the world's 'contras' than of its 'pros', of its misery, evil, cruelty and so on. Hersye's *Hiroshima* was shattering confirmation of this. If her new baby had previously seemed to be one of life's 'pros', it now became a 'contra', since it must have seemed unfair to bring a child into such a cruel world.

What was broken was her *will*. She would now flinch at everything, like a terrified animal. There would be no courage to go forward, and momentary flashes of pleasure would be regarded with suspicion, as deceivers. Since perception of meaning is intentional, a reaching-out, the world would strike her as meaningless. The appearance of grass and leaves—as imitations—would be a perceptual expression of this mistrust (for we have seen that perception is a transaction, in which the currency is energy): they were not alive, and therefore meaningful, but dead.

To grasp that perception of meaning *is* a transaction is important for the understanding of the blue flower episode.

She was rather happier than usual as she walked up the garden, and the blueness of the flower caused her to stop and stare, to double the energy she had been putting into perception. This was enough to break the internal deadlock: to admit meaning, and to start a positive chain-reaction of trust, effort and further perception of meaning.

Now the neurotic may have certain symptoms in common with the schizophrenic. In a case that has recently come to my notice, a married woman has been seriously neurotic for the past twenty years. It began as a tendency to be dominated by fear; if she saw a horror film on TV, she would wake up having nightmares. The tendency to fear has slowly developed, so that now her husband has to censor the newspaper before she reads it, and cut out anything he knows would upset her. (Similarly, Larry Cassidy's brother had to get into the habit of censoring his speech before the lobotomy.) But there is no sign of the neurosis developing into schizophrenia. That is to say, although she has become a perpetual victim of 'the partial mind', unable to escape a feeling of inadequacy and vulnerability, she is more-or-less in control of the illness. It is rather like a person who feels sick, but can keep it under control with a certain effort, and avoid actual vomiting. That is to say, there is not yet an emergency situation, where her 'essential self' abdicates, and leaves control to the robot.

In schizophrenia, this is precisely what happens. A state of emergency is declared. The robot takes over most of the vital functions. And, like an accountant taking over a bankrupt business, *he* doles out energy. But the realm of the robot is the subconscious, which is also the realm of dreams. This explains schizophrenic hallucinations and distortions. With the robot in charge, dreams are allowed to stroll in and out of the conscious mind. And they appear to challenge the real world, to possess a self-subsisting reality (as vivid dreams do).

Long-standing neurosis *can* develop into schizophrenia, particularly in highly intelligent people, whose powers of imagination may act as an amplifier to the fears and depressions. (Strindberg is an interesting case in point.) Fortunately, this seldom happens; neurosis acts as a vaccination, which increases the mind's resistance to psychosis.

One of the most interesting observations to arise out of all this is that when the mind falls below a certain energy-level, its capacity to *receive meaning* drops abruptly; the control cable goes slack. And so although schizophrenia is an altogether more serious illness than neurosis, its milder forms occur every day to almost everyone. You might say that your sense of meaning is suddenly cut by a half; a grey, chill wind seems to blow in the mind. But then, like a water cistern, your energy tank refills, the cable tightens, and life appears normally pleasant and meaningful again.

I would identify this as by far the most important question for the psychology of the future. Until its phenomenology is fully understood, we are still missing the vital key. I would only suggest here that we are dealing with the psychological equivalent of quantum theory. The disconcerting thing about 'life failure' (which would probably serve as a synonym for schizophrenia) is its unexpectedness. One minute, William James is just feeling rather low; the next minute, as if he has walked into an elephant trap, he has crashed into a 'panic fear of his own existence'. And the 'quantum leap' out of it is equally sudden, as in Margaret Lane's case. Psychotherapy will not be a true science until we understand the mathematical laws governing this problem. Peak experiences may be the important clue, for they are sudden energy 'spurts', when the mind seems to receive a shock of meaning. Meaning-perception is the key to the evolution of our species. And this is one of the great mysteries. Human beings surely waste about 99·9% of their time in meaninglessness, aimlessness. We plod through the ritual of everyday living like a gramophone needle in its groove; it is as if we were blindfolded or blinkered most of the time. We are capable of boredom—a sullen refusal to be interested in anything—when surrounded by meaning. And poets experience sudden storms of 'meaning' when they seem to catch a glimpse of an endless staircase stretching beyond the stars. I can state this with confidence: there is something bloody fishy about human existence.

The one thing that is quite clear so far—and I suppose this is the main contribution of existential psychology to date—is the peculiar interdependence of the will and the sense of meaning. We know the will depends on the sense of meaning; a bored man soon becomes apathetic. But it is equally true that the sense of meaning depends upon the will. Maslow's healthy subjects had regular peak experiences because the will was alive and active. Hoffer's alcoholic subjects were cured when the whole will-meaning cycle was reactivated by a psychedelic peak experience. (Similarly, Larry Cassidy's brother, who had fallen into a neurotic state of guilt about the lobotomy operation, was cured by psychedelic treatment, which presumably lifted him completely *above* his guilt, revealing James's 'distant horizons of meaning'.)

The central need, at the moment, is to develop a psychology of man's higher consciousness, a complete breakaway from Freudian pathology. When he was a young man, the 'clairvoyant' Edgar Cayce lost his voice, and was cured by a hypnotist (who recognised the illness to be psychosomatic). But if Cayce had wanted to go on and become an opera singer, the hypnotist would not have been much use; Cayce would have had to go to a good voice teacher. Psychology at the moment is concerned chiefly with the sub-normal; never with the higher ranges of human possibility. Maslow's *Principles of Abnormal Psychology* needs to be supplemented with a *Principles of Supernormal Psychology*. And the starting point of such a psychology would be the study of the relation between the will and the sense of meaning. For this is quite clearly the key to self-actualisation.

Let me be more specific about this. The will and the sense of meaning are capable of mutual stimulation. If I want something badly, what happens is the exact reverse of Stavrogin's sense of meaninglessness. My will begins to build up a certain weight, a certain thrust. If I want it badly enough, and it is difficult to achieve, the sense of meaning may become so powerful that everything in the world seems to vibrate with meaning. The ruby laser provides a good analogy. An intense flash of light causes the atoms in the ruby to vibrate at a high rate, and the light emitted by the ruby is 'phased'—its waves march in step. The beam of phased light bounces back and forth between two mirrors, one partly-silvered and the other fully-silvered, becoming steadily more powerful as more and more atoms are excited by it: finally, it emerges as an intense beam through the half-silvered mirror, capable of punching a hole through a pack of razor blades.

We recognise a similar process when something interests us deeply. If nothing disturbs the concentration, the 'temperature' of the beam of interest rises steadily. And in the case of strong desire, the will and the sense of meaning seem to act like two mirrors, intensifying the vitality. In such experiences, we become aware that the properties of such a beam of intensity may be as remarkable as the properties of phased light. (Does this, for example, explain the curious problem of Ted Serios, who can apparently cause images to appear on a photographic plate by concentrating on the camera?[1]) When the first laser was constructed (in the early sixties) it produced only brief pulses of intense light. Is the peak experience the mental equivalent of such a pulse?

The novelist Stendhal suffered from an embarrassing psychological disability. Although highly susceptible to female charms, and capable of normal sexual excitement, he was unable to offer the ultimate proof of his devotion: on the point of making love, he would suddenly experience 'le fiasco', and become totally incapable. I have already mentioned Maupassant's description of a similar 'fiasco' in his story *The Unknown*, where the hero's ardour is extinguished by the sight of a fine line of dark hair down the young lady's back. (p. 53.)

Such examples reveal something of the mechanism of the will. 'Le fiasco' is the opposite of the 'laser'. The intensity explodes harmlessly before it achieves its object. And this makes us aware that the will is focused by the sense of meaning. And its 'grip' must be adequate to the sense of meaning.

Here is an illustration. My daughter, age ten, was reading a story about witches; she got bored halfway through and gave it up. I asked her what she was reading, and she started recounting the plot. When she reached the halfway mark she said: 'Telling you has got me interested again', and she went and finished it.

Everybody has noticed this kind of reaction. Somebody returns a book you had thought lost, and you read it with avidity, although before you lent it (and forgot all about it) it had been lying around unread for months.

In order to get an adequate return from a book—or any

[1] See *The World of Ted Serios* by Jule Eisenbud (1967).

other activity—you have to put an adequate amount of energy
into it. If you don't, it will prove unexpectedly boring. But
the mechanism of 'gripping' is also important. If I intend to
chop a log, I make sure it is standing firmly on its end; otherwise it may fall over before I raise the hatchet, or it may fall as I
hit it so the force of the blow is lost. If I intend to drill a piece
of metal, I lock it firmly in the vice first. This act of *preparation*
is as important as the actual drilling. And where mental activities are concerned—reading, listening to music, even making
love—the preparation consists of an initial act of *focusing*, of
weighing up the value of the prospective activity. If there are
half a dozen new books at the side of my armchair in the even-
ings, I shall almost certainly get less pleasure out of them than
if there was only one. Because I shall be inclined to chop and
change, and I shan't put sufficient 'preparedness' into any one
of them. If I am going on a long train journey, I make sure that
the book I take with me is moderately hard work—*Arabia
Deserta*, or Hogben's *Mathematics for the Million*—so that I am
forced to put a certain effort into it. I have learned by experience that when I make such an effort, the journey passes easily
and quickly; whereas if I give way to the temptation to indulge
in softer mental fare—perhaps a Maigret—I shall be bored and
restive before it is half over. The lack of mental effort has the
effect of letting down my inner pressure as you might let the air
out of a tyre. And once it is down, it is not easy to pump it up
again.

Living, as we do, in a fairly hectic world, there is not all that
much time for the quiet act of thinking and 'preparing'. But as
an excuse, this is actually rather dishonest. Even for a city
business man, there are probably several hours every day when
he doesn't have to think about business—for example, travelling to and from work. In fact, these tend to get wasted in
passivity—in staring out of the window, or idly scanning the
newspaper. It is simply that we have got into a habit of gulping
down experience unprepared as we might gulp down a quick
meal in a self-service restaurant.

There seems to be no harm in this; it would be unreasonable
to expect a man to meditate for five minutes before opening a
newspaper, like saying grace before a meal. But the truth is that
the long-term effect of continually 'taking life as it comes' is

much like the long-term effect of gulping quick meals and rushing back to work. The general mental health suffers. This is why sensitive souls daydream nostalgically about monastic life or a quiet weekend cottage, and why a whole generation— of 'beats' and 'hippies'—has tried to develop a way of life with the emphasis on leisure rather than on success. 'Preparedness', tightening the control cable, is an instinctive hunger in human beings.

The concept of 'preparedness' explains Frankl's law of reversed effort. The stutterer stutters because he is nervous, and he is nervous because he feels life is rushing him. (After all, what is stage-fright but a kind of 'unpreparedness'?) When he is told to *try* to stutter, *he is being asked to put preparedness into his stuttering*. But stuttering is due to 'unpreparedness', and as soon as he stands back from it and prepares to stutter, the root cause of the stutter vanishes. In the same way, Tom Sawyer's friends would find it boring to paint the fence if he asked them as a favour, because the knowledge that they were allowed to do it would lead them to do it in a casual, unprepared frame of mind. As they stand watching Tom—who declines to let them have a go—they have time to build up 'preparedness'. And their enjoyment—when they are allowed to paint—is not an illusion, some kind of trick, but the same genuine pleasure they would get on setting out on a holiday.

The way of life in a modern city may encourage 'unpreparedness', but it does not actually prevent 'preparedness'. Our ancestors had more leisure than we have, but they did not necessarily make use of it. The human race has always been inclined to live in the present, to put the minimum effort and preparation into living. The proof is that man has always been driven by boredom, and boredom is another name for being stuck in the present—for unpreparedness.

Unpreparedness is, on the whole, a neutral thing; but it develops easily into a nuisance or a danger. In the case of Maupassant's hero, certainty of achieving his objective has led him to relax and take it for granted, until there is a minimum of preparedness. A minor obstacle—the curious line of dark hair down the girl's back, arousing unpleasant associations (animal? devil?)—is enough to reveal the extent of his un-preparedness, and to set up a panic that makes him impotent.

Anyone who has followed this argument closely will see that all I have done is to apply Husserl's concept of intentionality to some of the paradoxes of 'attitude psychology'. Intentionality *is* preparedness. But the idea of preparedness brings to light new subtleties and complexities in the Husserlian concept. To say, 'All perception is intentional' is enlightening, but it seems to be a statement of a *static* situation, like saying, 'All grass is green.' To call it 'preparedness' is to reveal that it is a dynamic situation. The difference between life-failure and the peak experience is a difference in preparedness. Frankl called his book *Man's Search for Meaning* as if man went around looking under flat stones; but meaning is *revealed* by intensifying 'intentionality'.

This in turn leads to another basic insight, which needs to be incorporated into the foundations of phenomenology: that consciousness is also *relational* by nature. By which I mean that just as perception depends upon a subjective 'reaching out' towards the object, so the object-as-perceived is not a simple thing, but a complex structure depending upon the relation between the object and the rest of the contents of consciousness.

The simplest way to explain this is to describe how the insight came to me. Driving through the Lake District some years ago, I was struck by my intense awareness of 'otherness'— not only of places that were out of sight on the other side of the hills (with which I was familiar), but of many other times and other places. It was as if some kind of spider's web stretched from my brain to these other places behind the hills. The spider's web analogy made me aware that the basic structure of consciousness is web-like. At the centre of consciousness there are things I am immediately aware of; then further out, there are memories, ideas, hopes, stretching into a kind of outer darkness. The lighted area in the middle of the web is consciousness, and when I am tired, the area gets smaller, and vanishes altogether as I fall asleep. When I wake up, the lighted area proceeds to expand for a while, particularly if I am on holiday, or in an excited or hopeful frame of mind. The wider it expands, the greater my awareness of 'otherness', and the stronger my general *sense of reality*. And, what is more, my 'preparedness' increases automatically. I get the sense of detachment from my own life, the 'bird's eye view', the sense of control and serenity that Wordsworth meant when he talked about 'emotion recollected in tranquillity'. My sense of 'relations' broadens.

But it is important to recognise that *all* perception involves a sense of relations, just as all perception involves intentionality. It is possible to imagine a very narrow and stifled perception, like Sartre's 'nausea', in which you look at a particular object without any sense of 'otherness', and it seems to block your field of vision, huge and boring. But if there was not a penumbral area of relations in your mind—a part of the web vibrating in the darkness—you would not see anything at all, because it would be meaningless to you. Your gaze would be blank, like an idiot's stare. Nothing can be perceived in true isolation; all perception is relational.

Relationality is the meaning experience; intentionality is the will experience. They are intimately related, in that relationality can be increased by an act of intentionality, and meaning, in turn, stimulates and guides intention.

All this, I think, makes a start on creating a phenomenology for the new psychology. And this, in general, is what the new psychology has lacked so far. This is not intended as a criticism: Boss, Maslow, Glasser, Laing, MacDougald, were practical or experimental psychologists. Only Binswanger regarded himself as a pure phenomenologist, and he stuck fairly close to Heidegger's descriptive approach. MacDougald's recognition of the 'blocking mechanism', for example, was an important step for Attitude Therapy; but it was, as I have shown, simply a restatement of transactionalism—which was, in turn, a restatement of the insights of Husserl and Whitehead.

With the concepts I have outlined above, it is possible to show logically that Maslow is more correct than Freud. Freud dismissed the 'oceanic feeling' as an infantile reversion; Maslow said it was proof of 'higher ceilings for human nature'. When we recognise that perception must be both intentional and relational, then the oceanic feeling is seen to be a wider state of relationality. (James had said the same thing in his 'Suggestion About Mysticism', but without the phenomenology to support it.) Freud is wrong; Maslow is right; but without a phenomenology that recognises the relationality of consciousness, Maslow cannot be proved right.

But the question that is asked by everyone who reads Maslow is: Can the peak experience be achieved at will? Quite clearly, it is *the* question. Maslow's psychology is basically optimistic, and this raises the question: How can it be *used*? If someone is in a state of nervous depression or neurotic self-contempt, what is the good of telling him that human nature has higher ceilings than Freud ever realised, or that all intelligent people are capable of self actualisation?

The phenomenology I have sketched goes a long way towards providing an answer. It is an objective fact of consciousness that depression is connected with 'the partial mind' and that the peak experience is invariably associated with wider relationality. One of the most dangerous things about depression is that its vision of the world seems objectively true—and therefore to offer no reason for effort. And the vicious circle of 'nausea' and despair can begin. MacDougald's Attitude Therapy has demonstrated how far a simple piece of *knowledge* of how the mind works can open up new horizons. 'Relational phenomenology' can offer a still broader foundation for optimism. One of the greatest problems of modern consciousness is what I have called 'ambiguity', a kind of uncertainty that leads us to stamp on the brake and the accelerator at the same time. It is due to self-division; one part of the mind wants to go forward, the other part hangs back. Genuine relaxation—the essence of the P.E.—is impossible. Ambiguity can only be overcome by certain knowledge. Until ambiguity has been overcome, consciousness is like a leaky bucket, continually losing the larger part of its energy.

The peak experience is a question of plugging the leaks.

And this brings me to my central point, the point I have explored, analysed and reiterated since *The Outsider*. *Human consciousness operates at too low a pressure for efficiency.* This has always been so—which explains why philosophers and poets have always taken a tragic view of human existence: 'All is vanity'. 'It is better not to have been born'. 'Misery will never end'. 'This dim vast vale of tears'. But balance against that the whisky priest's recognition that it would have been so easy to be a saint, or Raskolnikov's assertion that he would rather live on a narrow ledge for ever and ever than die at once. It also explains why vital men seek out challenges and welcome wars.

'I have no life except where the swords clash . . .' The state of intensity, of *concern*, of seriousness, brought to bear by the whisky priest on the point of death, is the correct operating pressure for the human mind. At lower pressures, we are un-economical to run. Our powers are wasted.

The human mind is a big gun, capable of driving its pro-jectile for a long distance; when it backfires, it is likely to wreck itself. All this emerges from my analysis of the 'artist-outsider'. Nietzsche, Van Gogh, Nijinsky, were men who taught themselves to work at a higher pressure than most men achieve; all of them glimpsed what Maslow calls 'further reaches of human nature'. Nietzsche, like Maslow, was obsessed by 'great health'. There was something superhuman about Nijinsky's dancing and Van Gogh's later painting. All three men were destroyed by their inability to reconcile this insight with the 'triviality of everydayness'. They were living at the end of a century of pessimism; the intellectual characteristics of the new age were ambiguity and confusion. (Musil gave it defi-nitive expression in *The Man Without Qualities*.) Freud told Jung that he felt himself menaced by a 'black tide of mud'— Freud 'who, more than anyone else' (says Jung), 'had tried to let down his buckets into those black depths'. E. M. Forster accused James Joyce of trying to cover the universe with mud. It was an age of mud; even its neo-Christianity insisted that man is firmly stuck in Original Sin. The healthy instinct of Nietzsche and Van Gogh was contradicted by the intellectual spirit of the age. There seemed to be no way *forward*, no way to express the best that was in them. It was the situation that killed off so many of Frankl's companions in Dachau: pro-visional existence.

If Nietzsche, Van Gogh, Nijinsky, were alive today, insanity would not be inevitable. The age of ambiguity is over. It may not be obvious yet, but it is.

The peak experience, the orgasm experience, the poetic experience, is the 'completion of the partial mind'. But let us look more closely into this question of the partial mind. It has its own peculiar phenomenology.

In *Being and Nothingness*, Sartre speaks about how you feel if you are caught doing something disgraceful—looking through

a keyhole, for example. The gaze of the other person becomes a
pin, and you are a butterfly being impaled by it, feeling yourself determined by it, *seeing yourself through his eyes*. Sartre is
fascinated by this concept of 'the gaze of others' and its power
to narrow our sense of identity. His enormous book on Genet
elaborates the idea. As a child, Genet was told he was a thief;
he decided to accept this estimate of himself and to live according to it. His work thereupon becomes a form of revenge against
the society that has imposed this identity upon him.

Blake devotes one of the 'memorable fancies' in *The Marriage
of Heaven and Hell* to describing the same mechanism. An angel
warns Blake that he will end up in hell, and shows him a vision
of the nether-world, complete with giant spiders and demons.
Blake then seizes the angel and shows him a vision of where *he*
will spend eternity—in an equally unsavoury pit, where
baboons tear one another to pieces. The angel says indignantly:
'You ought to be ashamed of yourself; your fantasy imposed on
me', and Blake replies: 'We impose on one another. It is a waste
of time arguing with you.' It is a kind of duel, in which the
'gaze' of the opponents takes the place of swords.

Shaw makes the same point in *Man and Superman:* 'We all
bully as much as we dare; we all bid for admiration without the
least intention of earning it'. It is only one step from this to
Adler's notion of the will to power—in which the fundamental
life-drive is ego-assertion. In *Being and Nothingness*, Sartre uses
this as the foundation of a philosophical system in which all
human relations are seen as forms of conflict—the attempt to
'impose on one another'. With Sartre, as with Adler, the
hierarchy of needs comes to an end with the need for self-
esteem. (This also explains Sartre's attraction to Marxism, with
its theory of the class war; it is the political version of his
psychological theory.)

But although the ego-domination theory may be inadequate
as an account of man's basic drives, it can still offer some important insights into what we might call the 'anti-peak experience'. In the peak experience, man 'completes his partial
mind'; or at least, the moon gets slightly larger: perhaps it
expands from a quarter to a half. On the other hand, if I slip on
a banana skin, or back my car into a lamp post, the opposite
happens: I feel, as Proust says, 'accidental, mediocre, mortal'.

But precisely *what* happens? Supposing, for example, someone calls me a liar in public? My *sense of myself* is diminished,
just as if I had suddenly shrunk to the size of a dwarf. A number
of reactions are possible. The simplest and crudest would be to
hit him, for this would make *him* feel accidental, mediocre and
mortal, and would establish me in my own eyes as powerful and
capable, thus restoring my normal stature—in fact, slightly increasing it. I might achieve the same result more subtly by
making some amusing and biting retort. But neither of these
methods answers his accusation that I am a liar. A more reasonable method of restoring my 'stature' and self-esteem would be
to explain, as clearly and briefly as possible, why I am not a
liar; at least, if he believes me and apologises. (Since his own
self-esteem is at issue, he may not want to apologise, even if he
knows I am right.) Finally, I might be mature enough to understand why he has called me a liar, and not to care in the least;
Glasser had to train himself to adopt this attitude with aggressive patients. But then, such an attitude is possible only because my idea of myself—my self-image—is too accurate and
objective to be altered by someone else's opinion.

It comes back, then, to the question of the self-image.
Miseries, humiliations, embarrassments, accidents, have the
effect of creating *partial self-images*—self-images which, since
they present themselves as complete, are bound to be false.
Consciousness narrows, and my self-image becomes as false and
distorted as if I was seeing myself in a trick mirror at a fair-
ground. But a trick mirror at least shows you your whole self,
from head to foot; the partial self-image is a pocket-size distorting mirror.

Sartre's theory of 'mutual conflict' is based upon misunder-
standing of the distorting mirror. It is true that my self-image
is eroded by the 'gaze' of the other, and that I, in turn, attempt
to attack his self-image. But this proves nothing about human
beings. My self-image may also be attacked and distorted by a
wet Monday morning, or by the sound of a fingernail scratching
a windowpane, or by the smell of a gasworks, or by the sight
of a tramp blowing his nose in the gutter. Anything that reminds me of something unpleasant may cause that inner
'shrinking' which is the reverse of the peak experience—i.e. is a
shrinking *of the self-image*. The wet Monday morning is not

hostile towards me, and under different circumstances—if I have just been reprieved from execution, for example—I may see it as delightful. If I analyse why it causes a shrinking of my self-image, I see that the fault lies with me; I *allow* myself to be depressed by it, and if I am honest with myself, I must admit that this is mere hypochondria—spoiltness, self-indulgence. My inner-pressure is so low that a mere unpleasant association is enough to start a chain reaction of gloom. And if two human beings cause the same reaction in one another, this proves nothing about the general hostility of human beings; only that they are a couple of hypochondriacs.

This argument may sound unfair to Sartre; for he claims that it is in the nature of things that human beings should try to 'impose' on one another—even lovers—just as it is in the nature of things that I exert a certain pressure on the ground when I walk, or displace a certain volume of water when I dive into a swimming pool. I am arguing, however, that Sartre's view of human relations is a false generalisation from a false state of consciousness; (I have said that partial-consciousness is bound to be false while it remains unaware of its own incompleteness.) And this can be seen clearly if we consider the mechanism of the peak experience. Suppose I am depressed for 'personal' reasons, and that, like Edmund Spenser, I take a stroll by the river to 'ease my pain'. The warm air and the sound of the water soothe away the tension; they have the effect of rescuing me from my subjectivity, from the shrunken and distorted self-image. Yeats asks:

'How in the name of Heaven can he escape
That defiling and disfigured shape
The mirror of malicious eyes
Casts upon his eyes until at last
He thinks that shape must be his shape?'[1]

The answer is that music, poetry, nature, philosophy, science, mathematics, can all free me from that 'defiling and disfigured shape' by *reminding* me that I am being taken in by a 'partial self', and that my 'real self' has an altogether wider range of response. The effect of the walk by the river is, oddly enough, a de-personalisation, 'escape from personality', a kind of de-

[1] A Dialogue of Self and Soul.

materialising of the sense of identity, like Aladdin's genie vanishing into thin air. This is accompanied by a sense of expansion and relief. Freud may have thought it a reversion to the irresponsibility of childhood, but nobody who has experienced it can believe this, for the sense of wider 'relationality' brings a feeling of profounder *involvement with reality* which is not in the least like a retreat into dreams.

When man 'completes his partial mind', he becomes aware of this wider relation with reality. There is no longer a question of him imposing himself on reality, or reality imposing itself on him. The Sartre view of universal conflict is seen to be a half-truth, which looks plausible only so long as one ignores man's curious passion for the 'objective'.

For the philosophically minded, let me explain that the Sartre position is based on his curious brand of Kantianism: his feeling that our minds *create* meaning and impose it on the world. According to Sartre, we human beings find ourselves huddled together in an alien universe; we have to draw warmth and comfort from one another, and create a comfortable little world of human values—rather like a country club in which everybody knows everybody else's business—and look at the universe through our warm, human-coloured spectacles. Occasionally, the spectacles slip, and we experience a feeling of nausea and horror as we confront the reality of the nightmare, Martian landscape in which we live. We *have* to cling together, to keep the illusion going, and protect ourselves from the meaninglessness that surrounds us like a void.

The phenomenological position is that meaning exists as a reality outside us, and would exist whether we were here or not. It is an inherent part of the universal organism. We breathe it in like air, and it keeps us alive. Sartre's nausea is actually a bad attack of catarrh.

What happens, for example, in the familiar childhood experience of getting absorbed in a book, until inner vistas seem to open and the world becomes a magical place? Sartre would say we have entered a world of *created* meaning, as artificial as Disneyland. The relational theory of consciousness would explain it as a perception of a wider 'net' of relations, and therefore as a valid experience of reality. And, what is more, as a genuine glimpse of the way the world could appear all the

time, if consciousness operated at its correct pressure. We see
the world through our casual, taken-for-granted, low pressure
consciousness, and our 'gaze' skims over its surface and fails to
extract its meaning. Perception is an arrow, fired outwards
from the eyes; if you fire it with a slack bow-string it will
bounce harmlessly off its object. When Cortez and his gallant
men looked at the Pacific from a peak in Darien, what they saw
was more meaningful than the view seen by a tourist who has
driven to the top in his Cadillac.

In the same way, if I try to write without putting any pressure
on the pen, the result will be feeble and spidery, and probably
only half legible. If I fail to put enough pressure on my perception, meaning becomes only half legible. Most human beings
have got into such a habit of writing without pressure that they
take the semi-meaningless universe for granted.

At this point I must make a vital distinction. There is a world
of difference between inner-pressure and mere nervous tension,
just as there is a world of difference between relaxation and
mere slackness. This must be borne constantly in mind. The
difference between positive and negative tension—or relaxation—is a question of the robot. A racing driver experiences
positive tension, because it is his real 'self' that is concentrating
on the driving; a worried businessman experiences negative
tension because it is the robot that has taken over the worrying,
and which keeps him in a useless state of general hypertension.
If I set out on a holiday, and every sight and sound strikes me
as fresh and delightful, this is because it is my real 'self' that has
relaxed: if I am bored on a long train journey, the robot has
taken over the relaxation.

Why does 'life fail'? Why does a man in love imagine he will
be happy for ever if he can marry the girl, and yet take her for
granted within a year of marriage? Clearly, the answer is the
robot. This raises another question: how does it happen? (for to
answer that would be to answer the question: How can we
prevent it happening?) Let us recognise first of all that there
is a constant intercourse or traffic between the 'self' and the
robot. If I am listening to a piece of music, I may listen intensely
for a few minutes, then my thoughts wander and the robot takes
over, then I 'pull myself together' again. On a train journey, I
may watch the scenery with interest for the first half hour, then

gradually allow the robot to take over. But with a certain extra effort, I can prevent the robot taking over. And here is the important point. You might suppose that the effort has to go on and on, because your attention will keep on wandering, and you will have to drag it back again. This is untrue, for an amusing reason. If you make a great initial effort to keep your attention from wandering—to prevent the robot taking over your perceptions—the robot himself will take over the effort, and will *himself* alert you before allowing himself to take over. And why not? He is a machine. You made him. It is only because you don't understand your own creation that he can be more trouble than he's worth.

The point is perfectly illustrated in the Rubinstein and Best experiment with planaria (cited by Ardrey[1]). Planarion worms (one of the most primitive members of the worm family) were trained to make their way down a plastic tube, and to choose a left- or right-hand fork which led to water. A high percentage of them learned this trick with ease; and then they got bored with doing it—so bored that they began choosing the wrong alleyway out of sheer cussedness, and then preferred to lie down and die rather than find the water yet again. (They need water to live.) Rubinstein and Best cured this by making the training far more difficult. They used two tubes, one made of rough plastic and one of smooth plastic (so the worms could sense the difference with their bellies), and in the rough plastic tube, the water was to be found down a lighted alleyway, and in the smooth plastic tube, it was down the dark alleyway. A much lower percentage of the worms learned this more complicated trick. But the ones that *did* learn never got bored. The experimenters would drain off the water from the main body of the tube by turning a tap; the worms would instantly rush off looking for water, and would choose the lighted or dark alleyway, depending on whether the tube was rough or smooth. And they would keep on doing it for ever. They had been forced to make a greater *initial* effort, and the robot obligingly incorporated a sense of urgency or danger into the habit.

You will note the same thing on a train journey; an enormous initial effort of will prevents boredom for the whole journey.

[1] *Territorial Imperative*, p. 327.

This observation explains the difference between 'peakers' and 'non-peakers'. We know, from Maslow's observations, that peakers tend to be healthier than non-peakers; but that is not the important part. There might be two people, both reasonably healthy and cheerful, and yet one is a peaker and one isn't. The non-peaker falls slightly short of the effort required to get the robot's full co-operation. It is obvious, for example, that there is a definite dividing line between the bore-able and non-bore-able planaria; worms above that line will remain forever un-bored with the effort of finding their way to water; worms slightly below it will, sooner or later, start taking the wrong turning for the sake of variety.

The importance of this—for post-Maslow psychology—is immense. It means that *anybody* can become a 'peaker', provided they are willing to put a certain amount of effort into it. Non-peakers are either the habitually lazy or the habitually *discouraged*—those who do not realise how easy it is to become a peaker.

And the general technique for inducing peak experiences is bound up with the psychology of the self-image. And at this point, some of the wider implications of this psychology become apparent. Machado's lieutenant in *The Looking Glass* demonstrates its simplest application; so do the prisoners in *The Roots of Heaven*. The purpose of the mirror is to prevent *amnesia*. It is true that Machado's hero can still recall the days when his aunt flattered him into a state of blissful egotism with her admiration; but this is not true memory, only a poor carbon copy, as different from the real thing as paste jewellery is from a diamond. But the sight of his uniform in the mirror evokes something closer to the real thing, restoring his self-esteem and sense of purpose. (After all, it also has its implications for the future; how many village girls are going to admire him as much as his aunt?) He is saved from 'provisional existence'—a form of provisional existence due to 'amnesia'. And in the same way, the game with the imaginary girl in Gary's prison camp 'reminds' the prisoners of happier days, of the self-esteem that comes from having a pretty girl on your arm, of the prospects for the future. We see that the 'nothingness neurosis' that arises out of provisional existence is caused by *forgetfulness*, which produces roughly the same kind of inconveniences as losing your address book, or losing your compass on a cross-country hike.

In the following passage from Simone de Beauvoir, the problem is only apparently more complicated:

'I look at myself in vain in a mirror, tell myself my own story, I can never grasp myself as an entire object, I experience in myself the emptiness that is myself, I feel that I am not.'[1]

Here we are apparently talking about something entirely different, the basic 'human condition' according to existentialism (at least, Sartre's variety)—consciousness is an emptiness, etc. But is this *necessarily* so? Can we imagine Mme de Beauvoir looking in a mirror and experiencing a strong sense of identity? Of course. It is merely a question of wider relational consciousness, induced, perhaps, by great emotional excitement or anticipation. In which case, we see that the trouble is 'low pressure consciousness' again, which she takes for granted and regards as inevitable. Her mirror fails to dissipate the 'forgetfulness of existence' because she is 'unprepared', has failed to make the preliminary effort.

The self-image, then, is not simply an arbitrary sense of identity, but a way of focusing powers that would otherwise find themselves deprived of an object. The orchestra plays badly in a soundproof studio because it cannot hear itself, and therefore has no way of judging how much effort is still needed. Even an artist painting a picture—with which he is in continual solid contact—has to keep standing back to judge the total effect. It is a question of giving one's efforts a certain continuity of objective. This also explains why the autobiographical novel has become so popular in the 20th century—Joyce, Wolfe, Kerouac *et al.*—because in times of social instability, when the artist can no longer use society as a mirror for his soul, he has to create his own mirror. The self-image serves the same purpose as the arrangement of microphones and loudspeakers that enabled the orchestra to 'hear itself' again.

We might consider psychotherapy as a process of encouraging the patient to seek for a suitable self-image—one that is consistent with the highest level of self-esteem and creativity. (I have pointed out, in a book on Bernard Shaw, that Shaw's five

[1] *Pyrrhus et Cinéas*, 1943, p. 67.

early novels may be seen as attempts to find a suitable self-image, almost as if he tried on a series of masks.) But it must be emphasised that the self-image is not a lie, or some kind of self-deception. When Maslow advised his female patient to go to night school, he had recognised that work in the chewing gum factory had eroded her self-image (by causing 'forgetfulness'); but the night classes only had the effect of *reminding* her that she possessed intellectual capacities. Similarly, when psychologists from the Yonan Codex Foundation treat hardened criminals as intelligent human beings, capable of changing their lives, they open-up unexplored areas of creativity in the prisoners.

But all this can only be adequately understood in terms of Husserl's *intentionality*. Perceptions are *acts*, and when I look at something or think of something, it is as if an arm reached out from my brain and grasped its object. Our minds differ from our bodies in that unused capacities tend to go 'dead' or latent; it is rather as if you had very bad circulation, and every time you sat down for five minutes, your arms and legs went to sleep. This is 'forgetfulness'. When Maslow sent the girl to night school, he persuaded her to engage in activity that brought the circulation back to 'dead' areas of the mind.

And this enables us to see clearly that what Maslow has done is to add an entirely new significance to the Freudian notion of the unconscious. The girl's creativity had passed into the un-conscious—i.e. been 'forgotten'. This suggests a re-definition of the unconscious as 'the home of man's latent powers and possibilities'. The unconscious mind may include all man's past; but it also includes all his future.

Man controls his physical environment by means of his physical powers. He controls his inner world by means of his mental powers—'intentions'. His future evolution depends upon increased ability to use 'intentions', these mental pseudo-podia that determine his thoughts, moods, ideas, emotions, insights. The intentions do not create ideas or insights; they only *uncover* meaning. They could be compared to the blind man's fingers that wander over Braille. But this image fails to bring out the most important aspect of the intentions: their power to *penetrate* into meaning. I have compared the relation between intentions and 'the world' to the relation between a gramophone needle and the record, but this image also fails to emphasise the *variable* nature of the relation—although it is easy enough to see, for example, that a very light needle would only skim over the surface of the grooves and produce a reedy, distorted version of the music. An altogether better image can be found in John Taine's[1] classic science fiction novel *Before the Dawn*, in which a scientist explores the idea that when light falls upon crystals, it 'registers' in much the same manner that sounds can be made to register on wax or magnetic tape. This means, in theory, that it ought to be possible to 'play back' the crystal records of the remote past, if the right playback equipment could be devised. Taine suggests that this could be done by exploring the surface of the crystal with a tiny needle of monochromatic light. When this is done correctly, each crystal reveals amazing pictures of the pre-human era on earth.

Think of 'intentions' as being needles of light, exploring the world's pitted surface; when used with delicacy and accuracy, and the results are sufficiently amplified by close attention, the result is a revelation of meaning. The simplest way to grasp the accuracy of this description is to take a picture—perhaps some coloured photograph of a landscape— and to look at it slowly and carefully, thinking of the eyes as the projectors of needle-like intentions. An ordinary glance at the picture seems to reveal most of its meaning; but after this first glance, treat the picture as a record of hidden meanings, waiting for the needle of light to search them out and re-create them in all their richness. We soon become aware that intentions *are* fingers that are capable of probing into meaning, uncovering meanings that are already present in coded form. We are living in a world of infinitely rich meaning, and we possess the equipment for 'playing it back'. The chief obstacle is our ignorance of the purpose of the equipment, and of the meaning waiting to be decoded. I imagine that my ordinary perception of the world is a perception of its meaning; this is like imagining that I can play back the music on a gramophone record by looking at it.

The rather mixed imagery of the above paragraph underlines another aspect of the self-image. When I can understand a mental activity in terms of definite images, I can also control it. Without such images, I am groping in a fog, with no idea which way to go or what to do. A scientist investigating the

[1] Actually the mathematician E. T. Bell.

behaviour of planaria uses words to embody his findings; but a psychologist exploring the intentional activity ·of the human mind finds images more useful, for in this shadowy realm, words lose their precision. When Simone de Beauvoir peers into her mirror, she is not really peering into the 'emptiness that is myself', but into a mental fog in which nothing is defined. The world of intentions operates through images, and is grounded in the self-image.

The discoveries I have tried to outline in this book are all so new that we have only just begun to explore their possibilities. Only one thing can be said with any certainty: the most interesting part is still to come.

SELECT BIBLIOGRAPHY

SELECT BIBLIOGRAPHY

GENERAL

BUGENTAL, JAMES F. T., *Challenges of Humanistic Psychology*, McGraw-Hill, New York 1967.

FLUGEL, J. C. and WEST, DONALD J., *A hundred years of Psychology*, Duckworth, London 1964.

HEBB, DONALD OLDING, *A textbook of psychology*, W. B. Saunders Co., London, 1962.

MARX, MELVIN H. and HILLIX, WILLIAM A., *Systems and Theories in Psychology*, McGraw-Hill, New York 1963.

MAY, ROLLO, ANGEL, ERNEST, and ELLENBERGER, HENRI, editors, *Existence. A new dimension in psychiatry and psychology*, Basic Books Inc., New York 1958.

PROGOFF, IRA, *The Death and Rebirth of psychology*, Routledge and Kegan Paul, London 1956.

ZILBOORG, GREGORY, *A History of medical psychology*, Norton, New York 1941.

* * *

ADLER, ALFRED, *Individual psychology*, Routledge & Kegan Paul, London 1955.

ASSAGIOLI, ROBERTO, *Psychosynthesis: a manual of principles and techniques*, Hobbs, Dorman & Co., New York 1965.

BOSS, MEDARD, *Psycho-analysis and Daseinanalysis*, A clinical handbook of Existential theory and therapy, Basic Books Inc., New York 1963.

BRILL, Dr A. A., editor, *The basic writings of Sigmund Freud*, Modern Library, Random House, New York 1938.

(CANTRIL, HADLEY) *Explorations in Transactional Psychology*, edited by Franklin P. Kilpatrick, New York University Press, 1961.

FRANKL, VIKTOR E., *Man's search for meaning*, An introduction to

Logotherapy, Washington Square Press, New York 1965. (Freud, Sigmund)

Glasser, William, *Reality Therapy*, A new approach to psychiatry, Harper & Row, New York 1965.

Goble, Frank, *The Third Force, the psychology of Abraham Maslow*, Grossman, New York 1970.

James, William, *Principles of psychology*, Constable, London 1950.

Jones, Ernest, *Sigmund Freud, life and work*, Hogarth Press, London 1954. 3 vols.

Jung, Carl G., *Psychological Types, or the Psychology of Individuation*, Routledge & Kegan Paul, London 1959.

Jung, Carl G., *Memories, Dreams, Reflections*, recorded and edited by Aniela Jaffe, Collins and Routledge & Kegan Paul, London 1963.

Laing, R. D., *The divided Self*, Tavistock Publications Ltd., London 1960.

Maslow, Abraham H., *Towards a psychology of Being*, Van Nostrand, New York 1968.

Maslow, Abraham H., *Motivation and personality*, Harper & Row, New York 1970. 2nd edition.

McDermott, John J., editor, *The writings of William James*, Random House, New York 1967.

Progoff, Ira, *Jung's psychology and its social meaning*, Grove Press, New York 1953.

INDEX

INDEX